# The Advent of
# the British Labour Party

# The Advent
## of the
# British Labour Party

by

PHILIP P. POIRIER

NEW YORK
COLUMBIA UNIVERSITY PRESS
1958

58-14891

PREFACE

This book is an attempt to account for the emergence of the Labour party as a major political force between 1900 and the General Election of 1906. The first four chapters on the later nineteenth century background do not pretend to give a complete picture. They deal briefly with the growth of trade union sentiment in favour of independent political action before 1900 and, at greater length, with the relative contribution of the main socialist groups and key figures in the labour movement to the earlier efforts to create a new party.

The emphasis throughout the book is on politics—on the tactics, bargaining and compromise that enabled socialists and trade unionists to work together in the Labour Representation Committee, and on the origins, the nature and the extent of the Committee's electoral collaboration with the Liberals. The trade union section of the Committee has received here less attention than it perhaps deserves, but I hope that the reader will agree that the prominence given to the socialist I.L.P. is justified, that the I.L.P., or certainly its leaders, played the crucial role in forging the socialist-trade union alliance and in guiding it to success.

While I regret that the papers of James Ramsay MacDonald for this period were not available, I very much doubt that they would have led to any appreciable alteration of my conclusions. The important question of MacDonald's dealings with the Liberals is, in any case, remarkably well covered in the correspondence of the Liberal Chief Whip, Herbert Gladstone.

I have cited the Gladstone papers frequently and have given considerable space to the Liberal party. From 1900 to 1906 the fortunes of the Committee and the Liberal party were so intertwined that a history of the Committee must of necessity be a study in inter-party politics, a case study in political opportunism.

I am especially grateful to Mr. Francis Johnson for making available the correspondence of J. Bruce Glasier and the minute books of the I.L.P., to the Passfield Trustees for permission to consult the Beatrice Webb diaries, to the Fabian Society for providing access to various correspondence and the minute books of the Fabian Executive, and to Mr. Victor Hull of the Colindale Newspaper Library for helping me find my way to files of both London and provincial newspapers. The staffs of the Fabian Society, of Labour party headquarters, of the British Museum and of the British Library of Political and Economic Science have assisted me in innumerable ways. I also wish to thank Professor David Owen of Harvard University for his encouragement and invaluable advice, and Professor Harry Coles of Ohio State University and my brother, Richard Poirier, for reading parts of the manuscript and making suggestions as to style and organization.

Ohio State University
*April,* 1957

# CONTENTS

# CHAPTER I

# The Trade Unions and Politics
# before 1900

ON a Tuesday morning in February 1900, while England was in the midst of the Boer War, delegates of British trade unions and socialist societies gathered in the gas-lighted library of London's Memorial Hall. In a conference lasting two days they resolved to join together in a federation to be called the Labour Representation Committee (the L.R.C.) and to co-operate nationally in running independent 'Labour' candidates for Parliament. Like earlier attempts to achieve increased Labour representation in Great Britain, the meeting was not expected to accomplish much and received scant attention in the press; the news of the hour was coming from South Africa where Cronje, the Boer general, had just been defeated and where the relief of Ladysmith was imminent. In 1901 the Committee held its first annual conference while the nation was mourning the death of Queen Victoria, and again it went almost unnoticed. It continued to work in such relative obscurity that when twenty-nine L.R.C. candidates emerged victorious in the crucial General Election of 1906, the result was widely greeted with a mixture of astonishment and dismay.

In the quarter-century previous to the Memorial Hall meeting, the growth of sentiment in favour of a separate and self-reliant Labour party was one manifestation of a widespread social and economic unrest. Politically Great Britain was adjusting to democratic suffrage, to the enfranchisement of the workers in the Reform Bills of 1867 and 1884; economically, to the loss of her former virtual monopoly of the export trade of the world. Competition from the seventies onward from newly emergent industrial powers, particularly Germany and the United States, and periodic slumps in prices and profits, linked together by a prolonged depression in agriculture, undermined the once buoyant faith in the Victorian free market. Reports of Royal Commissions on housing and sweated trades, investigations of poverty like those of Charles Booth in London, and the literature and agitation of various radical and socialist groups, all served to focus attention on wide areas of misery and abuse beneath the surface of Victorian prosperity. Though the vast majority of workers had shared in this prosperity—with real wages rising after 1850, pauperism appreciably declining and the fifty-four-hour week becoming as typical by the nineties as was the sixty-hour week some thirty years earlier—there was, nevertheless, a mounting impatience with economic hardship; the improvement in the material condition of the worker had not kept pace with the humanitarian conception of what that condition should be. While not yet fully aware of the powerful weapon he possessed in the vote, the working man dictated the course of legislative change as never before, and, as a long-range result of Forster's Education Act of 1870, he was at once more receptive to change than his untutored forebears and more articulate in expressing his discontent. Liberal and Tory Governments in turn vied for his support by sponsoring far-reaching measures of social reform.

Above all, it was the channelling of trade union discontent into political action that had paved the way for a Labour party. Although they accounted for only a small percentage of the working class—one adult male labourer in five in the early nineties[1]—the unions alone appeared capable of the financial outlay involved in seeking an appreciable increase in working class representation, and they were so massed in industrial constituencies and so organized nationally in the Trades Union Congress as to exert an important influence on the Parliament of the day. Contributing in varying degrees to the conversion of the unions to a broader and more independent role in politics before 1900 were (1) their loss of confidence in the established parties, and especially the Liberal party, as vehicles for reform and redress; (2) their growing doubts of the effectiveness of purely industrial action as industrial controls were tightened and their bargaining position deteriorated; and (3) their absorption of a more militant element from the late eighties onward after socialism had revived and 'new unions' had been organized among the heretofore neglected unskilled workers.

By 1900 disillusionment with the Liberal party among the trade unionists was widespread but by no means universal. Only a handful of Labour M.P.s sat at Westminster, and they were trade union officials for the most part, with miners predominant, elected as Liberals and accepting the Liberal whip. After the Trades Union Congress had been formed in 1868, when there were some half a million trade unionists in Britain,[2] the unions had successfully brought pressure to bear on the existing parties to secure a favourable legal status (1871) and the removal of criminal penalties attaching to strikes (1875). Thereafter they had been satisfied to look mainly to the party of Gladstone and to serve as an auxiliary of its Radical wing. A Labour party at the time was considered impossible until there could be payment of members of Parliament by the state and of election expenses out of the rates, and such reforms were deemed unattainable without Liberal support. Gladstone, venerated by the working classes, had championed their right to vote and in his first administration from 1868-1874 achieved a remarkable record of reforms. The organization of the Liberal party was not as inflexible as it later became, and especially in industrial areas working class elements aspired to gain control of local Liberal machinery and perhaps in time to dictate party policy. Most important of all, the radical elements in the party were gaining steadily in strength. In the early eighties it appeared that Joseph Chamberlain, the chief Radical spokesman, would inherit the mantle of leadership.

Gladstone's espousal of Irish Home Rule in 1886 had changed this situation, for it insured that henceforth the Irish problem would colour and obscure all other questions in domestic politics. In Chamberlain's words, it 'relegated to the dim and distant future any serious attempt to deal with the social problem.'[3] It drove Chamberlain himself into opposition and eventually into the Conservative camp, and the only man of

11

stature who might have filled his place as Radical leader, Sir Charles Dilke, soon lost his political promise in the divorce courts. The Liberal party was rent asunder over Ireland and, except for a brief return to office from 1892 to 1895, was reduced to twenty years of barren opposition and internal wrangling. Finally, the appearance in Parliament of a disciplined Irish party under Parnell revealed the tremendous power that a small group could wield when it held the balance in the Commons and encouraged demands from trade union ranks that Labour follow the Irish example.[4]

By 1900 it was obvious that the local Liberal associations, despite the defection of disgruntled Whigs over Home Rule and despite the urgings from Liberal leaders, were generally averse to Labour bids for seats and interested mainly in candidates with strong financial backing and, further, that those wealthier Liberals who frequently financed local contests were seldom amenable to candidates of advanced views. While in office from 1892 to 1895 the Liberals lost their last good chance to forestall a Labour break-away by a timely response to working class demands, hampered in such a pursuit by a precarious majority, a Tory-dominated House of Lords and by Gladstone's determination to push Home Rule to the detriment of reform legislation in general. The promises held out to Labour in the Liberal Newcastle Programme of 1891 could thus be dismissed as mere election bait. In any case, after going down to crushing defeat in the Election of 1895, the Liberals appeared hopelessly ineffectual if not indeed moribund. The party chieftains were increasingly at odds, and while Lord Rosebery sulked in retirement, Sir William Harcourt and then John Morley abandoned the command of a divided rank and file. In 1898, the year of Gladstone's death, the leadership fell to a member of the Scottish gentry, Sir Henry Campbell-Bannerman. When the outbreak of the Boer War split the party even further, Sir Henry's task seemed well-nigh insurmountable and the prospects of a Liberal majority, extremely remote.

If the Liberals were found wanting in trade union circles by the turn of the century, even less was expected from the Conservatives or Unionists. When they took office in 1895 under

Lord Salisbury, there were grounds for expecting at least a few major contributions in the field of social reform, for Joseph Chamberlain had been appointed to the Cabinet as Colonial Secretary. His reputation as the country's most effective practitioner of municipal socialism while Mayor of Birmingham, his Radical Programme of 1885 and his attacks on selfish wealth were still remembered. He was, to be sure, in the Liberal Unionist minority of a Conservative government and, by choice, his efforts centred on colonial matters, but his prestige and strong personality enabled him to impress his preferences on general policy. There was a wide field in 1895 for whatever reformist zeal he still felt. Aside from charity, only the Poor Law took cognizance of those without livelihood, and in its operation there was a strong odour of disinfectant and a tendency to treat need as an offence as well as a misfortune. No insurance for the sick or the unemployed yet existed. There were no pensions for the aged, no effective assistance for the victims of industrial accidents. Yet in spite of the Conservatives' firm control in Parliament, the only major piece of social legislation their party put through was the Workmen's Compensation Act of 1897 covering injury to the workman in a limited number of trades. [5] The demand for old age pensions also drew Chamberlain's attention, but after long-drawn-out inquiries by Royal Commissions, plans in this direction were sidetracked. The cost of the South African War precluded such expenditure, but perhaps more to the point, Chamberlain, the author of the 'doctrine of ransom,' was losing interest in matters wholly domestic, intoxicated with the problems and possibilities of Empire.

Accompanying mounting impatience with the Liberals and distrust of the Conservatives by the later nineties was growing uneasiness among trade unionists in regard to their legal status and increasing strain in employer-worker relations. The owner-managed competitive private firms of the mid-century were giving way to larger combinations, making collective bargaining more impersonal and seemingly less profitable. With greater mechanisation, the skilled craftsmen became increasingly unrestful. The employer class, faced with recurrent trade slump and foreign inroads into the overseas market, bemoaned trade union practices as a serious hindrance to the nation's industrial advance and by forming employers' federations gave notice of a pending showdown with the unions all along the line. The changing atmosphere was reflected also in the courts where decisions apparently adverse to picketing were handed down and where in 1897 a judicial pronouncement, later reversed by the Law Lords, questioned the legality of strikes to secure the dismissal of non-union workers.[6] Even more ominous, in 1897 Britain's premier union, the powerful Amalgamated Society of Engineers, with 92,000 members and funds of more than £360,000, went down to defeat after an intense and costly strike.[7] Beginning in July 1897, the strike lasted for six months, ostensibly over the demand for an eight hours day but substantially over the determination of the engineer employer's federation to break down union restrictions (particularly those on the number of apprentices) and to secure mastery of their own workshops. The final surrender of the Engineers, the heavy depletion of their funds, was the worst setback that British trade unionism had experienced in a generation, and it seriously called into question the long held union belief in the efficacy of industrial as opposed to political action. As if to drive home the lesson, in 1898 the South Wales miners fought an equally gruelling and losing battle with the mine owners. Many trade union officials became convinced that with strikes now too costly, and with legislative redress and the clarification of trade union law unobtainable in the existing Parliament, their only recourse was to seek increased Labour representation.

The influence of the 'new unions' and of the socialists on this trade union change of attitude, though of great importance, has probably been over-stressed. It should be noted that the Trades Union Congress was passing essentially collectivist resolutions and that Congress delegates were demanding a more independent attitude in politics before the new unions or the socialists had any voice.[8] Furthermore, growing loss of assurance among trade unionists in regard to their legal status and industrial strength, and their irritation at legislative impasse would, in all likelihood, have dictated a new course of action even without socialist prodding. Admittedly the older unions were an 'aristocracy of Labour,' maintaining in many cases elaborate systems of friendly benefits which only the higher skilled could afford. Collectivists in practice, they nevertheless were usually suspicious of state intervention lest it be turned against them. With socialism quiescent and Chartism virtually dead after 1850, they lacked a clear ideology of their own, except in trade union matters, and were therefore inclined to think in purely Liberal terms. Given the prevailing sentiment among the governing classes in the mid-Victorian years, they correctly assumed that in order to obtain a secure and recognized place within the capitalist framework, they had to appear 'respectable' and to eschew violence and broad challenges to the established order. But they were never lacking in militancy when their own interests were endangered as bitter strikes and concerted lobbying attest, and they regarded dependence on the Liberals more as a necessity dictated by circumstances than as an ideal. Where they were most vulnerable to criticism was in their indifference to the problems of the vast body of workers, those outside the trade union fold.

The trade societies of the less skilled that had mushroomed in the early seventies were crippled or crushed out in the ensuing trade depression, but after 1886 agitation among the unemployed in London and the provinces enabled the socialists to stir unrest not only among non-unionists but practically everywhere in the trade union world. In 1888 a drive to organize the unskilled began in London. First came the successful match girls' strike, and then the victory of thousands of London gas workers in their fight for an eight-hour day and a slight increase in wages. In the latter part of 1889 the drive reached its peak in the Great London Dock Strike. Skilful generalship, that of socialists like John Burns and Tom Mann, and public sympathy won the day for the dockers. The first volumes of Charles Booth's survey of *London Life and Labour* had just appeared to spotlight abject poverty and squalor in London's working class districts. The lot of the docker was known to be hard, and his demand for sixpence an hour seemed eminently fair. The strike was

15

orderly, and the newspapers for the most part, friendly. Prominent figures, including Cardinal Manning, intervened on the dockers' behalf while the public subscribed generously to a strike fund.

The immediate result of these victories was a tremendous increase in trade union membership. New unions were formed, and the older unions, which had already begun to expand with business improvement in 1887, received a new influx of members, some revising their constitutions in order to sign in the lower paid in their trades. Trade union statistics are usually quite inadequate before 1892, but it is generally estimated that whereas just before 1888 there were not more than three-quarters of a million trade unionists in Great Britain, by 1892 there were over one and a half million.[9] It is clear, however, that it was the expansion of the old unions rather than the rise of the new that accounted mainly for the over-all increase. In the years 1892 and 1894 the annual average membership of the principal new unions was only some 107,000 compared with a total union strength of 1,555,000.[10] The newer unions, losing heavily in strength in the trade decline of the early nineties, made up some of their losses later as conditions improved.

From the start the masses from which the new unions drew their members were relatively free of the skilled workers' inherited bias for Liberalism. Not having shared so fully in the prosperity of the preceding years and frequently led by socialists, they were less inclined to identify their interests with those of capital. This is not to imply that they immediately took to socialism in any doctrinaire sense. There was little resort to abstract Marxian tenets, no waving of the red flag, by their leaders in the Dock Strike period, only a firm concentration on immediate objectives. It was by skill as organizers and administrators that these leaders inspired respect and so made socialism more respectable, and this held true even within the older circles.

In the Trades Union Congress the entrenched secretaries of the older societies, who controlled the Congress' executive, the Parliamentary Committee, soon found their leadership contested by the newcomers. Yet at no time prior to 1900 was there a clear-cut Congress majority in favour of an independent Labour Party or even for the creation of a general political fund to run candidates, and at no time did the more conservative elements lose control of the Parliamentary Committee. The socialists gained in influence, nevertheless, though at the very first they overplayed their hand and solidified opposition to their proposals by personal and vindictive attacks on prominent defenders of the Liberal connection, the 'Lib-Labs' as they were called.

The controversy over a legal eight-hour day has often been regarded as a test question in the struggle between the old and new men, but it was never argued simply on Socialist vs. Individualist lines, the objections of certain unions to an eight-hour day having little to do with opposition to state intervention,[11] and when an Eight Hours resolution did finally pass the Congress, in 1890, older unions like the Stonemasons, the Engineers and the Carpenters were staunch in their support. Socialist influence is best measured in the response of the Congress to resolutions in favour of the collective ownership of the means of production. Failing of acceptance in 1890 by 365 votes to 55 and in 1892 by 153 to 128, such a resolution was approved in 1893 by 137 to 97. But half the delegates did not vote in 1893, indicating indifference or inability to decide; some of those who voted in favour were, and remained, good Liberals, and the socialists cannot be said at this early date to have 'captured' the Congress. In 1894 a similar resolution passed by 219 to 61 with only fifty abstentions, but in 1895 the Congress amended its rules in such a way as to exclude many of the more prominent socialists from further attendance and rescinded the strongly worded socialist resolution. It still voted, however, in favour of nationalisation of land, mines, minerals, royal rents and railways and elected a socialist, Ben Tillett, to the Parliamentary Committee. In 1896 a resolution in favour of old age pensions was carried unanimously, and in 1897 a strong nationalization resolution was passed, though the miners abstained.[12]

An unequivocal declaration of political independence was the natural corollary to such decisions, but the Congress was never noted for its consistency nor even for seeing the implications of some of its own pronouncements. Moreover, it could still be argued that the problem of running candidates should best be left to individual unions since a firm declaration of independence or the setting up of a central political fund would only retard the chances of state payment of M.P.s. In 1893 a plan for setting up a voluntary fund to finance independent candidates had to be abandoned when only two unions expressed any interest in subscribing.[13] Succeeding Congresses voted down all proposals for similar funds.

In 1898 a well-informed though perhaps biased observer judged that the majority of the Congress delegates were socialist sympathizers,[14] but, even if this were so, non-socialists dominated the Parliamentary Committee, and the miners and the textile operatives, among whom the socialists had made little headway, were still in command when the votes were counted. The cotton operatives of Lancashire were usually Tories, partly out of opposition to their Liberal millowner employers, while certain miners' unions appeared protected forever from socialist capture by their hard Liberal shell. The obduracy of the miners stemmed in part from their having already turned the Reform Bills of 1867 and 1884 to wider use than any of the other unions. More frequently affected by regulatory law, their interest in having spokesmen in Parliament where the laws were made was therefore keener. In the homogeneity of the average mining constituency they had an initial advantage, for with miners overwhelmingly predominant the local Liberal association usually had no choice but to accept a miners' leader when one was put forward, and his return was virtually certain. In Northumberland, for example, Thomas Burt dominated the Morpeth division after 1874, Charles Fenwick the Wansbeck division from the time of its creation in the redistribution of seats in 1885. Long before the demands for an independent Labour party were well advanced the return of miners as Liberals from Durham, Northumberland, South Wales and parts of Lancashire had become an established custom. Even the Miners Federation, formed in 1888 in opposition to the policies of the Northumberland and Durham miners' leaders, was firmly attached to the Radical wing of the Liberal party. For their actions in Parliament, moreover, the miner M.P.s felt that they were answerable to no one but their own constituents; they refused to be bound by T.U.C. resolutions.[15]

The passage of Socialist resolutions by the T.U.C. did not mean that trade unionists generally in the nineties had experienced a Pauline conversion to socialism. Involved in the arduous administrative duties which his job entailed, the average trade union official devoted little time to economic or political inquiry, finding it easier to stick to old forms and to echo old slogans. Anti-capitalist or class struggle tirades left him unmoved, and he was too steeped in Liberal-Radical notions to have lost his respect for property rights. Yet, despite the fact that socialist zealots were often feather-heads in his eyes, he still had come a long way in freeing himself from the cult of Manchesterism so dominant in the mid-Victorian years when 'Lib-Labs' like Henry Broadhurst held sway, and he could with no shock to his conscience declare himself in favour of a broad collectivist proposal. It is probable, on the other hand, that such a declaration often meant little more to him than shouts of 'Come to salvation!' meant to a follower of General Booth. He was no fool, he knew that there were crying evils, and he was not necessarily opposed to extensive social change. But agitation for reforms, unless they directly affected his union, he was glad to leave to others.

There were many exceptions to this type, however, and in the Congress they constituted a vociferous and influential element. This was especially true among the new unionists, but in almost every union were a few young men keenly interested in politics and of sufficient intellectual curiosity to have immersed themselves in socialist literature. Quite often their fellow-workers raised them to positions of leadership even in the more conservative societies, but like the leaders of the unskilled in the Dock Strike period, they remained in the hierarchy of the trade union world mainly because they proved their worth as reliable and hard-working administrators. The influence of a moderate socialist element in the Congress was growing before 1900 and its conflicts with the older school subsiding. In the creation of the Labour Representation Committee this socialist-trade union agreement found formal expression.

## NOTES

1. Sidney and Beatrice Webb, *History of Trade Unionism*, London, 1911, 411.
2. J. H. Ludlow and L. Jones, *Progress of the Working Class: 1832-1867*, London, 1867, 205.
3. J. L. Garvin, *Life of Joseph Chamberlain*, 3 vols., London, 1934, vol. ii, 212.
4. On the need for Labour adopting the tactics of the Irish see speeches of delegates at the Trades Union Congress. *T.U.C. Annual Reports*, 1885, 33; 1888, 24.
5. This Act was criticized by some Labour members of Parliament and by those trade union leaders who feared it would undermine trade union administration of friendly benefits. The Fabian leader Sidney Webb regretted that these Labour critics were 'taking the anti-collectivist line of the Liberals' (Webb to Edward Pease, Jan. 19, 1897, Fabian Society Correspondence). The Act was a great advance over the abortive Liberal measure of 1894. It covered a larger number of accident cases and swept aside consideration of workmen's 'negligence.'
6. On these cases, Lyone vs. Wilkins (1896) and Allen vs. Flood (1897) see H. H. Schloesser and W. S. Clark, *The Legal Position of Trade Unions*, London, 1912, 5-17.
7. George Barnes, Secretary of the Engineers later wrote that after the strike 'of fourteen members of the Employers' executive, more than half were dead in a few months . . . and two of my immediate colleagues died soon after from the strain.' George N. Barnes, *From Workshop to War Cabinet*, London, 1924, 48.
8. D. W. Crowley in his doctoral thesis, 'Origins of the Revolt of the British Labour Movement from Liberalism, 1875-1906' (British Library of Political Science, 1952) concludes, after a close study of Trades Union Congress proceedings, that 1886 was the high mark of 'old unionist' discontent with the Liberal connection and of the 'old unionist' movement toward collectivism.
9. G. D. H. Cole, *A Short History of the British Working Class Movement*, London, 1948, 246.
10. E. J. Hobsbawm, 'General Labour Unions,' *Economic History Review*, series 2, vol. i, 1949, 124.
11. The Northumberland and Durham miners, for example, usually worked less than seven hours a day and so opposed a legal eight hours lest it become the minimum. See George Howell, *Trade Unionism New and Old*, London, 1894, 171.
12. *T.U.C. Ann. Rpts.*, 1890, 38; 1892, 46; 1893, 48; 1894, 53; 1895, 34 ff; 1896, 50; 1897, 54.
13. The plan for a fund was only half-heartedly pushed by the Parliamentary Committee. G. D. H. Cole, *British Working Class Politics: 1832-1914*, London, 1941, 111-112.

# The Trade Unions and Politics before 1900

14. James Keir Hardie in the *Labour Leader*, September 10, 1898.

15. The feeling of desperation with which some socialists responded to the conservatism of the miners is shown in the following excerpts from Beatrice Webb's diaries: The Angel, Chesterfield, Nov. 12, 1895; Away on one of my investigating tours. Attended a Derbyshire Miners Council meeting . . . a stupid, stolid lot of men characterized by fair mindedness and kindliness— but oh! how dense! The officials are the ordinary good type, hard working, narrowminded, whiskey drinking, self-complacent persons, excellent speakers on the question of Miners' Trade Unionism, and competent negotiators, but stupid, stupid, stupid like the men. Is it the abnormal quantity of whiskey these good fellows drink—without getting drunk—that deadens their intelligence—or is it brainwork carried on by an uncultivated and untrained mind that exhausts all the intelligence? How can anyone fear anything but unmitigated Conservatism from the English Democracy? The miners' radicalism is largely traditional made up of allegiance to the Party that gave them the vote. Of course there remains the fact that their real interests are on the side of Economic Collectivism and sooner or later they will, I suppose, perceive it in a dim sort of way. But it will have to be dinned into them—and they will depend exclusively on middle-class leadership for years to come.

# CHAPTER II

# Marxists and Fabians and the Idea
# of a Labour Party

WITH the collapse of Chartism at the end of the tense and troubled forties all the revolutionary tendencies of earlier vintage lay dormant for over thirty years. Though the International Working Men's Association—the First International —was founded in London in 1867 and British trade union leaders on its council came into contact with Karl Marx, there is no indication they they gained even a passing acquaintance with Marx's main theories.[1] What socialist groups existed before 1880 were small, scattered and of negligible importance.

Among the intellectual forces contributing to the revival of socialism in the eighties were the writings of the English Positivists who, though not socialists themselves, often argued for a complete reconstruction of the social system. John Stuart Mill, who enjoyed immense prestige, had expressed growing doubts of the validity of Benthamite individualistic doctrines in the years just before his death in 1873. Carlyle, Matthew Arnold and Dickens had protested against the ugliness and injustices of industrial England. In the churches Christian Socialism had left its mark, and there was a mild social protest that gave rise to the Guild of St. Matthew and the Christian Social Union. A reading of Comte had encouraged among the literate the idea of society as an organic whole rather than a mere aggregate of individuals. There was now an increased stress on scientific investigation which demanded statistics and social surveys, and these soon proved beyond question that Victorian prosperity was a chimera for a large part of the population. A new school of economists—including Cliffe Leslie, Arnold Toynbee and

## Marxists and Fabians and the Idea of a Labour Party

William Cunningham—emphasized examining long-range developments and current conditions rather than basing judgments on *a priori* theory, while in philosophy the neo-Hegelians —T. H. Green, Bosanquet and Ritchie—asserted that state interference could in some instances enhance rather than undermine individual freedom. Meanwhile, to those middle-class radicals who looked to America for guidance and inspiration, the growth of trusts and the unhealthy influence of big business in American politics weakened even further the faith in *laissez-faire*. Of major importance in helping to popularize the belief in the need for social and economic change was the American Henry George, who through his book *Progress and Poverty* and his lecture tours in England in the early eighties stirred a discussion that went far beyond his own infatuation with the 'single tax' on land. George's insistence that poverty was not caused by weakness of character or the working of inexorable economic laws but by defective arrangements of society that were correctible by state action was easily merged into a larger concept of collective ownership for community ends.

The revival of socialism had no immediate impact on the working classes in the eighties. It was rooted rather in middle-class disillusionment in the face of declining prices and profits, agricultural depression and growing foreign competition. But once the mounting criticism of the prevailing system became linked with the growing power of working-class opinion and with the efforts to organize it, the way was paved for a socialist-trade union political alliance and the emergence of a new party.

### THE SOCIAL DEMOCRATIC FEDERATION

The first of the new socialist organisations grew out of a group of radicals, positivists and anarchists who formed the Democratic Federation in 1881. Their purpose was to consolidate the Radical Working Men's Clubs in London and to agitate for a series of radical measures and for land nationalization. The moving spirit was Henry Mayers Hyndman, a well-to-do and widely travelled journalist and a graduate of Eton and Cambridge. In June 1881, having read *Das Kapital* and

23

talked with Marx, who then lived in London, Hyndman brought out *England for All,* the first clear exposition of Marxian socialism for English readers. By 1884, under Hyndman's domination, the Federation had adopted a clearly socialist programme and changed its name to the Social Democratic Federation. It numbered among its members such middle-class figures as William Morris, the poet and designer; Karl Marx's youngest daughter, Eleanor; Belfort Bax, the philosopher; and an ex-artillery officer, Henry Hyde Champion. It also attracted young working men including Tom Mann, Will Thorne and John Burns, future organizers of the new unions.

On street corners and at trade union meetings the S.D.F. members unfurled the red flag and sang revolutionary hymns, their speeches full of prophecy and violence as the speeches of a small and ineffectual crusading group are apt to be. 'Our militant socialism of the eighties,' writes one observer, 'although captained by poets, artists, anglican clergymen and ex-army officers was profoundly proletarian in speech and motto. Its scarlet banner blazed with the war cry "Workers of all nations, unite!" The "class-war" was vividly declaimed. The absurd titles "Mr." and "Esquire" were dropped like live coals, collars were turned down, cuffs sheared away. . . . The Middle-class could not be mentioned even by that unlovely title; they became the hated "bourgeois". . . .'[2]

Though the S.D.F. aspired to win mass support, from the outset it alienated a large segment of the working class, especially in the trade unions. In 1884 it issued a manifesto denying that the unions had any right to speak for Labour: their loftiest goals were raising wages and shortening hours when not improvement but revolution was wanted.[3] John Burns in the S.D.F. organ *Justice* in 1887 heaped scorn on the unions; they were, he asserted, 'mere middle-class and upper-class rate reducing societies.'[4] The Federation's policy in the later nineties of urging members to join unions in order to influence them from within did little to assuage the resulting bad feeling.[5] The average British worker, anti-revolutionary and conservative in temper, found much of the dour, dogmatic teaching of the S.D.F. incomprehensible or was repelled by its anti-religious bias. Hyndman, who in the eighties genuinely believed that 'The Great Social Revolution of the Nineteenth Century was at hand,'[6] chose to ignore the conservatism of the workers, being too inclined, as Shaw commented, to mistake hungry stomachs for intellectual conviction of the class war.[7] Such rigid orthodoxy was attacked by Friedrich Engels, Marx's chief disciple after the latter's death in 1883. Stress on revolution in England meant 'making phrases and doing nothing more,' Engels insisted; the Hyndmanites expected to convert the working man not 'through an evolution set in operation by class feeling' but by having them swallow Marxian doctrine whole.[8]

The S.D.F. found its chief support in London where it built up nearly half its branches. Elsewhere, outside Lancashire, the branches were scattered. Since as few as six persons could form a branch, many of them had but a nominal existence.[9] At the end of 1884 there was a split in the Federation when, in opposition to Hyndman's autocratic methods and his insistence on running candidates for Parliament, Morris and others formed a separate Socialist League. For a time this defection weakened the S.D.F. financially and intellectually, though it did gain something from increased unity after the split. In the late eighties when it encouraged and exploited the widespread agitation of the unemployed, it showed considerable promise, and in London during the riots of 1886 and the Trafalgar Square demonstrations of 1887 Hyndman, John Burns and others gained a wide notoriety as heroes of the mob. The Federation then grew rapidly, profiting still further from the industrial agitation that culminated in the Great Dock Strike. This was its high point. After the formation of the socialist body known as the Independent Labour Party (the I.L.P.) in 1893, its relative influence waned though it continued to grow numerically. It claimed about 4,500 paying members in 1894, some 9,000 in 1900 and added about 3,000 more over the following decade.[10] The Socialist League, after gaining some support in the provinces, primarily in Yorkshire and along the Clyde,[11] ceased to exist in the early nineties, having been taken over by anarchists. Morris, retiring to Hammersmith, gathered a small following about him until his death in 1896.

Restricted by the narrowness of its own definitions and indulging in arrogant disputation with other socialist groups, the S.D.F. contributed to its own isolation and impotence. Still its influence must not be underestimated. It preached a rigid doctrine in the days when socialism in most of England was but a sound and a rumour and when merely to attract attention was a gain. It thus helped to pave the way for the broader movement that followed. When Pease, the historian of the Fabian Society, wrote that the Federation propaganda in the eighties failed to attract the industrial districts in the North, George Bernard Shaw disagreed. 'I don't think that it had failed to attract them,' he wrote. 'It certainly had alarmed their consciences badly, and made them anxious to find a sensible and practical way out. That was where we came in. We should certainly not have done so well if the S.D.F. had not pick-axed the ground for us.'[12] Also, the S.D.F. provided a rostrum and training school for some of the new unionists and even for some of the Fabians. Shaw for a time considered joining it and spoke from its platform.[13] A nineteen-year-old Scot, James Ramsay MacDonald, when he came south in 1885, joined the Federation's branch in Bristol though he soon abandoned it. J. Bruce Glasier, a Fabian and a future Chairman of the I.L.P., helped form a Glasgow branch in 1884 and later followed Morris into the Socialist League.[14]

Once the development of a Labour Party on independent lines was under way the S.D.F. served as constant critic of those socialists who seemed to prize political success more than their socialism. Perhaps one of its greatest services, however, was a negative one: it served as a warning and example to other socialists of what not to do. At one moment Hyndman would appear to foresee the possibility of revolutionary and sudden change, at another, to support reforms which by their ameliorative nature delayed such change; the S.D.F. never solved the problem common to many socialist movements of whether revolution should be regarded as a cataclysmic overthrow of the capitalist order or as a long-term process. It did seem to demonstrate by its very weakness, however, that reformist methods alone could gain a mass support in England. In electoral policy the S.D.F. likewise showed indecision. Its strict interpretation of the class war logically pointed to treating Liberals and Tories as enemies of the same cloth, but in practice S.D.F. members showed a penchant for supporting Liberal Radicals whenever socialists were not in the running. In elections the S.D.F. played down theories which implied a final resort to the barricades. It had some success in municipal contests, especially in working-class districts like London's West Ham. On the other hand, it never won a single parliamentary contest in which it engaged. In 1885, when it boasted a membership of less than a thousand, it ran three men for Parliament and two of these three, running with the aid of Tory money to split the Liberal vote, attained the humiliating polls of twenty-seven and thirty-two. In 1892 there were two S.D.F. candidates who together secured only 659 votes; in 1895, four candidates with a total of 3,730 votes. In 1900 two S.D.F. men achieved respectable polls despite their defeat. In 1906 there were 22,000 votes for eight candidates.

In the meantime the S.D.F. alternated between criticizing and courting the I.L.P. Though some provincial members of the Federation encouraged close ties with the I.L.P. in running candidates for Boards of Guardians and other municipal posts, the leaders in London regarded the new body with a jaundiced eye, Hyndman calling it a 'conspiracy against the S.D.F.'[15] Posing as sole guardians of the socialist fire, they denied the need for Keir Hardie's organization; it existed simply because its leaders had to indulge their idiosyncrasies and in their eagerness for office were unwilling to submit to wholesome S.D.F. discipline.[16] This antagonism to the I.L.P. had weakened somewhat by the later nineties as the S.D.F. became less interested in street corner orations and self-imposed isolation and more concerned with focusing what socialist strength had been mustered.[17] In July 1897, the two bodies set up a court of appeal to adjudicate in cases where they coveted the same seat in local and national elections, and on Hardie's suggestion, they began polling their members with a view to uniting in a single organization. Nothing came of this, however. The I.L.P. leaders, despite a favourable rank and file response to the fusion proposal, drew back when faced with the imminence of Hyndman's embrace.[18] At the annual I.L.P. conference in 1898, J. Bruce Glasier denied the claims of the S.D.F. that there were no obstacles to unity and that the S.D.F. had come nearer and nearer to the I.L.P. 'alike in principle, in tactics, in organization and in method of propaganda.'[19] The I.L.P. showed greater sympathy with trade unions, co-operation and all earnest reform, Glasier asserted, 'If I may say so the ways of the S.D.F. are more doctrinaire, more Calvinistic, more aggressively sectarian than the I.L.P. The S.D.F. has failed to touch the heart of the people. Its strange disregard of the religious, moral and aesthetic sentiments of the people is an overwhelming defect.'[20]

When fusion sentiment persisted in some of the I.L.P. branches, Glasier again took up the cudgels against the Federation. If socialism was backward in London, he insisted, the S.D.F. was mainly responsible while in Yorkshire the I.L.P. stood alone so that fusion could serve no purpose. Even in Lancashire it was a perishing cause. Convinced by such arguments, the I.L.P. conference in 1899 voted against the merging of the two groups; only federation in which they would maintain their separate identities was considered feasible.[21] The followers of Hyndman at their next general meeting, arguing that they 'had been humbugged long enough,' refused even to consider the federation proposal.[22] The whole matter then hung fire until overshadowed by the combination of trade unionists and socialists in the L.R.C. Although the S.D.F. joined the L.R.C. it did so with considerable misgivings, as will be noted, and then withdrew in August 1901, after failing in efforts to impose a socialist test on L.R.C. candidates. It continued to act as if it considered isolation a proof of its own incorruptibility.

THE FABIANS

Though the Fabian Society, founded in January 1884, exerted considerable influence on the climate of social and economic change in Great Britain and helped shape the philosophy of the nascent Labour Party, the widely held notion that it played a deciding role in the creation of the new party, provided its brains and determined its basic outlook is quite untenable and owes more to Fabian-sponsored myth than to a close examination of the facts. In accounts that overestimate both the influence and the foresight of the 'old-guard' Fabians in Labour politics, Fabian writers have expounded the thesis that the Webbs, Shaw and their colleagues imposed the Fabian conception of society on the early Labour movement, insuring that it would be gradualist, practical, and constitutionalist when, in reality, the movement was all of these things before Fabianism was even invented.[23] What rescued the movement from the massive domination of Karl Marx was not the attractiveness of the Fabian alternative so much as the attitude of the already firmly entrenched British trade unions which, for ethical and empirical reasons, were almost wholly impervious to doctrines of violence and sudden change and fully convinced of the desirability of the parliamentary method. The Fabians helped to clarify, systematize and disseminate collectivist demands and to make them more respectable and so accelerated the Labour party's acceptance of a collectivist programme, but this programme was not uniquely Fabian; one need only note that it embodied most of the short-term objectives of the Marxists. In seeking collectivist remedies, moreover, the early Fabians chose to work through existing parties, leaving the task of mass recruitment for a new party to others. The Fabian contribution remained peripheral and advisory and was at no time decisive. Far from looking to the Fabian Society as their main source of inspiration, the chief organizers of the Labour party, the architects of its first electoral triumph in the General Election of 1906, were often sharply critical of the Society, and, after 1900, at odds with its leaders on practically all the major political issues of the day.

The idea that British socialists might profitably organize as a separate party preoccupied the Fabians of the eighties only briefly. A separate Fabian Parliamentary League formed in 1886 with this end in view soon lost its identity and was merged with the Society.[24] Though Edward Pease, later the Society's Secretary, could write in 1887 that the chief aim of the Fabian plan was 'the formation of a distinct Labour Party in Parliament,'[25] it soon became obvious that the Fabians were neither themselves making efforts in this direction nor encouraging others to do so. Of the trade unions from whose ranks the mass support for a Labour party was to come, they evinced a singular neglect. The first Fabian tracts contain no mention of the trade unions; Webb admits that in the eighties the Fabians did not sufficiently appreciate trade unionism as a political force or even as an essential part of the social structure;[26] the famed *Fabian Essays* written in 1888 scarcely allude to it. By choice remaining small and exclusive, a group of middle-class intellectuals centred in London, the Society was quite averse to organizing on a national scale. It sought its ends by other methods, firstly, by platform propaganda and the circulation of 'topically powerful' tracts,[27] secondly, by 'permeating' Liberal and Conservative organizations and strategically placed individuals and enlisting them, however reluctantly, in Fabian causes.

In the realm of Fabian myth is Sidney Webb's claim that *from 1887 onward* the Fabians were looking to a Labour party to take over from the Liberals who 'could not satisfy the aspirations of those who stood for change.'[28] Rather than looking to a Labour Party, Webb and Pease, George Bernard Shaw and Graham Wallas, indeed the majority of the Fabian hierarchy, were all actively and hopefully engaged at the turn of the decade in trying to convert the Liberal party to their point of view. They were encouraged in this pursuit by the successful cooperation achieved between Liberals and Socialists on the London County Council. In 1889 Webb himself had little doubt that the Liberal party would choose to become the Labour party rather than be superseded.[29] He gives every indication of having regarded permeation as a substitute for a new party. 'This permeation is apparently destined to continue,' he wrote, 'and the avowed Socialist party in England will probably remain a comparatively small disintegrating and educational force, never itself exercising political power, but applying ideas and principles of social reconstruction to each of the great political parties in turn, as the changing results of English politics bring them alternately into office.'[30] Such permeation

was not confined to London. Once the Home Rule split had rid
the Liberal party of its more incorrigible Whigs, there was a
growing demand in party ranks, in part Fabian inspired, for
a programme of constructive social reform. To some extent this
demand was reflected in the broad promises of the Liberal
Newcastle Programme of 1891, for the acceptance of which by
the National Liberal Federation the Fabians claimed a goodly
share of the credit.[31] As late as 1893 it seemed to Webb
probable that the old-time capitalists would drop away from the
Liberal party and that it might have then to be reconstituted
'mainly as a working-class organization on a practically
Collectivist basis.'[32]

While some of the Fabian leaders regarded permeation as
merely a temporary expedient,[33] the majority appear to have
shared Webb's attitude. Steeped in the Progressivism of the
Metropolis, they showed little appreciation of the problems of
socialists in the northern industrial centres where Liberal
Radicals of the London type were rare, where a narrow Liberal
caucus spirit often prevailed and where permeation at the local
level frequently held no promise.[34] When in 1891 the Yorkshire
*Workman's Times* was advocating the immediate formation of a
Labour party, it was not surprising, therefore, that the Fabian
leaders only offered discouragement. It was apparently impossible as yet to get an 'effective' party together, Webb noted,
while Pease could see little hope of rapid progress in this
direction and, as proof, pointed to the disastrous failures of
earlier socialist attempts at independent political action.[35]
'We realized,' writes Webb, 'more vividly than most of our
colleagues that, at any rate in Britain, no political party,
however "proletarian" its composition or its sympathizers, and
however attractive its programme, could ever carry far-reaching
reforms in Parliament by the support merely of the members it
enrolled or even of its sympathizers at elections.'[36] A handful
of socialists or stubborn Independents in the Commons
appeared far less conducive to the immediate Fabian objectives
than two-hundred or so 'imperfectly and unwillingly socialized
Radicals.'[37]

In the meantime, however, a mass pressure for independent

31

Labour representation and, to a lesser degree, for a vague sort of socialism, was building up in the provinces. Finding no outlet in the Social Democratic Federation, whose arguments the average worker could not fathom, nor in the Fabian Society, whose interests lay elsewhere, it sought to express itself in various local organizations that in 1893 were finally drawn together in the socialist Independent Labour Party. As permeators of the Liberal party toward which these provincial elements nursed the liveliest distrust, the Fabians as early as 1892 were feeling some uneasiness lest they come to be regarded as merely a Liberal left wing, and at a meeting in London, attended by Fabians from the provinces, in February of that year, it had been agreed that a Labour party which would act independently was desirable. According to Shaw, permeating had passed its peak.[38] In its Election Manifesto of 1892, moreover, the Society was ready to blast the Liberals for trying 'to stifle English questions by an agitation about Irish grievances' and to call on the working classes to plan for a party of their own, financed by the trade unions. The rise of the new unions in the wake of the Great Dock Strike of 1889 had aroused the keenest Fabian interest—the trade unions were no longer to be ignored—and though by 1892 these new unions were suffering a setback due to trade decline, it is against the background of this seemingly revitalising force in the Labour world that the ideas set forth in the manifesto are to be understood. There was no reversal of Fabian policy, however, no abandonment of permeation in favour of class pressure through the vote. The 1892 proposal is clearly one for the future, and working-class elements are specifically cautioned not to abandon their efforts to force socialists and strong radicals on the Liberal caucuses (in other words to 'permeate' the Liberal Party) and in no case to boycott the polls simply because Labour candidates are not in the field.[39]

The Fabians did not expect legislative triumphs from the Liberal party when it came to power in 1892, for this was patently impossible in view of the narrow Liberal majority and the centring of party energies on Irish Home Rule. Administrative reforms, however, not needing the sanction of

Parliament, were expected, especially in the treatment of labour within the various government departments. Here the Fabians had an intimate knowledge of what went on, and here they suffered acute disappointment. Shaw has asserted that even before the Election of 1892 he and Sidney Webb had 'foreseen and discussed the discarding of the Newcastle Programme when it had served its electioneering purposes,' and 'had known beforehand that the Government would lay itself open' to a Fabian attack combined with a renewed demand for a Labour party.[40] That there was some such premeditation is not unlikely. Yet the timing and nature of this vigorous attack—which took the form of a manifesto written by Shaw and Webb in November 1893, entitled 'To Your Tents, O Israel!', and which was later issued in revised form in January 1894 as a Fabian tract, 'A Plan of Campaign for Labour'—owed much to more immediate considerations.[41] It is worth noting that the resolutions of the Fabian Executive which led to the preparation of the manifesto were prompted by Fred Hammill who was also an adherent of the I.L.P.[42] Also noteworthy is Beatrice Webb's admission of 'some truth in Graham Wallas's observation' that the Fabians were rushed into its issuance by 'fear of being thought complacent and apathetic by the Independent Labour Party.'[43] There was another consideration. The trade unions seemed receptive to a call to action in 1893. In September the Trades Union Congress had passed a resolution calling for a political fund to assist independent candidates and had approved a broad collectivist resolution. The manifesto mentions that as a result of this the larger unions had formally acknowledged their responsibility to finance candidates for Parliament. This was not, however, the case, and in placing so much store in Congress resolutions the Fabians had misjudged the situation. The proposed financing scheme was never implemented by the Congress while the strong socialist resolution was later rescinded.[44]

Regardless of what considerations lay behind the manifesto its call for the immediate formation of a labour party and its tirade against the Liberals did mark a significant shift in Fabian policy. Some of the more ardent Liberals in the Society were incensed by its issuance. 'I had hoped,' wrote one of the members who resigned in protest, 'that, with an occasional fling at official Liberalism—to please the gallery—the Society intended to continue its useful work of permeating Liberalism with Socialism and . . . its no less useful work of turning useless or mischievous *intransigeant* Socialists into practical Socialistic Radicals.' Liberals like Gladstone and Morley, the writer asserted, might not 'swallow every formula of the dogmatic new unionism,' but they were men whose intellect and character was 'a greater security for sure and steady political and social progress than a whole wilderness of . . . fanatical Keir Hardies. . . .'[45]

The issuance of 'To Your Tents, O Israel!' meant that Fabian permeation of the Liberal party, nationally at any rate, had been pretty well abandoned. True, the advent of a supposed friend of the London Progressives, Lord Rosebery, to the Prime Ministership in 1894 was regarded by the Fabians as 'significant in the progress of Collectivism,'[46] and the Parish Councils Act of that year and Harcourt's Death Duties revealed a greater propensity for reform in the party than many Fabians had thought existed. But Fabian influence on the Liberals could never be what it had been. Nor did it seem to matter much. When the Liberals were decisively defeated in the General Election of 1895 the feeling was widely shared that Liberalism had reached its demise and that henceforth the political line of cleavage would be between Conservatism on the one hand and an advancing Socialism on the other.[47]

The advice to the trade unions in the *Plan of Campaign*—to groom fifty Labour candidates and raise £30,000 for the approaching General Election—having gone unheeded and the efforts of the Independents in the Trades Union Congress seemingly abortive, Fabian hopes in the possibility of a Labour party were soon much chastened: The Webbs' *History of Trade Unionism*, which appeared in 1894, has a distinctly non-political note. The practical advice in the *Plan* on the financing and handling of elections was no doubt widely read and of no little influence. Yet its influence was probably nowhere near as great as Fabian writers have asserted. There was nothing novel in the assumption that a Labour party had to be securely anchored in the trade unions. From the outset an alliance with the trade unions was a star-point of the I.L.P. objective, and pleas for a trade union political fund and for a truly self-reliant Labour party had long been raised in the Trades Union Congress. The Fabians in their disillusionment with Liberalism, were, in fact, echoing a demand that already had been made and giving advice that already had been given. For this reason, even the claim of the cautious Pease that the *Plan of Campaign* 'did much to prepare the ground for the Labour party'[48] would appear to be an exaggeration while Shaw's statement that, as the *Plan's* joint authors, he and Webb 'laid the foundation of the I.L.P. under Keir Hardie'[49] may be dismissed as completely without basis. The I.L.P. was founded and its programme formulated before the *Plan of Campaign* was even written.

The impatience of the provincial Independents with the London Fabians was strikingly demonstrated when with only a few exceptions Fabian branches outside the London area broke with the mother society in 1893 to join the I.L.P.[50] Pease states that the Fabian leadership did not resist the breakaway, its connection with these branches having always been rather tenuous, while Shaw asserts that the break was actually encouraged.[51] Actually the Society had little choice. For some time previous these branches had shown themselves more I.L.P. than Fabian in sentiment. Some seventy to eighty had been formed by 1893. Chiefly working class in membership—a condition lamented by the Fabian leaders who, though never guilty of snobbery, were possessed of a strong middle-class bias[52]—they had begun to neglect education work, which the Fabian Executive considered of primary importance, to devote themselves exclusively to politics.[53] Also, to the irritation of the London Fabians, they tended to sever their connections with the local Liberal associations in favour of a rigid independence.[54] Even those branches which survived the 1893 debacle were often critical of the 'permeation' tactics advocated by the London leaders and were determined to support I.L.P. and other socialist candidates regardless of the type of men, 'progressive' or otherwise, put forward by the two older parties.[55]

That in issuing the Election Manifesto of 1892 and later 'To Your Tents, O Israel!', the Fabian leaders were identifying themselves with a movement over which they had little control and which they only vaguely understood can be seen in their response to the conference in Bradford (Yorkshire) which founded the I.L.P. When on the eve of this conference, the London Executive decided to send two representatives, Fabian branches had already begun to organize in preparation for the meeting.[56] Chosen to speak for the Society were George Bernard Shaw and W. S. De Mattos, the latter of whom had gained a wide acquaintance with the provincial Independents as a Fabian lecturer.[57] Though Shaw has portrayed himself as a master influence at Bradford, no one else, as far as this writer can determine, has corroborated his claims, and all that can be said with certainty is that he had some share in drawing up the list of socialist objectives in the I.L.P. programme.[58] To many of the delegates he was an object of suspicion, as was any London permeator, and when it was learned that under no conditions would the Society join the new party, the conference came close to refusing Shaw and De Mattos the right to take their seats.[59] The suspicions attaching to Shaw were not unfounded. He had written to Pease on the eve of the Bradford meeting, 'My present intention is to go uncompromisingly for Permeation, for non-centralized local organization of the Labour Party, and for the bringing up of the country to the London mark by the supplanting of Liberalism by Progressivism. I feel like forcing the fighting as extravagantly as possible; so as to make it clear to all the new men that the Fabian is the lead for them to follow. . . .'[60] The Fabian lead was not followed, however. Shaw, with no faith in achieving socialism through mass enlistments, was thinking less in terms of a separate national party determined to find its own way than of local organizations, sanely socialist, pushing potentially progressive elements of all parties in the direction of further reforms. Keir Hardie and his colleagues, though by no means 'impossiblists,' were ready to neglect piecemeal reforms for the moment in order to concentrate on recruiting a mass following.

No matter what Shaw intended, the Fabians were unfitted by

temperament and by past experience to lead the I.L.P., a movement essentially working class and strongly Nonconformist. The Webbs certainly in the early nineties had hopes of finding some working-class leader to whom they might serve as mentor, and in particular they had their eyes on John Burns, who, it should be noted, was first of all a Londoner engrossed in London problems and one of the I.L.P.'s most avid critics. But Burns would not be managed; the Webbs' plan to become 'the clerks of the Labour movement' did not come off; and by March 1894, Beatrice Webb could see 'no signs of any real leader' in the Labour camp.[61] Meanwhile, the I.L.P. was attracting a following in the northern factory towns through an appeal at once more emotional and more class conscious than that of the Fabian in London and based less on hard Fabian facts than on a general indignation with suffering and with the inertia of those in power. Its spirit, moreover, was shaped by works more utopian and idealistic than the *Fabian Essays*.[62]

One cannot speak in any all-inclusive terms of a Fabian attitude toward the I.L.P., individual members of the Society being allowed to follow their own bent in such matters.[63] It is possible, however, to determine wherein the prevailing views of each group were essentially in conflict and at times diametrically opposed. Most of the leaders of the I.L.P. and many of its rank and file had some connection with the Society through Fabian branches or through Fabian lectures and literature. Only a few I.L.P. members in the nineties, however, were active on the Fabian Executive or had much success in determining Fabian policy, except, perhaps, in the decision to publish 'To Your Tents, O Israel!' For much of the Society's propaganda they had the greatest respect; with particular Fabian methods they expressed the sharpest disagreement.[64] When I.L.P. leaders criticized London Progressivism as inimical to the socialist cause[65] and I.L.P. candidates, polling poorly themselves, opposed Liberal candidates whom the Fabians considered 'progressive,' Beatrice Webb became convinced that the I.L.P. was a 'wrecking party,' an 'unknown force of irreconcilables' utterly checkmating the more reasonable policy of permeation.[66] Especially galling to some of the Fabian 'old guard' was the presence on the Fabian Executive of a spokesman for the I.L.P. viewpoint, James Ramsay MacDonald.

To the I.L.P. which he joined in 1894 MacDonald brought the moderating influence of a political realist and an essentially Fabian dislike for extremism. Like the London Fabian he was at first critical of the I.L.P. excesses and its rigid separatism. But of Fabian indifference to the provincial movement he was even more condemnatory, and years later he rather ungenerously described the Fabians of the nineties as 'smart people who held weekly meetings, published pamphlets, and drafted resolutions, the passing of which by a list of societies and Liberal Associations was to transform politics and the world.'[67] 'Pottering little pennyworths of boiled-down law' must not become 'the end and aim of Fabian existence,' MacDonald argued. The Society was out of touch with anything but London socialism and, smug in its own wisdom, neglected the opportunity to build up socialist organization throughout the country.[68] 'Whether we sneer or not at the S.D.F. and the I.L.P.,' he warned the Fabian Executive, 'these bodies are alive and doing work without us. The work is all the poorer for that, and the ultimate interests and prospects of Socialism all the more uncertain.'[69] But MacDonald's pleas that the Society pioneer and organize went unheeded. 'The truth is,' Beatrice Webb confided to her diary, 'that we and MacDonald are opposed on a radical issue of policy. To bring about the maximum amount of control in public administration, do we want to organize the unthinking persons into Socialist societies, or to make thinking persons socialistic? We believe in the latter process.'[70]

Fabian hostility to the I.L.P. was not confined to diaries. It came to the surface in official pronouncement. In the *Plan of Campaign*, in remarks obviously aimed at the I.L.P., those who indulged in 'a violent and indiscriminate denunciation of the Liberal party' were described as the worst type of Labour candidates, since they alienated working-class voters who formerly had voted Liberal.[71] *Fabian Tract* 70, issued in August 1896, went still further, suggesting that the Society should oppose 'frivolous' third candidates who called themselves 'socialist' but, not well supported, often involved in their own defeats the better of the two candidates competing with them. An organized demand within the Society that *Tract* 70 be withdrawn was led by MacDonald but was overwhelmingly voted down in general meeting.[72]

Since the I.L.P. did not win a single parliamentary contest in the nineties and remained weak both financially and numerically, the Fabian inability to appreciate its potentialities is certainly understandable. At times the I.L.P. appeared little more than a belligerent sect centred in Lancashire and Yorkshire, preaching a crude socialism and almost totally lacking in political acumen. Yet it was peculiarly suited to be the vanguard of a broader movement. From the vantage points which its members occupied in many of the trade unions, it could zealously advocate a trade union-socialist alliance, and, unlike the other socialist societies, it was willing to risk absorption in an essentially trade union party in order to cement this alliance. To compensate for its dismal showing nationally, moreover, it had considerable success in placing I.L.P. men on municipal bodies. This practical administrative experience in local administration and in the give-and-take of local politics robbed the I.L.P. of much of the intransigence of its earlier years when it was struggling for the merest recognition. As it lost interest in what the Fabians considered 'frivolous' parliamentary candidatures and became more sympathetic with the problems of the London Progressives,[73] I.L.P.-Fabian relations became less strained. The two bodies were brought together above all by their common interest in municipal reform, and in 1899 they co-operated in setting up a Local Government Information Bureau under joint Fabian-I.L.P. supervision.[74] Although the Fabians had lost much of their earlier interest in Labour politics, as permeators they were as one with the I.L.P., and in opposition to the Marxists, in encouraging close ties with the trade unions.[75] In 1900 they were willing to join the Labour Representation Committee, mainly because it embodied this trade union-socialist connection.

If they joined the L.R.C., however, the Fabians had not the slightest intention of submitting to its discipline to the detriment of their main preoccupation, permeating those in power. In a sense, as the I.L.P. leader Philip Snowden later pointed out, they were hampering themselves for their special work by joining the Labour party.[76] Aside from this consideration, the fact remains that the Fabian luminaries showed a remarkable lack of enthusiasm for the Labour Representation Committee. Only Edward Pease, who appointed himself to the L.R.C. Executive, displayed a real understanding of its purpose and promise. The Webbs, on the other hand, were almost completely out of touch with the Committee; there is not a single mention of it in the Beatrice Webb diaries. There is surprisingly little reference to it in the Fabian Executive Minutes, usually brief references to the fact that Pease reported on the Committee's doings. And whenever any clear attitude is expressed it is mainly one of criticism, for the Fabian leaders differed from the L.R.C. majority on practically every major issue of the day. On the South African War, on the education question, on free trade vs. protection and on the question of Liberal-Labour co-operation, they parted company with the spokesmen for the L.R.C.

## NOTES

1. George Howell, a member of the council, notes that 'some of the theories connected with his (Marx's) name were not then known to his colleagues,' and adds that he 'is not sure that they had at that date even been propounded.' George Howell, *Labour Legislation, Labour Movements and Labour Leaders*, London, 1902, 150-151.
2. S. D. Shallard in *I.L.P. News*, Aug. 1901. Apparently the S.D.F. terrified many of the well-to-do at this time. See Henry S. Salt, *Seventy Years Among Savages*, New York, 1921, 79.
3. Quoted in *Justice*, Sept. 6, 1884.
4. *Justice*, Sept. 3, 1887.
5. Tom Mann, *My Memoirs*, London, 1923; Max Beer, *A History of British Socialism*, London, 1948, 2 vols., vol. ii, 271-272.
6. *Justice*, July 18, 1885.
7. Shaw in the *Clarion*, Nov. 4, 1904.
8. Engels to F. A. Sorge, April 19, 1890, quoted in *Socialist Review*, vol. i, Aug. 1918, 32; Engels to Sorge, May 12, 1894, in *Briefe und Auszuge aus Briefen von Engels, Marx, Sorge und Andere*, Stuttgart, 1921, 412.
9. For a list of S.D.F. London and provincial branches in 1896 see *The Labour Annual*, 1897, 92-94. Pamphlet, *Program and Rulers of the S.D.F.*, 1898.
10. *Annual Report of the S.D.F.*, 1894, 16; Beer, *Br. Socialism*, vol. ii, 266; see also *Labour Year Book*, 1895 and 1900.
11. H. W. Lee and E. Archbold, *Social Democracy in Britain*, London, 1935, 122.
12. Shaw annotation to manuscript of Edward R. Pease's *History of the Fabian Society*, British Library of Political Science.

Marxists and Fabians and the Idea of a Labour Party

13. Shaw, *Fabian Tract 41*, 'The Fabian Society: It's Early History,' London, 1892, 4.

14. Lee and Archbold, 66.

15. Quoted in Gustav Mayer, *Friedrich Engels*, London, 1936, 253.

16. *S.D.F. Annual Report*, 1894, 25-27.

17. As early as the summer of 1895 Hyndman was writing to an S.D.F. member that the time had arrived to concentrate on organization, the old forms of agitation being no longer necessary. Hyndman to George Lansbury, Aug. 28, 1895. Lansbury correspondence, British Library of Political Science.

18. *I.L.P. Ann. Rpt.*, 1898, 4; *I.L.P. News*, Dec. 1897; Minutes of the National Administrative Council of the I.L.P., Jan. 7 and 8, 1898.

19. S.D.F. circular included with *S.D.F. Ann. Rpt.*, 1898.

20. *I.L.P. Ann. Rpt.*, 1898, 27-28.

21. *ibid.*, 1899, 38-41.

22. *S.D.F. Ann. Rpt.*, 1899, 14 and 25.

23. An extreme example of the thesis is contained in G. D. H. Cole, *The World of Labour*, London, 1920, 2-3: 'The first leaders of the Fabian Society, and in particular Mr. and Mrs. Sidney Webb, were able so completely, through the Independent Labour Party, to impose their conception of society on the Labour Movement that it seemed unnecessary for anyone to do any further thinking. . . . The progress of Labour was beautifully resolved into the gradual evolution of a harmony divinely pre-established by the Fabian Society in the early nineties.' In a more popular work one encounters the statement that 'the Webbs and George Bernard Shaw had done more than anyone to found the parliamentary Labour party.' Hesketh Pearson, *G.B.S.: A Post-script*, London, 1951, 129.

24. Shaw, *Early History*, 12-14.

25. Pease in *Today*, quoted in Beer, vol. ii, 298.

26. Webb's introduction to the 1920 edition of the *Fabian Essays*. It is reprinted in the 1931 edition, p. xxi.

27. The phrase is Webb's. In a letter from Webb to Pease, Feb. 3, 1902.

28. In *St. Martin's Review*, Feb. 1929, quoted in Mary Agnes Hamilton, *Beatrice and Sidney Webb*, New York, 1933, 31.

29. Sidney Webb, *Socialism in England*, London, 1889, 130.

30. *ibid.*, 25.

31. G. B. Shaw, 'Early Days,' a chapter in *The Webbs and Their Work*, edited by Margaret Cole, London, 1949, 11-12.

32. Introduction to an 1893 edition of *Socialism in England*, p. xv.

33. Particularly Hubert Bland, a Tory Democrat, who as early as 1886 was preaching the need of a 'socialist party on practical lines with a definite policy, aims and proposals. . . .' *Practical Socialist*, Oct. 1886.

34. On the difficulties encountered by the provincial socialists see the article by H. Russell Smart in the *I.L.P. News*, Sept. 1898.

35. Quoted in Eric Hobsbawm, editor, *Labour's Turning Point: 1880-1900*, London, 1948, 121-122.

36. Quoted in Hamilton, *Beatrice and Sidney Webb*, 32.

37. See lecture of H. W. Massingham to the Society, Feb. 5, 1892, reported in *Fabian News*, Mar., 1892.

38. Shaw, *Early History*, 20.

39. *Fabian Tract 40*, 'The Fabian Election Manifesto,' London, 1892. At the

41

conference with Fabians from the provinces in Feb. 1892 proposals to deny membership in the Fabian Society to officials of the older parties has been voted down, while Webb argued that, even if a Labour party were formed, the Fabians would remain independent of it, *Fabian News*, March, 1892.

40. Shaw annotation to the manuscript of Pease's *History*.

41. *Fortnightly Review*, new series, vol. 54, Nov. 1893, 569–589; *Fabian Tract 49*, 'A Plan of Campaign for Labour,' Jan. 1894.

42. According to the *Fabian News*, Aug. 1901.

43. Beatrice Webb, *Our Partnership*, ed. by Margaret Cole and Barbara Drake, London, 1948, 110.

44. One member of the Fabian Executive declared of the manifesto 'that the flabbiness, apathy and disorganization of the trade union world as a whole, made the threat held out to the Liberal party a pure piece of bluff.' H. H. Sparling in the *Workman's Times*, Nov. 25, 1893, quoted in William K. Lamb, *British Labour and Parliament: 1865-1893*, doctoral thesis, British Library of Political Science, 1933.

45. Letters of D. G. Ritchie to Edward Pease, Oct. 31 and Nov. 1, 1893.

46. *Annual Report of the Fabian Society*, 1894, 13.

47. For an expression of this view see Edward Pease, *History of the Fabian Society*, London, 1925, 117.

48. *ibid.*, 117.

49. Shaw, 'Early Days,' Chapter I in M. Cole, *The Webbs and Their Work*, 8.

50. Friedrich Engels was of the opinion in early 1893 that five-sixths of the Fabian branches were antagonistic to the London Executive and predicted— rightly as it turned out—that they would drop away at a critical moment. Engels to F. A. Sorge, Jan. 18, 1893, quoted in *Socialist Review*, Aug. 1918, 31.

51. Pease *History*, 103, and Shaw annotation to the manuscript of Pease's *History*.

52. The *Fabian News* in Mar. 1892, argued that the most successful branches were those closest to London in type of membership. Sidney Webb urged a Fabian provincial lecturer to do all he could to get middle class elements into the Fabian branch at Newcastle. Webb to W. H. Utley, Aug. 16, 1892.

53. W. H. Utley in *Fabian News*, Nov. 1892.

54. See criticism of the Manchester Fabian branch for its having excluded from membership affiliates of the established parties, in *Fabian News*, Dec. 1892.

55. Particularly the most important surviving branch in Liverpool. See *Fabian News*, Aug. 1896.

56. Webb to Pease, Dec. 23, 1892.

57. Robert Blatchford, in defending the Fabians against the charge of indifference to a Labour Party, related how some years previous to the Bradford meeting, de Mattos had come to Manchester and had urged him to organize a national Labour party. *Clarion*, Jan. 21, 1893.

58. Shaw has written that when the conference was in danger of wasting time on an unnecessarily detailed programme he met Keir Hardie on the stairs one afternoon and 'settled that programme in just two minutes in such a style that it passed without a word to the entire satisfaction of every delegate present.' Shaw in the *Clarion*, Feb. 23, 1906. Possibly Shaw made the suggestion that there be no list of purely political demands. See page 52. What he was clearly responsible for was the insertion of a fiscal clause demanding 'The

taxation to extinction of unearned incomes.' *I.L.P. Inaugural Conference Report*, 1893, 12. He spoke also against the so-called Manchester Fourth Clause, a proposal of the Manchester I.L.P. group to require that members abstain from voting in elections for any candidate of the older parties. The proposal was defeated. Shaw later asserted that it constituted an attempt by 'A section of the I.L.P. . . . to exclude the Fabian Society and its Permeation Policy' and 'to keep out Radicals and Tory Democrats.' Shaw Memorandum to the Fabian Executive, Dec. 13, 1911, as contained in the Society's Minutes.
59. *I.L.P. Inaugural Report*, 1 and 2.
60. Shaw to Pease, Jan. 11, 1893.
61. Entry in Beatrice Webb's diary, Mar. 2, 1893.
62. Such works were Edward Bellamy's *Looking Backward*, 1887; Laurence Gronlund's *Cooperative Commonwealth*, 1884; Robert Blatchford's *Merrie England*, 1894 and the writings of Thoreau and Walt Whitman.
63. *The Fabian Annual Report* in April 1893, welcomed the I.L.P. as 'a promising attempt to form an Independent Labour Party with an essentially socialist basis.'
64. The semi-official journal of the I.L.P., the *Labour Leader* on Aug. 18, 1894, dealt with the Fabian Society in this way: 'The Fabian Society is composed of very dear and charming ladies and gentlemen of good education and undoubted social standing. They speak with an aristocratic drawl, and are very backward in coming forward. They call this permeation. But none the less we confess a sneaking liking for the dear creatures. They are very conscientious in their work and everything they do is well done. They have done a vast amount of economic and social research, and we like their publications.'
65. Keir Hardie in addressing the Society in 1895 predicted that in the coming election the Liberal party would be 'wiped out' and that 'if it were not, the responsibility would be on the Fabian Society of London.' *Fabian News*, Feb. 1895.
66. *Our Partnership*, 117, 126-7.
67. The foreword by MacDonald to Arthur Compton-Rickett, *I Look Back: Memoirs of Fifty Years*, London, 1933.
68. Letters of MacDonald to Pease, Mar. 6 and April 8, 1896. Fabian correspondence.
69. Minutes of the Fabian Executive, June 5, 1896.
70. *Our Partnership*, 132.
71. *Fabian Tract 49*, 23.
72. *Fabian Tract 70*, 'A Report on Fabian Policy', July 1896; *Labour Annual*, 1897, 231; Pease, *History*, 127.
73. By Sept. 1898, H. Russell Smart could write in the *I.L.P. News*, 'The advanced London Progressive is a good fellow; in fact he differs in no important respect from our own I.L.P. members on provincial bodies.'
74. Webb welcomed the setting up of this bureau as a means of increasing Fabian influence over members of the I.L.P. Webb to Pease, April 7, 1899.
75. In 1899 Keir Hardie was writing the Fabian Secretary, 'In the best interests of Socialism we should seek every opportunity of fraternizing with the trade unions and breaking down the barriers between us and them.' Hardie to Pease, Jan. 19, 1899.
76. Snowden to W. Stephen Sanders, Jan. 13, 1912. Fabian Correspondence.

# CHAPTER III

# The Independent Labour Party (the I.L.P.)

•••••••••••••••••••••••••••••••••••••••••••••••••••••••••••••••••••••••••••••••••••••••••••••••

As the core of inspiration and leadership in the Labour Representation Committee, the I.L.P. proved remarkably flexible, displaying a readiness to compromise and a sense of the possible quite in contrast with its earlier unyielding attitude. Basing its own national hopes on the alliance with the trade unions, it was willing to play down its socialist proselytizing and to sacrifice clarity of programme and doctrine for breadth of appeal. Once the crippling of the strike weapon by the employers and the courts had convinced even the most lethargic trade unions of the need for increased Labour representation and had led them to join the Committee, the I.L.P.'s keen sense of how far the trade unionists would go contributed appreciably to making the socialist-trade union alliance a continuing success. At the same time the I.L.P.'s insistence that the principle of independence be respected or at least not openly flouted helped keep the L.R.C. from reverting to the 'Lib-Labism' that had characterized the movement in the past.

On the eve of the founding of the I.L.P. in 1893 the new movement on its industrial side was losing momentum. Business recession with resulting unemployment was sapping both the strength and the spirit of the new unions, and they turned increasingly to friendly benefits and other security measures once scorned as curbs to militant action. In the political sphere, however, the movement showed no signs of subsiding. Many local organizations for independent Labour representation were increasingly active—primarily in London, Scotland, Lancashire, Yorkshire and on the North-east coast—and frequent proposals had been made for welding these local efforts into a single effort national and sustained. The nineties were in many ways unfavourable to the formation of a new party with advanced views. This was not a decade of great issues or great changes; political life was relatively calm, the electorate apathetic, and toward the end of the decade a mounting imperialistic tide swept socialism into the background. Yet in some respects the early nineties seemed a not inauspicious time for launching a new organization. No longer did agitation among the working classes strike terror in the hearts of the privileged, and 'Socialism of a very mild type was beginning to be indulged in even by duchesses.'[1] Thanks partly to the new unionism, the vast body of wage earners were becoming increasingly familiar with collectivist ideas. The main appeal of the new party, moreover, was to the young, to men and women who had been to school and had read Carlyle, Ruskin and Morris.[2] A great boost had been given to scattered Labour associations by the return to Parliament of three independent Labour candidates in the Election of 1892. Municipal successes also seemed a portent; in the ten years prior to 1892 the number of Labour representatives on public bodies had risen from twelve to two hundred.[3] The Liberal party, from whose apostate members the new party would gain most of its supporters, was again in office, but it maintained the allegiance of many wage earners only by drawing heavily on the party's main asset: the veneration felt for the ageing Gladstone. The trade unions, if Trades Union Congress resolutions were of any significance, were moving leftwards under socialist prodding and were ready to accept a more active political role. Encouraging as were the signs of a trade union awakening, however, the pace was too slow to satisfy the more ardent proponents of independence. At the Glasgow Trades Union Congress of 1892, Keir Hardie convened a private meeting of trade union delegates and representatives of various independent Labour associations. It arranged for calling a conference to form a new party.[4]

James Keir Hardie, who was to be the dominant figure in the I.L.P., had been born to gruelling poverty in Lanarkshire in Scotland in 1856. He entered the mines at ten. Self-taught, except for reading learned from his mother, and brought up an atheist, he was converted to Christianity in 1878, after which he preached for the Temperance League and the Evangelical Union.

He first gained notice in Scotland through his efforts to re-organize the Lanarkshire and Ayrshire miners, earning part of his living at the time by writing for Scottish newspapers. In 1887 he started his own monthly, *The Miner*, which he later named the *Labour Leader*. This paper failed in the early nineties, but Hardie was able to revive it, turning it into a weekly in 1894 as the semi-official organ of the I.L.P. When he first appeared in the Trades Union Congress where he sat from 1887 to 1895, at first as representative of the Ayrshire miners, Hardie regarded himself as a Liberal though he was ready to deride the most prominent of the Liberal-Labour M.P.s, Henry Broadhurst, then Secretary of the Parliamentary Committee. In 1888 he ran for Parliament as a miners' candidate in a by-election in the Scottish constituency of Mid-Lanark. Refused Liberal support, Hardie went forward as an Independent. His defeat and the Liberal victory in the resulting three-cornered contest dramatically demonstrated, perhaps more than any election up to that time, the obstacles in the way of Labour candidates within the Liberal fold, and Hardie registered his resentment by helping to form a Scottish Labour Party. Supported by a few socialists and advanced Liberals and by members of the Scottish Land Restoration League, the party remained weak and ineffectual. Though its programme included nationalization of the railways and the establishment of a national banking system, Hardie as yet had worked out no clear set of objectives.[5]

In attracting a following in the North, Hardie never owed so much to systematic socialist doctrine as to the moral, evangelical nature of his appeal. The larger socialist movement of the nineties—outside London at any rate—was a religion, its meetings frequently revivalist, reflecting the needs of a people whose lives had centred around the Nonconformist chapel. The Marxists obviously could not satisfy their need. A Webb or a Shaw would have found such emotional exhortation distasteful. John Burns, though the most prominent Labour figure of the period and one of the greatest of mob orators, was not a religious man, at least in the narrower sense, and could never have said, as did Hardie, that the teachings of Christ were the source of his inspiration.

## The Independent Labour Party (the I.L.P.)

Hardie knew his Bible well. Carlyle, Ruskin, John Stuart Mill and, above all, Robert Burns also shaped his philosophy. He never read Marx and deprecated the class war creed of Hyndman. 'Socialism makes war upon a system, not upon a class,' he wrote.[6] His command of economics was meagre at best, and his socialism was not analytic. His power lay rather in conveying to others his own terrible impatience with suffering and with the inertia of the older parties. To many he was a charlatan and a demagogue, but not to the downtrodden elements of the miserable factory towns to whom he brought hope of a better life. The very vagueness of his appeal added to his effectiveness as he worked to detach from the Liberal fold its strongly Nonconformist labour section. This was especially true where men were turning from the chapel, as in Yorkshire, in search of a substitute faith.

Hardie had a bitter tongue and a stubborn self-assertiveness that did little to assuage disunity in a movement noted for its sectarian bias. With Burns at one time or another he exchanged scurrilous insult. Robert Blatchford, the famed editor of the *Clarion*, disliked Hardie perhaps more than any man he ever knew, thought him narrow and puritanical and a detriment to the socialist cause.[7] Ramsay MacDonald in 1906 privately regarded him as an impossible leader in Parliament.[8] But in the creation of the Labour party none of his detractors was as steadfast in the faith as he, none had such abiding hope in the working classes finding their way. The singleness of purpose which Hardie as much as anyone stamped on the I.L.P. had its drawbacks from the socialist point of view. Like MacDonald he seemed at times obsessed with the idea of building an effective political force, not at all the same thing as making socialists, as Blatchford clearly saw. The primary requisite was a mass following organized to get out the vote and, as Hardie admitted, the march of such an army had to be regulated to suit the pace of the slowest.[9]

The conference which founded the Independent Labour Party met in the Labour Institute in Bradford on January 13th and 14th, 1893. Some 120 delegates attended. They represented eighty local I.L.P.s, nine branches of the Scottish Labour Party,

47

four small trade unions, four trades councils including the Labour Representation League of the London Trades Council, six S.D.F. branches, mostly from Lancashire, the London Fabian Society and eleven Fabian branches, two socialist societies, and an Eight Hours League. The majority of the delegates came from the North, mainly from the textile areas. Yorkshire sent 48 delegates and Lancashire and Cheshire 32, these together making up over half the total number.[10] By April 1895 when the third annual conference of the party was convened, this geographical distribution had altered little. In a claimed total of 305 I.L.P. branches, 102 were in Yorkshire, 73 in Lancashire and Cheshire, 41 in Scotland, 29 in London, 23 in the Midlands, 18 in the North-East, eight in Kent, four in the Eastern Counties, three in Ireland, three in the South of England and one in Wales.[11] Three years later the I.L.P. branch with the highest membership was Halifax with 350 paying members. Next came West Bradford, then East Bradford.[12] All were in Yorkshire.

Except for a few isolated centres the party remained feeble in the South. Its weakness in Wales stemmed partly from isolation and differences in language, partly from pressing local questions which Welshmen felt could best be solved through the Liberal party. Still, the party made a steady if slow progress in South Wales, raising funds for the striking South Wales miners in 1898, forming many I.L.P. branches and paving the way for Hardie's return to Parliament in 1900 from the Welsh constituency of Merthyr Tydfil.[13] One of the most discouraging areas was London. If socialist opinion grew there in the nineties it was in a Fabian or Progressive direction, the I.L.P. and the S.D.F. invariably doing poorly in L.C.C. elections. Part of the difficulty lay in a lack of cohesion among London working men as contrasted with those of Manchester, Bradford and other provincial centres. The complexity of London local government was also a factor, according to Tom Mann.[14] Still another obstacle was the political activity of London Liberal and Radical Working Men's Clubs to which the Fabians devoted much attention. Hardie and others in the I.L.P. hierarchy tended to regard the Metropolis with suspicion and to bemoan its corrupting influences and the lack of moral fibre in its labouring classes. An active member of both the Fabian Society and the I.L.P., James Ramsay MacDonald, partly expressed this feeling when he wrote to Edward Pease, the Fabian Secretary, in 1896, 'You are altogether out of touch with anything but London Socialism, which, I can assure you, is about as sickly now compared with provincial robustness as London life itself is.'[15]

The numerical strength of the I.L.P. in the nineties is difficult to determine. In all probability the central office never knew the total membership except by shrewd guesswork, and in making computations it was hindered by the lethargy of branches in providing it with information. In 1899 only 75 branches sent in annual statements, 200 others failing to do so. The following year only a fourth of the branches complied.[16] In the Fall of 1894 Hardie claimed between 40,000 and 50,000 members. In April 1895, he claimed 35,000 *paying* members. This latter figure appears wildly inaccurate. Only a few of these could have been paying dues at the central office, for the total affiliation fees as 3d. per member for the year ending in March 1895, amounted to little over £153.[17] In the following year even the I.L.P. Executive itself claimed a *total* membership of only 20,000.[18] By 1898 the party had temporarily ceased to grow. In 1899 there was a fall in the paying membership to 5,277, over 700 less than in the previous year,[19] and the I.L.P. was in desperate financial straits. Though no accurate figure of I.L.P. membership is possible, on the basis of affiliation fees, there were probably at the turn of the century about 7,000 paying members. The total membership was in the neighbourhood of 20,000. It is not unlikely that some of the branches not sending delegates or paying fees had little more than a paper existence merely serving to provide a façade of power for the purpose of platform propaganda.

The I.L.P. drew almost all of its recruits from the working classes. Many of its most effective propagandists were union officials and included J. R. Clynes, Ben Turner, James Sexton, Robert Smillie, Pete Curran, Tom Mann, G. N. Barnes and Ben Tillett, most of whom were in time to enter Parliament. For its leadership, however, for its intellectual outlook, and for its definition of purpose and policy, the new party owed as much, if not more, to professional men and middle-class adherents. Had it been possible for the I.L.P. to gain the official support of the trade unions at the outset, the influence of these men in the inner circles of the party would undoubtedly have been weakened. As it was, the I.L.P., though ever anxious to achieve an alliance with the unions, stubbornly resisted the suggestion that Labour candidatures be limited to men actually engaged in a trade. The I.L.P. frowned upon this 'hoary-handed son of toil' idea of a Labour party. Thus, paradoxically, the I.L.P. socialist despite his more vociferous insistence on a strict independence was quite often far less class-conscious in his attitude toward parliamentary representation than his non-Socialist trade union ally. The majority of I.L.P. candidates were indeed active trade unionists. But all classes were represented. R. M. Pankhurst was a lawyer; John Lister, a landlord and a member of one of Yorkshire's oldest families; Fred Brocklehurst, a university man who had studied for the ministry; Russell Smart, a professional actor and commercial traveller; Edward Marsden, a manufacturer; A. E. Fletcher and James Ramsay MacDonald, journalists. Philip Snowden was a civil servant and like many other I.L.P. parliamentary candidates—F. W. Jowett for example—an outstanding administrator in municipal government. Dr. Stanton Coit, who came into the movement later than these others, was an American, a graduate of Amherst and Columbia, who in England became a leader in various ethical societies.[20] The emancipated female was also a familiar figure in the I.L.P. Sometimes women formed their own branches. Though they laboured under many disabilities, they were able, after the passage of Fowler's Local Government Act of 1894, to be elected to Parish Councils.

At the initial I.L.P. conference, because of the disparity of opinions, with many organizations not at all clearly socialist, federation rather than amalgamation had been decided upon. Still neither the S.D.F. nor the Fabian Society would federate. Their branches that chose to do so broke with the parent organizations. Moreover, Hardie's dearest wish, that the trade unions be brought into the movement, showed no signs of imminent realization. By the time the second conference met in 1894, therefore, only local I.L.P.s were being summoned, and the party became not so much a federation as a united body with local branches. The I.L.P. executive known as the National Administrative Council, or N.A.C., consisted of six members elected at the annual conference plus a President, a Secretary and a Treasurer who were members of the Council by virtue of their offices. A few I.L.P. branches were so opposed to the policy of the N.A.C. that they broke from the party, some joining the S.D.F. The vast majority, however, were willing and eager to follow N.A.C. advice, for the movement, to a remarkable degree, reflected the character and viewpoint of its leaders. The members of the N.A.C. could be re-elected and usually were, men like Hardie, Glasier, MacDonald and Snowden being returned year after year. Criticism was early raised against this condition as unhealthy and undemocratic and especially at Hardie and his office of President. At the 1896 conference the title was changed to Chairman, even the retention of this office being favoured by only little over half the delegates.[21] The unquestioned predominance of Hardie and his ownership of the party's semi-official organ, the *Labour Leader*, continued to encourage arguments against too great a dependence on leaders, especially from Robert Blatchford in the *Clarion*. By the end of the nineties the question of the chairmanship was again to the fore, and in 1900 Hardie relinquished the office to Glasier.

The stated object of the party was clearly socialist, 'the collective ownership and control of the means of production, distribution and exchange,' in 1895 re-worded to read, 'An Industrial Commonwealth founded upon the Socialization of Land and Capital.' Yet with that peculiar blend of idealism and prudence that characterized the I.L.P. all efforts to include the word 'Socialist' in the party's title met with failure. The word 'Labour' identified it with working-class aspirations and traditions; the word 'Socialist' might retard the party's development. Ben Tillett was even more outspoken. 'He wished,' he said, 'to capture the trade unionists of this country . . . he would sooner have the solid, progressive, matter-of-fact, fighting

51

Trades' Unionism of England than all the hare-brained chatterers and magpies of Continental revolutionists. . . . If the Labour Party was to be called a Socialist Labour Party he would repudiate it.'[22] His point made and the title he favoured adopted, Tillett saw no incongruity in later accepting the party's clear statement of socialist objective. Blatchford was not satisfied with this outcome. 'What is the chief danger of the Independent Labour Party?' he wrote early in 1894. 'It is the danger of being bought, or captured, or cajoled by Liberalism. In every town the Liberal agents hang upon the flanks of the I.L.P. and try to capture stragglers. The outside masses, the great body of the workers who have not yet joined the I.L.P., can see no reason for forsaking what they call The Party of Progress. . . . But once let the I.L.P. declare itself the Socialist Party and all this danger and confusion will cease.'[23] Year after year motions to change the name of the party failed of acceptance. For sentimental as well as for tactical reasons the majority were satisfied with the name as it stood.

The programme of the I.L.P., as laid down in 1893, underwent few important alterations. In 1895 a rather detailed list of agricultural reforms was added, but this had no appreciable effect in winning rural support and was abandoned when the programme underwent some weeding-out and condensation two years later. In most respects the programme differed little from that of the S.D.F. One marked difference was its neglect of political aims. At the inaugural conference a committee had drawn up a list of such aims including adult suffrage, the second ballot, payment of members, and the abolition of the monarchy and the House of Lords. When the Committee presented its suggestions, however, it was moved and adopted that these items be deleted and replaced by a general statement to the effect that the Independent Labour Party was 'in favour of every proposal for extending electoral rights and democratising the system of Government.'[24] Hardie was ever wary of purely political issues, impressed rather with emphasizing social and economic questions.[25] All the purely political demands were already embodied in Radical programmes, and giving them prominence would only court suggestions for a Labour-Radical

## The Independent Labour Party (the I.L.P.)

alliance. At its advent the I.L.P. was too weak and too little known to risk submergence in a larger group; only a strict separatism could make its identity and its special purpose unmistakably clear.

The social and economic demands of the I.L.P. included a maximum eight-hour day, a sixpence per hour minimum, various powers for local bodies to acquire land and capital to undertake projects to insure employment, state pensions for those over fifty and free education to the university level. Also stressed were raising the age of child labour, municipalization and public control of the drink traffic, abolition of indirect taxation, and the taxation to extinction of unearned incomes. The party never made a major issue of any of these points, however. In its propaganda it was always stronger in preaching a general gospel than in elaborating specific proposals, except, perhaps, in its insistence on provision of work for the unemployed. In the later nineties under the influence of men like Glasier and MacDonald, there was an impatience with 'programme' schemes and a greater willingness to accept piecemeal reform as inevitable. 'The Social Revolution is accomplished by patient toil,' said the *I.L.P. News* in October 1897, an attitude encouraged by the experience of members of the party on numerous public bodies where they witnessed socialism without fanfare making sustained and fruitful progress. Municipalities were acquiring land, running railways, reducing the hours of their employees and curbing the privileges of landlords. Doctrinaires might dismiss this as 'gas and water' socialism or as merely social reformism, but many members of the I.L.P. were impressed.

Though financial assistance sometimes came to the party from friendly outsiders like George Cadbury, the Quaker Liberal and chocolate manufacturer, and Joseph Fels, the American Jewish philanthropist, such contributions were infrequent and moderate, and the I.L.P. usually led a hand to mouth existence surviving electoral setbacks and stunted growth, not through such windfalls, but through the fanatical devotion and self-sacrifice of many of its members. Probably about a quarter of the members were active workers for the cause, and considering the extent of I.L.P. proselytizing their efforts must have been tremendous. Often giving the party all their spare time from their regular work and speaking by day and night, these were dedicated men and women seeking converts to a new faith. Many of the I.L.P. propagandists had, in fact, gained their platform experience as lay preachers of one of the dissenting religions. Despite setbacks, their efforts had a perennial pre-election zest. Long journeys and uncertain receptions must have exacted a fearful toll in physical strain, and it is not surprising that the I.L.P. was an organization of young members, chiefly between the ages of twenty-two and thirty-three, according to Mann.[26] Hardie, after his defeat in 1895, spent most of his time in propaganda work writing his articles for the *Labour Leader* on trains and in the homes of party supporters. In 1896 a new prophet arose in the West Riding of Yorkshire in the person of Philip Snowden whose popularity and platform skill soon brought him to the forefront. In many places the Fabian Society, the S.D.F. and the I.L.P. co-operated and shared platforms to cut down expenses, and in a few cities, the I.L.P.-S.D.F. understanding was very close. The Clarion groups were usually ready to assist and to help in distributing literature. Millions of I.L.P. pamphlets and broadsides were distributed or sold for a penny.

The politico-religious aspect of the early propaganda found its most extreme expression in the Labour Churches. The first such church was founded in Manchester in October 1891 by John Trevor, a Unitarian minister, who was convinced that 'the real God was more at work in the Labour movement than in the Historic Churches,'[27] 'working through it, as once He had worked through Christianity, for the further salvation of the world.'[28] The monthly paper of the new body, the *Labour Prophet*, appeared in January 1892. In 1898 it was replaced by the *Labour Church Record* published quarterly. Some twenty towns had Labour Churches by 1895; by 1907 there were over thirty. Untheological in its teachings, Nonconformist in its spiritual ancestry, the Labour Church preached a creed that was vague and materialistic. The after-life was not stressed, emphasis being placed rather on 'enjoying a foretaste of the Fatherhood of God and the Brotherhood of Man here and now.'[29]

## The Independent Labour Party (the I.L.P.)

'The Labour Church,' Trevor wrote, 'shifts the religious question from the historic value of the Fourth Gospel to the rights and wrongs of the Miners' Lock-out, from the question whether the people can be "brought to Jesus" to the question whether they can be brought to Socialism, and to understand all that Socialism means to them and demands of them.'[30]

In some cities, such as Birmingham, the Labour Church became the centre of the socialist movement. Often it published a local paper, the church in Bradford being responsible for the *Bradford Labour Echo* which for a time was among the best edited and most flourishing of local labour weeklies. Included in the Sunday services were readings from Ruskin, Carlyle and Walt Whitman and Labour hymns sung to old chapel tunes. Trevor himself wrote a hymnal. Among others were the *Chants of Labour* of Edward Carpenter and the *Socialist Songs* of J. Bruce Glasier. A frequent speaker was the Rev. Stewart Headlam, a Fabian and founder of the Guild of St. Matthew.[31] The Rev. Philip Wicksteed, a noted exponent of the Jevonian theory of value, gave active support. Blatchford of the *Clarion* was a favourite as was his brother Mont, organizer of Clarion vocal unions which sang at Labour Church gatherings. Ben Tillett, Tom Mann, Hardie, Glasier, and other members of the I.L.P. supported the Labour Church and spoke from its platform. Undoubtedly one of its greatest contributions to the movement was affording a place of assembly for Sunday propaganda. 'With a prayer and a couple of hymns thrown in you get a Socialist lecture to thousands whom otherwise you'd never see,' one observer was heard to say.[32] The Executive of the I.L.P. urged its branches wherever it was practicable to run Sunday meetings on Labour Church lines,[33] and the church thrived where the I.L.P. was strongest—in Yorkshire—its three most active centres there in 1896 being Bradford, Leeds, and Halifax. In many places it tended to become a mere auxiliary of the I.L.P. increasingly engrossed in the organization of the movement.

As the I.L.P. entered a more practical, administrative phase in its development and had less need for the religious unction which the church dispensed, the Labour Church lost much of its spark. The average Labour M.P. or trade union executive was a member of one of the older churches. Very often he was a local lay preacher, indifferent to any new or exotic creed. By 1912 the principles of the Labour Church had so altered that they contained no reference to God at all,[34] but long before this it was a dying institution merely serving to recall the high-pitched fervour of the socialism of the nineties.

The I.L.P. and later the nascent Labour Party complained of the lack of an adequate voice in the public press. There were friendly journals in the nineties, however, aside from the regular Labour and socialist publications. Hardie thought that two London Sunday papers, the *Weekly Times and Echo* and the *Weekly Dispatch*, took such a kind attitude toward the I.L.P. that they could be virtually regarded as party organs.[35] The *Daily Chronicle* was another London paper alive to labour and socialist questions, and its editor until 1897 was A. E. Fletcher who was close to I.L.P. doings and even ran as an I.L.P. candidate. *Reynolds's Newspaper*, though radical rather than socialist and critical of I.L.P. electoral tactics, reported I.L.P. activities at some length. Of socialist papers the *Clarion* and the *Labour Leader* were at the top after 1894, with the *Leader* possessing neither the circulation nor the literary merit of Blatchford's weekly. Of local I.L.P. organs one of the most effective was the *Bradford Labour Echo*. There were numerous other small sheets of varying merit including that of the Keighley Labour Union, which Snowden edited for a time. In April 1897, the monthly report of the I.L.P. gave way to an eight-page monthly called the *I.L.P. News* which sold for a penny. For years it was printed at a deficit, and requests for its discontinuance were frequent. Bruce Glasier, who served as its editor, was its staunchest defender.

Of all these newspapers, none was more influential in winning converts to socialism than the *Clarion*. Its editor, Robert Blatchford, had been born in 1851 of an English father and an Italian mother who earned their meagre living from the stage. Apprenticed to a brush factory in Halifax, Blatchford ran away to enlist in the Dublin Fusiliers. On his release in 1877 after six years service, he began work as a factory clerk and timekeeper in Northwich. He married in 1880 and shortly afterward turned to writing. In 1885 he obtained a position with *Bell's Life* in London. Later he wrote for the Manchester *Sunday Chronicle* under the pen name 'Nunquam.' Having read a pamphlet of Hyndman and Morris and long having brooded over the horrors of the Manchester slums, in 1889 he announced himself a socialist. When work with the *Chronicle* did not give him adequate freedom for his socialist writings he quit his lucrative post, and after a short stint on Joseph Burgess's *Workman's Times*, founded the *Clarion* in Manchester in December 1891. Associated with him in the venture were his old associates in journalism, E. R. Fay, Alexander M. Thompson and Blatchford's brother, Mont. All were socialists.[36]

The *Clarion* was a delightful hodge-podge of literary, dramatic, political and other writings written with intimate candour, bluntness and gaiety. Its socialism was humanitarian, ethical and warm-hearted. The movement was brightened and humanized by the *Clarion*. It appealed to all camps, S.D.F. and I.L.P. alike. It also reached out to people to whom Hyndman's class war doctrines, the Fabian emphasis on bureaucratic efficiency, and the Nonconformism of the I.L.P. had little appeal. Its following especially included young artisans of Lancashire and the West Riding, but it was not strictly working class by any means. Blatchford thought that only half of its readers were working class and the rest clerks, writers, business men, teachers and professional men.[37]

Blatchford was a brilliant writer of a simple, lucid prose. He urged a common-sense socialism and made no use of Marxian terminology—he had not read Marx and as a socialist owed most to Morris.[38] At the root of his plea was a deep love of England and a bullish patriotism that later led him to support the South African War and to warn of the menace of imperial Germany. With *Merrie England*, addressed to John Smith, practical working man, Blatchford became for a time the most effective propagandist of socialism that England had produced. Hundreds of thousands of penny copies were sold in England alone.

Around the *Clarion* grew up a variety of organizations—

Mont Blatchford's Glee Clubs in the North, Clarion Cinderella Clubs to feed thousands of hungry children, Cycling Clubs and Clarion Scouts—all helping to spread the word and to sell *Merrie England*. Clarion Vans were organized and reached remote sections of Durham, Northumberland, Yorkshire and other counties with Bruce Glasier and Tom Mann among the speakers and with Vanners distributing thousands of Fabian, Clarion, I.L.P. and Land Nationalization leaflets. In the wake of the vans I.L.P. branches were formed and I.L.P., Fabian, and S.D.F. supporters drawn closer together. Later Clarion followers were gathered into one great Clarion Fellowship, its sections loosely knit and locally autonomous.

After withdrawing as the candidate in an East Bradford by-election in 1892 and failing to get the I.L.P. to embody the word 'socialist' in its title, Blatchford remained averse to any personal involvement in politics and not wholly in sympathy with Hardie's singleness of aim in building a political party. The I.L.P.'s determination to co-operate with the trade unions for political ends and in time to convert them did not greatly impress Blatchford, for he felt that the average trade unionist was slow, uninformed and ungrateful material interested primarily in getting more pay for less work and that, in any case, a Labour party and a socialist party were not the same thing.[39] Blatchford wanted to make real socialists first, not being willing, as was Hardie, to accept potential socialists as they were, rather than as he wished them to be. He was patient enough to forgo party-making, but not patient enough, as it turned out, to persist in the slow, seemingly hopeless task of converting the cloddish British worker.

The fault of thinking that simplicity of statement was synonymous with honesty was strong in Blatchford, and himself free from the sweat and compromise of creating an effective party, he was apt to concern himself solely with proposals while ignoring the possibilities of their realization. Thus he called on the S.D.F. and the I.L.P. to unite, without fully appreciating that the origins of the I.L.P. lay in part in a lively distrust of S.D.F. methods.[40] He resented the power of officials in the I.L.P. and called for a democratic movement without leaders, ignoring the fact that he too, idolized by thousands, enjoyed the advantages of a leader.[41] The *Clarion* squabbles with the *Labour Leader* grew more acrimonious. Operating on a more Olympian level than Hardie and his colleagues, Blatchford was nevertheless more impatient when his hopes and vision and his lucid exposition did not convince the average Englishman. He grew weary of waiting for John Smith to see the light as he saw it. His support of the South African War, his supposed atheism in works like *God and My Neighbour* lost him a considerable following, and the reaction to his *Britain for the British* in 1902 was only a weak echo of the apothesis he had achieved with *Merrie England.*

## NOTES

1. Canon James Adderley, *In Slums and Society: Reminiscences of Old Friends*, London, 1916, 170.
2. '... it is not boasting to claim that the growth of the Labour party has been owing to the rise within Labour organizations of an intellectual class of workmen who were influenced a good generation later than the intellectual classes were by the literary and spiritual movements of the Mid-Victorian time embodied in the works of Carlyle and Morris.' James Ramsay Mac-Donald, *A Policy for the Labour Party*, London, 1920, 47-8.
3. A. W. Humphrey, *A History of Labour Representation*, London, 1912, 97.
4. Cole, *Working Class Politics*, 137.
5. Godfrey Elton, *England Arise!* London, 1931, 182; G. D. H. Cole, *Keir Hardie*, Fabian Biographical Series, No. 12, London, 1941. William Stewart, *Keir Hardie*, London, 1921, 37-47.
6. Hamilton Fyfe, *Keir Hardie*, London, 1935, 70.
7. This is stressed in Laurie Thompson, *Portrait of an Englishman: A Life of Robert Blatchford*, London, 1951.
8. MacDonald to J. Bruce Glasier, July 21, 1906. Glasier correspondence. Courtesy of Mr. Francis Johnson.
9. Hardie in the *Labour Leader*, Dec. 21, 1902.
10. A list of the delegates and the organization they represented is given on the cover of the *Inaugural Conference Report*.
11. *I.L.P. Annual Report*, 1896, 10.
12. *ibid.*, 1898, 1-3.
13. Stewart, 143; *Labour Annual*, 1899, 71; *I.L.P. Ann. Rpt.*, 1899, 14-15
14. Mann in the *Clarion*, Nov. 17, 1894.
15. MacDonald to Pease, April 3, 1896.
16. *I.L.P. Ann. Rpt.*, 1899, 26; 1900, 15.
17. Hardie in *Labour Leader*, Sept. 15, 1894, *I.L.P. Ann.*, 1895, 5-6.
18. *Report of I.L.P. National Administrative Council*, 1896, 11.
19. *I.L.P. Ann.*, 1899, 2.
20. For sketches of these people see *Labour Annual*, 1895 and after.
21. *I.L.P. Ann.*, 1896, 7-8.

22. *I.L.P. Inaugural Rpt.*, 1893, 3. Edouard Bernstein who spoke to the conference as a representative of the German Social Democratic Party protested against Tillett's remark about continental socialists, *ibid.*, 5, and later in London, at a meeting of the Fabian Executive, Fred Hammill argued for Tillett's expulsion from the Fabian Society for his anti-socialist outburst. Minutes of the Fabian Executive, Jan. 27, 1893.

23. In the *Clarion*, Jan. 27, 1894.

24. *I.L.P. Inaugural Rpt.*, 12.

25. Hardie expresses this viewpoint in a letter to Charles Dilke, May 23, 1894, Dilke Papers, vol. xxviii.

26. Mann in the *Labour Annual*, 1898, 100.

27. Trevor in the *Labour Annual*, 1896, 41.

28. John Trevor, *My Quest for God*, London, 1897, 271.

29. *Labour Prophet*, Feb. 1895.

30. Trevor article in the *Clarion*, Aug. 18, 1894.

31. Fred G. Bettany, *Stewart Headlam*, London, 1926, 82.

32. According to Percy Redfern, *Journey to Understanding*, London, 1946, 71.

33. *Labour Leader*, June 30, 1894.

34. Rev. Gilbert Clive Binyon, *The Christian Socialist Movement in England*, London, 1931, 183; The *Labour Church Record* in April, 1899, stated that 'the Labour Church folk do not bother much about God.' Quoted in Donald O. Wagner, *The Church of England and Social Reform since 1854*, New York, 1930, 266.

35. Hardie in the *Labour Leader*, May 19, 1894.

36. See besides Laurie Thompson, A. Neil Lyons, *Robert Blatchford*, London, 1910.

37. In the *Clarion*, Oct. 12, 1901.

38. Blatchford's emphasis was never on mere material considerations. 'My ideal is frugality of body and opulence of mind.' *Merrie England*, London, 1895 ed., 38.

39. *Clarion*, Sept. 14, 1901; Thompson, *passim*.

40. Like Hyndman, he saw Hardie as the main obstacle to the proposed unity. *Clarion*, Feb. 7, 1902.

41. For Blatchford's list of those who should not lead in the Labour party see *Clarion*, Mar. 14, 1902.

# CHAPTER IV

# Toward the Great Alliance

THROUGHOUT the nineties one of the most interesting features of I.L.P. proceedings is the neglect of larger problems, of programme issues, and the absorption in prolonged and inconclusive discussion of such matters as fusion with other socialist bodies, the attitude to be taken toward non-socialist candidates, the abolition of the chairmanship and the changing of the name of the party. If the I.L.P. had returned even one of its members to Parliament after Hardie's defeat in 1895 it would, in all likelihood, have been far less absorbed in its own inner workings and more concerned with defining its position in regard to specific legislative proposals of the day. As it was, it remained for some time primarily a propagandist society with a platform message 'divided about half and half between a crude advocacy of Socialism and violent abuse of political opponents.'[1] Since at times it contested obviously hopeless parliamentary seats, even its electoral attempts were in part for advertisement and propaganda only.

The most effective publicity for the party until the Election of 1895 was Hardie's presence in the House of Commons. Hardie knew a few tricks of the showman—Engels called him a 'super-cunning Scot'[2]—and he arrived at his first session in 1892 in cloth cap and workman's clothes. Immediately he gained a notoriety that was to follow him for years. Aside from advocacy of the eight-hour day, he gave much of his time in the Commons to demands for various projects to insure work for the unemployed. During the Hull Dock Strike and the strike of the Miners' Federation in 1893 he condemned the government's employment of troops. In 1894 he created a sensation in the House and was angrily denounced for his manner of insisting that formal sympathy be expressed for victims of a Welsh mining disaster.[3] Hardie's speeches both in and outside the House were well worded and well delivered but often rather weak in information. John Burns and others were annoyed by his varied guesses as to the number of unemployed, and many felt that he had muddled this question in Parliament. Nor was his effectiveness as a parliamentarian conceded even by some in profound sympathy with his efforts. When trying to convince George Lansbury that he could work better for socialism outside the S.D.F., an advanced radical and consistent supporter of Labour named J. A. Murray MacDonald attributed the want of vigour of Labour's friends in Parliament not so much to fear of embarrassing the Liberal government as to want of forcible leading. 'I have never known Keir Hardie take a step,' he wrote, 'in which, as to aim, he was not in the right, but he has not always been wise in the course he pursued to effect his purpose—at least it seems to me. And for effective work wisdom as to the practical course is at least as important as general rightness of aim.'[4] One need only read some of Hardies' statements and writings on the unemployment question to be convinced that more attention to the careful preparation and briefing of his case would have made him a more effective champion in obtaining specific legislation. But Hardie's main concern in Parliament in the early nineties was to force public attention on what he considered crying evils, even if it meant flouting the decorum of the House. It should be remembered that he was virtually alone in Parliament in maintaining the principle of a strict independence. Had he been 'practical' and courted Liberal favour, had he been quick to make concessions to achieve specific ends, his effectiveness as the lone advanced guard of a new and independent party would have been undermined. In fulfilling his isolated role it was inescapable that Hardie should be more the propagandist with his eyes on the movement outside than the parliamentary tactician engrossed in blue books and in interminable planning and compromise.

The Parliament which Hardie entered in 1892 had twelve Liberal-Labour men and three independent Labour men, Hardie for South West Ham, John Burns for Battersea and J. Havelock

Wilson, the Seamen's leader, for Middlesbrough. There was still no Labour party, however, although it was often styled as such. It was simply a group, weak in leadership, in cohesion and in programme. Occasionally the Labour members met in formal meetings, at other times they exchanged views in the lobby of the House. In voting they tended to follow the Liberal whip, except, of course, on purely Labour questions. Even on these they were not united, disagreeing as to the limitation of working hours and not even unanimous as to the partial application of this principle in the case of the miners. Not even the independents could achieve a close co-operation. Wilson, once elected, gradually turned towards the 'Lib-Labs,' never having been anti-Liberal except in opposition to the local Liberal association. Also Burns and Hardie were soon at cross-purposes. Cunninghame Graham, the Liberal Radical, who was a friend of both, might have served to balance their conflicting personalities in the House, but he had not been re-elected.[5] Hardie alone seemed anxious to don the garb of the defiant independent.

John Burns, now in his early thirties, was no longer the demagogue of Trafalgar Square, but he still professed himself a socialist and was ready to throw his support behind socialist resolutions in the Trades Union Congress. He had quit the S.D.F., he told a colleague, because 'he felt more good could be done by working on practical lines and by effecting changes gradually than by making leaps which bring as much evil as good.'[6] Profoundly influenced by his experience as a Progressive on the London County Council, to which he had been elected in 1889, he had become decreasingly class conscious. Moreover, in the Great Dock Strike which had made him a national figure he had enjoyed the warm support of all classes, and this must have impressed him forcibly. Engels felt that if Burns had only once led a strike toward which the public was antipathetic his attitude would have changed.[7] As it was, he prided himself on being severely practical and ready to work with the Liberals if they would concede certain demands. To those who warned that the Liberal embrace was fatal, he answered that 'people stand more from their friends than from their enemies.'[8] By 1894 Beatrice Webb thought Burns was suffering from 'severe disillusionment with labour and an equally excessive admiration for the brain working classes.'[9]

Robert Blatchford once wrote to Burns that he considered him 'the most useful and hopeful man in London and the head and front of the great Labour Movement in England.'[10] This estimate Burns undoubtedly shared. A colossal egotist, he would brook no rivals, and where he could not lead he would not, it appeared, play the game. When after the election in 1892 Hardie, without consulting Burns, announced his intention to sit in opposition, the latter took umbrage. He disliked Hardie's unilateral action. He felt that by sitting with the Tories nothing was accomplished except the alienation of the fourteen or fifteen Liberals who were most sympathetic to Labour. His four years on the L.C.C., he said, had convinced him of the futility of manifesto-issuing and party-making.[11] 'We can do much better for the present,' he wrote to Graham, 'by sitting with the Radicals—with whom Hardie has expressed political agreement to a needless extent—and let them give us reason to compel us to sit in opposition if they ignore our social demands, a much stronger position than that assumed by Hardie.'[12]

Despite these feelings Burns finally joined Hardie on the opposition benches. Given Hardie's firm stand, there seemed no other course. Burns' own revolutionary past and his socialist utterances, even more militant than Hardie's, would have made sitting with the 'Lib-Labs' exceedingly difficult. At the beginning of 1893 Burns was willing to consult with Hardie before expressing any opinion on Labour matters brought before the House. Yet he ignored Hardie's call to take the lead in forming a new party,[14] and he did not attend the inaugural conference of the I.L.P. Many urged him to join, Graham pointing out that he, Hardie and Mann together would constitute a great power —but to no avail.[15] Burns' main interests centred in London and the problems of his own constituency, Battersea. The heart of the movement in the nineties was in the North, just as London had been its centre in the later eighties. Graham begged Burns to realize this and to get into Lancashire and Yorkshire,[16] but he paid no heed. In all probability he never understood or appre-

ciated the import of the new developments, and he apparently
long nursed the hope that a strictly trade union Labour party
would gain strength and turn to him as its leader.[17] The movement took a different turn and passed him by. He had little
respect or liking for the I.L.P. and labelled it 'badly led, worse
organized and wrongly inspired.'[18] Hardie in his counter-attacks
in the *Labour Leader* harshly lampooned Burns and so helped
kill any hope of understanding. More and more Burns concentrated on the path that led to the Liberal Treasury Bench.
His hold on a vast body of workers, even outside London, made
him a thorn in the side of the ardent independents and, at the
same time, a main Liberal asset in wooing the working-class
vote.

With Hardie's defeat in 1895 the I.L.P. had no representative
in the House. From 1893 to 1899, in fact, it failed to elect a
single candidate to Parliament, Hardie having been elected
before the I.L.P. was founded. Moreover, in all such contests
the I.L.P. man came in at the bottom of the poll. In by-elections
in the nineties, nine I.L.P. candidates polled 20,981 votes or an
average of 2,331. In the General Election of 1895 twenty-eight
candidates polled 44,594—an average of 1,592. In constituencies
where there was no socialist candidate, I.L.P. voting policy
remained ill-defined. The so-called Manchester Fourth Clause,
originating with the Manchester and Salford I.L.P., formed in
1892, required abstention from voting for non-socialists. Had it
been incorporated into the I.L.P. constitution, as Blatchford
wished, the party would have had a clear-cut policy but only at
the expense of virtually disenfranchising loyal supporters in
hundreds of constituencies and alienating a large segment of
trade union sympathy. Many considered the Fourth Clause a
suicidal proposal, and Hardie thought the movement would
stultify itself by its adoption.[19] According to Blatchford, these
opponents overstressed the parliamentary method and put
too much store in proceeding on the lines followed by Parnell
in bidding for the favour of the established parties. 'Now, in the
first place, I do not attach as much importance to the presence of
Labour members in the House as some of our friends do;' he
wrote in the *Clarion*, 'and in the second place, I do not like the

idea of adopting the tactics of the Home Rule Party. . . . Given a leader as clever as Mr. Parnell, and a willingness to be led, our party might find his methods effective. But I don't see any Parnell in the Labour movement, and I would not follow him nor advise my comrades to follow him could one be found. . . . We want no leaders and should be ill-advised to tolerate any.'[20] The Fourth Clause remained a live issue throughout the nineties, but it was never formally accepted. Instead in by-elections, in the absence of a socialist candidate, party members were to vote as the local branch decided. In General Elections the problem was to be dealt with by an official conference. Prior to the 1895 election such a conference voted almost unanimously in favour of voting only for avowed socialists,[21] and the Fourth Clause, for all practical purposes, was for a time in operation.

An accusation frequently aimed at the I.L.P. was that it was simply bent on splitting the Liberal vote in the Tory interest. Lord Rosebery in May 1894 even spoke of the I.L.P. as a 'blow to be struck at Liberal party' and denied that the I.L.P. could capture a single Tory vote.[22] Such notions stemmed in part from the widely held myth that the Tory working man was an anomaly, though the continued return of Conservative members from industrial centres and especially from textile areas in Lancashire belied this. The majority of I.L.P. candidates in the nineties contested Liberal seats, it is true, but results often revealed that they drew as many Tory as Liberal votes. On occasion an I.L.P. branch would officially support a Liberal Radical candidate. But a local I.L.P. was equally ready to throw its weight behind a Tory when the Liberal aspirant was regarded as an enemy of Labour. With 'Lib-Lab's in general the party had little sympathy. It relentlessly pursued Henry Broadhurst, supporting the Liberal Unionist who defeated him in 1893[23] but failing to defeat him with its own candidate either in 1894 or in the General Election of 1895. Against another 'Lib-Lab' the I.L.P. issued a manifesto denouncing him as 'the nominee of manufacturers and employers,' though an I.L.P. trade unionist, James Sexton, was against opposing trade unionists no matter what their political stamp.[24] Hardie's response in 1897 to the election of a miner's leader, Sam Woods, who was put forward by the Liberals, was a jibe at Woods as 'a hooded falcon guaranteed to return to rest when called upon by his keeper.'[25]

Before the 1895 election, the I.L.P. engaged in five by-elections. Then in the General Election seven of its twenty-eight candidates were in Yorkshire, eight in Lancashire and Cheshire, and seven in Scotland. In all of Northumberland and Durham, where the party had made little progress among the predominantly 'Lib-Lab' miners, there was only one I.L.P. candidate. The total defeat of the party in 1895 was extremely disheartening, especially with Hardie out, and though the total vote was no cause for shame, the independent vote in London and Scotland was embarrassingly low. All the I.L.P. candidates but three were opposed by Liberals.

The Labour group in Parliament after the 1895 election numbered twelve, an equal number of 'Lib-Labs' having been defeated, four by failing of re-election. There were five miners in the House. Three Irish Labour men were returned, including Michael Davitt. To the condemnation that fell upon the I.L.P. from trade unionists and 'Lib-Labs' who blamed it for Labour set-backs in general was added the lashing tongue of Burns. Even in late 1893 he had denounced 'the arrant frauds that, in the name of independent labour and Socialism, were going about the country doing everything to disintegrate Labour and the trade unions,'[26] and in November 1894 he was criticizing the movement in the North as 'impulsive, intolerant and wildly propagandistic.'[27] Attacks on Burns as a Liberal hack in the *Labour Leader* only incensed him further, and he was ready to thwart the party wherever he could. On the eve of the General Election he was warning members of the Amalgamated Society of Engineers not to let Tom Mann and the I.L.P. capture the society as a base of operations.[28] The dismal showing of the I.L.P. in the election only seemed to prove his worst predictions. When someone commented to Burns that a party which could expend over £5,000 on an election could not be considered dead, he retorted that it was the most costly funeral he had known since Napoleon was buried.[29] In a speech to his own supporters in Battersea, he heaped scorn upon Hardie and the I.L.P. 'Parliamentary anarchism always meets with its fate, and unscrupulous demagogy whether in a Tory or a Labour leader is soon found out,' he said. Hardie's unemployment agitation he dismissed as the most 'senseless, sentimental, anti-Socialist and futile movement' Labour had ever witnessed. If the Socialist party showed such little promise it was the Socialists who were at fault. 'So anxious are they to reach the millennium that they sacrifice each other on the way.'[30]

The enmity of some of the more conservative trade unionists toward the I.L.P. reached a new high in 1895. Leading 'Lib-Lab' members of the Congress had been defeated, many of whom had held seats in the outgoing Parliament, including Sam Woods, the Secretary. For this set-back and for the death-knell of the Labour Electoral Association, which had been closely linked to the Liberal Party and could not survive its defeat, the I.L.P. offered a convenient scapegoat. The party's policy of voting only for avowed socialists and its anti-Liberal rantings probably had, in fact, cost Labour a considerable number of Liberal votes. At the Cardiff Congress in September a Cardiff unionist named Jenkins, who presided, delivered a blistering attack on the I.L.P. 'Whatever good intentions the members of it harboured,' he said, 'the outcome of their hopeless electioneering campaign was to undermine some candidates most in sympathy with the demands of the Congress, to cover themselves with the discredit of overwhelming defeat, to convert the name "Labour" candidate into a by-word of reproach and mistrust, and finally to unmistakably demonstrate that the worst enemies of the advancement of labour might be those of their own household.'[31]

Such an attack was as nothing, however, compared to another blow which befell the leftist bloc in the Cardiff Congress. This was the revolutionary revision of the Standing Orders of the Congress, excluding trades councils from representation, requiring that every delegate either be an active worker in his trade or a salaried official of his union, and inaugurating a system of voting, by which, instead of one vote per delegate, each delegate was to have one vote for every thousand members in the union he represented. An I.L.P. and radical element, strong in the trades councils, was thus greatly weakened in the Congress; smaller societies were given less voice, and by the adoption of the 'card vote' the larger unions like the miners and the textile operatives were placed in practically undisputed domination.[32] The order limiting membership to active trade unionists meant that Tom Mann and other leaders of the new movement were henceforth ineligible to attend the Congress. Hardie could not be a delegate, because he had some time previously relinquished all official positions in the Miners' Federation. It also eliminated Burns,[33] who was quite ready to depart, and Broadhurst, who left with reluctance after trying to thwart those responsible.[34]

James Mawdesley, the Tory leader of the Lancashire cotton operatives, and John Burns were the instigators of this coup, and the coal miners and textile workers gave them the necessary support.[35] Burns in his manoeuvre was partly motivated, in all probability, by a desire to get rid of Hardie and to undermine the influence of the I.L.P. He had continually attacked the party. He was a man of colossal ego and strong hatreds, with Hardie one of his chief tormentors, and he had sufficient prestige not to be dependent himself on his Congress connection. Amidst hisses, according to one observer,[36] Burns informed his Cardiff listeners that it was in the interests of Labour that he and Broadhurst had to leave because—as the *T.U.C. Annual* reports it—'through the gate through which they passed every impostor could go.'[37]

Though the I.L.P. was more eager than ever for trade union sympathy after Cardiff, its warfare against 'Lib-Lab' candidates continued, and its by-election policy added further fuel to trade union criticism. The I.L.P. engaged in four by-elections between 1895 and 1900, and in the last of these, the by-election in Barnsley, a Yorkshire mining constituency, in October 1897, it ran against a Liberal in the face of stiff opposition from the miners and their leaders. Yorkshire was the centre of the Miners' Federation, and its salaried officials were good Liberals almost to a man; only in the chapters in Scotland were the Socialists powerful. Beatrice Webb, in attending miners' conferences, had been disappointed to discover how completely the Federation was dominated by its Executive. She found

Ben Pickard, the President, 'an extreme party Liberal' while the other officers including William Parrott and Sam Woods, appeared intensely conservative and difficult to win even to step by step reform.[38] Already the I.L.P. had aroused the ire of these men by opposing the Liberals elsewhere in Yorkshire, especially in Halifax and East Bradford. To introduce the same 'splitting tactics' to Barnsley, the very headquarters of the Federation, was the ultimate audacity. With Pickard offering no quarter, it took an iron will for I.L.P. men like Robert Smillie of the Scottish Miners to challenge his authority. According to Pete Curran, the I.L.P. candidate, Pickard was in communication with the deputy foremen of the various mines, and they attended meetings in the villages to discover who among their men held up his hand in Curran's favour.[39] The I.L.P. men had to provide their own chairmen at meetings, Hardie later recalled, and seldom found a supporter with sufficient courage to move the resolution of confidence in the candidate.[40] One day the miners in one village stoned Curran and drove him from his platform.[41] Even then, when the final count was tallied, he had 1,091 votes. The Liberal, at the top of the poll, had 6,744.

Barnsley had been costly, not only financially but in estranging from any possible sympathy with the party a large section of the miners. Hardie was heartsick. 'Barnsley, altogether, is the worst thing we have done,'[42] he wrote to a member of the *Labour Leader* staff. The party's appetite for propaganda candidatures temporarily waned, and in the next two years it took no part in parliamentary contests, devoting its attention rather to municipal matters and to preparations for the next General Election.

In contrast with its poor showing nationally, the I.L.P., toward the end of the decade, had one great solace—its increasing success in implanting the new type of civil administrator in the organs of local government. In April 1896, it claimed to be represented by four County Councillors, thirty-five Town Councillors and Aldermen, thirteen District Councillors, forty Parish Councillors, three Vestrymen, twenty-seven Guardians and thirty-nine members of School Boards. The following year there was a notable increase in the municipal socialist vote, and of some sixty I.L.P. and thirty S.D.F. candidates fifteen and eight respectively were elected, the socialists polling over thirty-three per cent of the votes in the wards they contested. The number of persons of I.L.P. persuasion on public bodies at the end of 1897 was estimated at 246. From April 1898 to April 1899, the net municipal gain of the party was over fifty, and in West Ham the combined S.D.F., I.L.P. and Labour vote was in a majority.[43]

Sobered by defeat in running candidates for Parliament and by trade union criticism, the I.L.P. leaders, immediately after the 1895 election, had issued a circular letter to members which cautioned, 'The movement has now reached that stage at which we can afford to dispense with much of the wholesale denunciation which hitherto has been almost a necessity. To our knowledge tens of thousands are looking towards us more or less kindly disposed. It must be our aim to enlist those under our banner, not by any sacrifice of principle, but by avoiding unnecessary offence.' A feeling had grown that perhaps even the Constitution was too rigid, especially the declaration binding upon members, 'to sever all connection with any other political party,' and at the Easter Conference in 1896, this membership pledge was deleted from the Constitution, and in its place by a majority of four to one the delegates accepted the simple declaration that membership was to be 'open to all Socialists who endorse the objects and methods of the party, and are accepted by the particular branch they desire to join.'[44]

Even in the discouraging aftermath of the Cardiff Congress, Hardie and his associates had never despaired of achieving an alliance with the trade unionists. Their goal was to harness the funds and the votes of the trade unions by means of a Socialist-Labour combination, the 'Great Alliance' as Hardie called it. Unlike Blatchford and some of the followers of Hyndman, they did not assume that trade unionists must become socialists before there could be a close and effective collaboration. The bridge of agreement was to be political independence, not some socialist abstraction. As would-be party builders, wooing the trade union giant, the group around Hardie approached their task with a spirit of give-and-take. They were willing that

71

'Independence' be stamped larger than 'Socialism' on their rallying standard.

Hardie, after Cardiff, had toyed with the notion of a separate Trades Union Congress made up of members of trades councils and others who had been barred from the older organization,[45] but he soon abandoned this idea, and in May 1896, the N.A.C. was suggesting that the Parliamentary Committee co-operate in convening a Joint English Socialist and Trade Union Congress.[46] In the I.L.P. leadership itself Hardie wanted a larger infusion of the trade union element, and with this in mind, urged Fred Jowett of the Bradford Trades Council to accept nomination to the N.A.C. in 1897.[47] At the I.L.P. annual conference in the same year, John Edwards read a paper in which he urged a Socialist-Trade Union Alliance. 'The unions must be won,' Hardie wrote, 'which means that the officials of the lodges and branches should be Socialists. A fighting lead is all that is needed to bring this to pass, and . . . a [socialist-trade union] conference repeated yearly would bring this about.'[48] When the party soon afterwards collaborated with the London Trades Council in the L.C.C. elections this seemed proof to Hardie that it was 'quite within the limits of possibility to secure hearty co-operation between the most advanced Socialist and the average Trade Unionist.'[49]

By 1898 dissatisfaction with the failure of the Parliamentary Committee in getting old laws amended or new bills promoted was becoming quite general, and in the Congress the leftist section was regaining its strength. Hardie judged that the majority of the delegates were of socialist sympathies in 1898 and that three-fifths of that majority were I.L.P.[50] Uneasiness as to the exact legal position of trade unions was by this time in evidence and on top of this came the defeat of the striking Amalgamated Society of Engineers. Then when the German socialists in 1898 polled over three million votes and won 50 seats in the Reichstag, their victory served at once as a stimulus and challenge to many British socialists, and as a reminder to many still doubting trade unionists that the proponents of a separate working-class party were not perhaps impractical dreamers after all. Many unions, by the late nineties, had begun to levy their members to send representatives to Parliament. Aside from the miners, the National Union of Seamen and Firemen, the Amalgamated Society of Engineers, the Boot and Shoe Operatives, and the Amalgamated Society of Railway Servants, among others, had voted such levies. The question was, could these and other unions be brought together in a joint political effort with the socialist bodies? Assuming this were possible, would it be accomplished within or outside the Trades Union Congress?

The primary function of the Congress was to serve as a forum for expressing trade union opinion while its Parliamentary Committee sought to give legislative expression to its demands through lobbying in the House of Commons and by other means of advertisement. But the T.U.C. itself could not legislate or enforce its decisions on its member bodies, and heretofore it had displayed an unwillingness to broaden its functions to include concerted political action aimed at sending men to Westminster. This it had left to organizations outside the Congress such as the Labour Electoral Association. Congress activities thus seemed stereotyped and unchanging, and a precedent existed for not enlarging its sphere of operations. This precedent was further strengthened in 1898 by the formation of a separate General Federation of Trade Unions to which about thirty per cent of the trade unions adhered and whose primary function was to administer a general strike fund.

While the Federation discussion was at its height, the ideas of the I.L.P. leadership regarding the 'Great Alliance' were, under the pressure of events, taking clearer form. In October 1898, Hardie suggested that it had to be based on 'trade Unionists, Socialists, and Co-operators each selecting their own candidates, a joint programme having been first agreed upon, and the expenses of the campaign also jointly borne.'[51] Early in 1899 an I.L.P. spokesman was predicting 'startling developments' at the forthcoming Trades Union Congress at Plymouth.[52] Working through the Amalgamated Society of Railway Servants whose Secretary, Richard Bell, was then in closer sympathy with the socialists than he was in later years, the I.L.P.

prepared a resolution to be introduced at Plymouth. It was drafted in the offices of the *Labour Leader* by MacDonald or Hardie, or perhaps by both in collaboration,[53] and it was put forward by James Holmes, the Railway Servants' delegate. It read as follows: 'This Congress, having regard to its decisions in former years, and with a view to securing a better representation of the interests of Labour in the House of Commons, hereby instructs the Parliamentary Committee to invite the co-operation of all the Co-operative, Socialistic, Trade Unions, and other working organizations to jointly co-operate on lines mutually agreed upon, in convening a special congress of representatives from such of the above-mentioned organizations as may be willing to take part, to devise ways and means for securing the return of an increased number of labour members to the next parliament.' The resolution was debated for three hours. James Sexton, Pete Curran, Ben Tillett and Margaret Bondfield were among those speaking in favour. Thomas Ashton of the Amalgamated Spinners belittled the resolution. Even if it were passed, he warned, 'not one trade unionist in ten thousand would take notice of it.' When the results of a card vote were finally announced—546,000 for the resolution, 434,000 against[54]—there was an outburst of cheering. The supporters of a new party had won a major victory.

## NOTES

1. Philip Snowden, *Autobiography*, 2 vols., London, 1934, vol. i, 70.
2. Engels to Sorge, Nov. 10, 1894, *Briefe*, 414.
3. For Hardie in Parliament see Stewart, 81-88; 90-95 and 105-109.
4. J. A. Murray MacDonald to George Lansbury, June 18 undated, but between 1893 and 1895. Lansbury correspondence.
5. Engels regretted Graham's not being in the House to bring Hardie and Burns together. See article on Engels, on the occasion of his death, by Edward Aveling in the *Labour Prophet*, Sept. 1895. Engels had a great admiration for Burns. See Edouard Bernstein, *My Years in Exile*, New York, 1921, 208.
6. Wallace Bruce reports this in a letter to George Lansbury, Nov. 23, 1893. Lansbury correspondence.
7. Engels to Schulter, Jan. 11, 1890, in *Briefe*.
8. Burns to Graham, July 29, 1892. Burns papers.
9. Beatrice Webb's diaries. Entry of Mar. 2, 1894.
10. Blatchford to Burns, Mar. 19, 1892.
11. Burns to Graham. No date.
12. Burns to Graham, July 29, 1892.

# Toward the Great Alliance

13. Burns to Hardie, Jan. 29, 1893.
14. See letters of Hardie to Burns in Burns papers dated May 23 and Nov. 2, 1891, and Jan. 12, 1892.
15. Graham to Burns, April 14 and Sept. 29, 1893.
16. Graham to Burns, May 19, 1893.
17. Joseph Burgess. *John Burns: The Rise and Progress of a Right Honourable*, Glasgow, 1911, 177.
18. Quoted in *Labour Leader*, Oct. 20, 1894.
19. *I.L.P. Ann. Rpt.*, 1894, 5.
20. *Clarion*, Feb. 11, 1893.
21. *I.L.P. Ann. Rpt.*, 1896, 14.
22. As reported in *The Times*, London, May 3, 1894.
23. *I.L.P. Ann. Rpt.*, 1894, 3.
24. In the Brightside by-election in 1897. *Labour Leader*, Aug. 14 and 28, 1897.
25. *I.L.P. Ann. Rpt.*, 1897, 15-16.
26. *T.U.C. Ann Rpt.*, 1893, 48.
27. In the *Clarion*, Nov. 24, 1894.
28. Letters of Mar. 8 and April 15, 1895, in the Amalgamated Society of Engineers papers of the Burns correspondence.
29. David Lowe, *From Pit to Parliament: Life of Keir Hardie*, London, 1923, 86.
30. *South Western World*, April 10, 1895, quoted in Humphrey, 137.
31. *T.U.C. Ann.*, 1895, 28.
32. See *Standing Orders of the T.U.C.*, 1896.
33. Though no longer an official nor an active member of the Amalgamated Society of Engineers, Burns was receiving £100 a year from the Society towards his Wages Fund as an M.P. He continued to receive it for some years until, on the grounds that he was not affiliated to the L.R.C., to which the Engineers were affiliated, the Society voted to end it. See *A.S.E. Monthly Journal*, Mar. 1905, 12.
34. Hardie wrote to Broadhurst asking him to resist the coup (Letter dated Dec. 28, 1894 in Broadhurst correspondence). Broadhurst sought the aid and advice of the Webbs. See *Our Partnership*, 49-50.
35. For description of the intrigue see *Our Partnership*, 47-50.
36. Joseph Burgess in the *Clarion*, Sept. 7, 1895.
37. *T.U.C. Ann.*, 1895, 38.
38. Beatrice Webb's diaries: Entries of Jan. 15 and 17, 1896.
39. Curran in the *I.L.P. News*, Nov. 1897.
40. Keir Hardie, *The I.L.P. and All About it*. I.L.P. Pamphlet, undated, 11.
41. R. Page Arnot, *The Miners: A History of the Miners' Federation of Great Britain: 1899-1910*, London, 1949, 302.
42. Hardie to Lowe, Nov. 4, 1897, quoted in Lowe, *From Pit to Parliament*, 117.
43. *N.A.C. Ann. Rpt.*, 1896; *I.L.P. News*, Nov. and Dec. 1897; *I.L.P. Ann.*, 1899, 11.
44. *I.L.P. Ann.*, 1896, 15 and 28.
45. *ibid.*, 5.
46. Minutes of the Fabian Executive, May 1, 1896, *I.L.P. Ann. Rpt.*, 1897, 8.
47. Fenner Brockway, *Socialism Over Sixty Years: The Life of Jowett of Bradford*, London, 1946, 63.

75

48. John Edwards, *Politics and the I.L.P.* Pamphlet, 1897; *Labour Leader* Jan. 22, 1898.
49. *Labour Leader*, Mar. 5, 1898.
50. *ibid.*, Sept. 10, 1898.
51. *ibid.*, Oct. 1, 1898.
52. *I.L.P. Ann.*, 1899, 10.
53. Godfrey Elton, *The Life of James Ramsay MacDonald: 1866-1919*, London, 1939, 99.
54. *T.U.C. Ann.*, 1899, 64-65.

# CHAPTER V

# The Establishment of the Labour
# Representation Committee

FORTUNATELY, perhaps, for the success of the conference that founded the Labour Representation Committee, the Parliamentary Committee of the T.U.C., in carrying out the instructions of the Plymouth Congress, largely confined itself to issuing invitations and arranging an agenda; its control went no further. 'The Parliamentary Committee in its heart pooh-poohed the whole project,' wrote Ramsay MacDonald with some exaggeration years later, 'and handed over the work to be done by others. Its co-operation was less than nominal. It was sure that nothing would result, and it would not nominate a joint secretary for the proposed new body, because it was not keen in sharing in the failure which it confidently anticipated.'[1]

Also contributing to the constructive results of the conference was a series of meetings beforehand among leaders of the various parties concerned. The co-operative societies did not participate; they had no mandate from their membership and were pursuing the question of parliamentary representation on lines of their own. The preliminary committee, therefore, consisted of representatives of the trade unions and of the three main socialist bodies. The former were represented by four members of the Parliamentary Committee present in London—Sam Woods of the Lancashire Miners, an M.P.; W. C. Steadman of the Bargebuilders, also an M.P.; Will Thorne of the Gasworkers' Union; and Richard Bell of the Railway Servants, whose union had introduced the Plymouth resolution. Keir Hardie and J. Ramsay MacDonald represented the I.L.P.; H. R. Taylor and Harry Quelch, the S.D.F.; and Edward Pease and George Bernard Shaw, the Fabian Society. The socialists outnumbered by six to four the trade unionists, one of whom, Thorne, was a member of the S.D.F. Lib-Labs, I.L.P. men, permeators and Marxists were thus attempting to reach some common ground of agreement. Shaw was skilled at performing on a verbal tight rope when confronted with conflicting opinions, but it is difficult to say what part he played, since the preliminary committee apparently kept no record of its proceedings. There can be no doubt, on the other hand, that a major contribution to eventual understanding was the readiness of the I.L.P. to refrain from injecting the question of socialism into the discussions and its clear idea of the main objective, namely, independence of other political parties. The I.L.P. leaders knew that the socialist mouse had to come to the trade union mountain, not the reverse. By the time the first meeting of the preliminary committee took place on December 6, 1899, this position had been made perfectly clear. The *I.L.P. News,* of which J. Bruce Glasier was editor, had stated, '. . . the I.L.P. must not enter the Conference with a view to "capture" it, but to work with it provided a working basis can be found. We are not going there with a fine Socialist oration up our sleeves and an economic treatise on surplus value in our heads. . . . The party ought . . . to make up its mind to support its delegates in opposing any attempt that may be made to make the abstract question of Socialism pure and simple a test.'[2]

MacDonald, in the meantime, was negotiating with the trade unionists on the basis of a rough 'scheme' which he had drawn up and which he hoped would prove acceptable as a basis for the discussion.[3] 'All that we are trying to do,' he wrote to Pease on November 29, 'is to ascertain how far the T. Unionists are willing to meet as we are suggesting: 1. That the candidates be run by Trade Union, Socialist and other Labour bodies and have no connection with either Liberal or Tory parties. 2. That each party run its own candidates and find its own money. 3. That a joint committee of the organizations running candidates should be the political committee of the combined forces.'[4] MacDonald also presented his plan to the Fabian Executive, which generally approved, having itself no important suggestions to put forward.[5] Just before the December 6 meeting, MacDonald gave a copy of his proposals, drawn up in some detail, to Richard Bell,[6] and undoubtedly he did likewise with other members of the preliminary committee.

After a series of meetings, this committee finally agreed upon an agenda, including a proposed series of resolutions, and commissioned MacDonald to write up the results in a final form. Essentially it embodied those basic points set forth in MacDonald's 'scheme.' On December 27 the Parliamentary Committee of the T.U.C., as sponsor of the coming conference, sent out printed copies of the agenda to societies expected to participate. Hardie later complained that before doing this it had, without authorization, made certain material alterations in the preliminary committee's recommendations.[7] The N.A.C. hoped that the original and the altered agenda might both be printed, but this failing, it was decided that efforts be made to get some trade union to send in amendments to the Conference, or if necessary, that the I.L.P. itself should submit amendments.[8]

Some seven weeks before the Memorial Hall conference, occurred the formation of the Scottish Workers Parliamentary Election Committee on a basis quite similar to that of the L.R.C. A resolution of the Scottish Trade Union Congress of April, 1899, had led to a gathering at Edinburgh on January 6, 1900, presided over by Robert Smillie of the Scottish Miners, with 226 delegates present—116 trade unionists, 29 trade councillors, and 28 co-operators, plus 34 delegates from the I.L.P., and 19 from the S.D.F. The Scots in acting separately were largely motivated by nationalist feeling but also important was the fact that the Scottish miners, unlike most of the miners in England, were not tied to the Liberal party. Then too the Co-operative movement in Scotland was more socialist and more politically minded than its English counterpart. Once formed, the Scottish Committee made a rather dismal showing in elections, remained largely an appendage of the Scottish Miners, and resisted frequent invitations to join with the L.R.C.[9]

In many ways the Edinburgh Conference paralleled the London meeting of the following month and revealed more precisely, if there was still any doubt, what the I.L.P. attitude would be. Hardie, Glasier, John Penny and Joseph Burgess were among the I.L.P. men who attended. A resolution in favour of independent representation was carried by a heavy majority against an amendment to remove the word 'independent' and against a further amendment by a Glasgow member of the S.D.F. to require candidates to support the nationalization of the means of production. Joseph Burgess spoke against this S.D.F. proposal, and when it lost by 145 votes to 23, the I.L.P. voted solidly for its defeat. 'The idea that, within certain lines, a give-and-take policy is possible without any sacrifice of principle,' wrote Hardie, 'has not yet begun to soften the rigidity of some of the S.D.F. members, and their threat to withdraw from the [Edinburgh] Conference unless the amendment was carried was in the worst possible taste.'[10] The S.D.F. weekly *Justice* heaped ridicule on this not-here-and-now-but-sometime socialism and accused the I.L.P. of having become 'a "reform" party, pure and simple.'[11] Significantly for the coming meeting in London it was the trade unionists at Edinburgh who had argued against the emasculation of the resolution for independence and the I.L.P. men who had deprecated the introduction of the socialist amendment. 'This speaks well for the spirit of abnegation, without which common action is impossible,' commented the *I.L.P. News*.[12]

One hundred and twenty-nine delegates came to London's Memorial Hall on February 27. Twelve represented socialist bodies. The I.L.P. sent seven—MacDonald, Hardie, Snowden, Fred Brocklehurst, F. W. Jowett, Joseph Burgess and James Parker. The S.D.F. sent four including Harry Quelch, the editor of *Justice*, and James MacDonald, a member of the London Trades Council, The Fabian Society was represented by its Secretary, Edward Pease. Sixty-seven trade unions were represented, the largest, the Amalgamated Society of Engineers, having 85,000 members and sending in its delegation both G. N. Barnes, its Secretary, and John Burns, who still maintained his Engineers connection. Others included the Railway Servants with 54,000 members, the Gasworkers and General Labourers (48,038), the Boot and Shoe Operatives (31,000), the Lancashire and Cheshire Miners (29,000), the Ironfounders

(17,887) and so on down to the smallest, the Waiters' Amalgamated Society, with a membership of only 200. Some of the most important unions held aloof, including the boilermakers, the cotton operatives, most of the building trade unions and all of the miners, except for the Lancashire and Cheshire group. About two-thirds of those usually represented at the Trades Union Congress were not represented at Memorial Hall.[13] Perhaps the absence of the miners was a blessing in disguise. Had the Miners Federation, its many votes controlled by staunch Liberals like Ben Pickard, sent delegates to Memorial Hall, the results of the Conference might have been far different. As it was Pickard assailed the meeting as a method of tapping trade union cash boxes for those unwilling or unable to pay their own way.[14]

In calling the Conference, the Parliamentary Committee had decided that voting should be according to the standing orders of the Congress, therefore, one vote for every one thousand members or fraction thereof. On this basis the socialist societies commanded but 23 votes out of a total of 591. Actually this was no true measure of their influence, one great advantage from the I.L.P. standpoint being the presence of its own members on various trade union delegations. On many questions some delegates abstained or were bound by instructions from their unions, and it is impossible to say just how they voted, but it is worth noting that a member of the I.L.P., George Barnes, as Secretary of the Amalgamated Society of Engineers, was in a position to influence its 85 votes,[15] and that among the delegates of the new unions—no longer 'new' in fact— were such I.L.P. men as James Sexton of the Dock Labourers, Ben Tillett of the Dock, Wharf, and Riverside Union, and J. R. Clynes of the Gasworkers. The support of the Railway Servants, whose resolution had sown the seed of the Conference and who commanded 54 votes, was probably taken for granted; G. J. Wardle, the editor of the *Railway Review*, was a member of the I.L.P.

There were present, to be sure, Lib-Labs, anti-socialists and proponents of 'working men' candidates only, who were hostile to almost all of the resolutions brought forward. There were trade union officials who came with a 'watching brief' and who were sceptical of the whole procedure. But out-balancing these were those trade unionists and moderate socialists sincerely interested in creating some new and effective instrument. Especially was this apt to be true among those unions already active in plans to run candidates. The Engineers had agreed to run three candidates at the next General Election, and the members were paying a special levy to meet expenses. The Railway Servants had nominated their General Secretary, Bell, to run for Parliament and had agreed to pay his expenses. The Gasworkers were doing the same by Will Thorne, and the Steel Smelters had voted an annual shilling levy for their candidate, John Hodge.[16]

After a speech by the Chairman of the Parliamentary Committee and the election of W. C. Steadman to preside, the Conference turned to a consideration of the items of the agenda. The first of these asked for:

> A resolution in favour of working-class opinion being represented in the House of Commons by men sympathetic with the aims and demands of the Labour movement.

This held implications too broad for those trade unionists who were fearful of socialists or of middle-class adventurers, and a delegate of the Upholsterers' Union moved that such representation be confined to 'members of the working classes.' Such a motion found no support among the socialists who, in theory at least, preferred a socialist peer to a Liberal or Tory ploughman, nor among those trade unionists who were thinking in terms of furthering their own demands rather than of a party based on status. G. N. Barnes urged in its stead the agenda resolution, adding one important qualification: that the candidates must be promoted by one of the affiliated organizations. With John Burns seconding, the Barnes motion was accepted by 102 votes to three.

Since the Cardiff Congress of 1895 Burns had played a minor role in trade union and political gatherings of this kind, and his willingness to attend the Conference was deemed a good omen.

Outwardly at any rate, his antagonism toward Hardie had somewhat subsided,[17] and late in the previous September two members of the I.L.P., John Penny, its Secretary, and G. J. Wardle, had called on Burns to discuss the coming meeting. 'I gave my opinion as to past follies and bad tactics in which they generally agreed,' he wrote in his diary. *'Let the new men mark the compass, but let the old men steer the ship,* that was my advice.'[18] Hyndman thought that Burns at this time was using his influence to 'hoodwink his fellow Trade Unionists in the interest of the Liberals.'[19] Burns, however, made no secret of his willingness to support some sections of the Liberal party and he shared, very likely, in the not uncommon assumption that the new organization, if it amounted to anything, would develop in a Liberal-Labour direction. If he himself had ambitions to 'steer the ship' he was not doing so at the Conference. He seemed, indeed, a little perplexed by the proceedings, and at a critical juncture in the debate, when a series of amendments had left him confused, demanded, 'Where are we now?' An irreverent cry came from the balcony, 'In Memorial Hall!'

It is doubtful if any speech of the whole Conference rivalled in oratorical effectiveness the Burns broadside against narrow class representation. It contained his famous remark about growing tired of 'working-class boots, working-class trains, working-class houses, and working-class margarine.' Although he was on the same side as the socialists, it should be noted that, unlike them, he was speaking against party as well as class restrictions and advocating the support of men who, in most instances, had no ostensible connection with the new body being formed. 'He was also getting tired,' he said, 'of working-class candidates for working-class constituencies. He believed that the time had arrived in the history of the labour and social movement when they should not be prisoners to class prejudice, but should consider parties and policies apart from all class organizations. . . . Let them take men like Charles Booth, Sidney Webb, J. A. Hobson and Leonard Courtney. These four men, although they could not see eye to eye with them on economic subjects, from the general point of view of the interests of the working classes, would be better representatives in Parliament than any engineer, however good he might consider himself.'[20]

The second and the main item in the conference agenda proposed that there be:

A Resolution in favour of establishing a distinct Labour Group in Parliament, who should have their own Whips and agree upon their policy which must embrace a readiness to co-operate with any party, which for the time being may be engaged in promoting legislation in the direct interest of Labour, and be equally ready to associate themselves with any party in opposing measures having an opposite tendency.

This was too mild for the S.D.F. which, as at Edinburgh, asked for a party based upon the recognition of the class war, with nationalization of the means of production, distribution, and exchange as its objectives. Ever sensitive to the trade union aversion to such an extreme declaration, Hardie's supporters considered the S.D.F. resolution impossiblist and disruptive. 'Very magnificent, very heroic, but it is not war,' exclaimed Sexton. Hardly less discouraging to the I.L.P. men was a substitute amendment expressing the attitude of the more cautious trade unionists. It was introduced by Alexander Wilkie, a Scotsman, well known for his success in building the powerful Shipwrights' Union. The Labour Group, Wilkie felt, should be agreed on a 'platform' of four or five 'planks' embracing questions on which the majority of workmen were agreed; no more could be accomplished, and to try to bind Labour M.P.s on other than purely Labour questions would be a mistake. Wilkie's amendment was carried by 59 to 35 and became the substantive proposition.

The I.L.P. was thus confronted with the problem of steering a middle course between the hard rock of socialist dogma and a loose and informal declaration that went no further than existing Lib-Labism. Hardie, therefore, moved an amendment which repeated, word for word, the agenda resolution quoted above but added the further important requirement that no member of the Labour Group must oppose a candidate of the L.R.C. Not only was the definition of a very limited Labour programme in this way avoided; it was also laid down that no trade unionist could oppose a socialist candidate, or vice-versa, when both were in societies adhering to the L.R.C. Apparently the I.L.P. leadership considered this the maximum area of effective socialist-trade union collaboration attainable at the time. Wardle of the Railway Servants seconded Hardie's amendment, and Wilkie agreed to accept it. Burns also gave his backing but in his remarks revealed how little he had fathomed the possibilities of the proposal and how very much out of touch he was with the progress that had been made by the Independents. He wanted it understood that there was already a distinct Labour group in Parliament with Sam Woods and himself as its Whips. 'They had not called themselves independent. They had not worn the trilby hats and red ties, but they had done the work.' He warned the Conference against too much dictation and of the mistake of thinking the Labour party could be united on all questions, citing the Miners' Eight Hours Bill to prove his argument. The Hardie resolution was then put and was carried without opposition.

For constituting a central executive committee the agenda had suggested 18 members, 12 from the trade unions and two each from the three socialist societies. The I.L.P., through Burgess, now proposed that this be changed and that, for reasons of economy and efficiency, there be only twelve members, seven from the trade unions, two from the I.L.P., two from the S.D.F., and one from the Fabian Society.[21] Wilkie protested that the socialists were being over-represented, but the Burgess proposal was accepted by 331 to 161 on a card vote. Thus the conference was willing to give the socialist section of the new federation five of the twelve executive seats even though that section commanded but a twentieth of the numerical strength that the trade unions commanded. Nothing indicated better how fully it was recognized that the problem was not simply one of counting heads. When the S.D.F. withdrew from the Committee in 1901, the official socialist representation dropped to only three, but since the trade unions, especially in the unskilled trades, were often represented by socialists or their close sympathizers, something close to a balance between the two salient viewpoints was maintained.

There was some suggestion that the seven trade union members on the Executive should be selected by and from the Parliamentary Committee. This would have meant representation for trade unions not necessarily affiliated to the L.R.C. and might have resulted in stifling, at the very start, the L.R.C.'s growth along independent lines. Ben Tillett condemned the proposal, and, with socialists abstaining, the trade union delegates themselves defeated it on a card vote by 344 to 165. Those trade unions which were enthusiastic about running candidates and joining the L.R.C. could do so. Those indifferent or opposed need not. In this way the Congress could maintain its traditional disassociation from the disruptive influence of party politics. But the Congress was not to be ignored. When George Barnes opposed the agenda resolution calling for an annual report to the T.U.C. on the grounds that the Committee would be busy enough with the report for its own annual conference, John Ward of the London Navvies reminded him that if the movement were to be entirely separated from the T.U.C. the Navvies would not affiliate and that this would, he believed, be the attitude of the trade unions in general. A card vote on this question resulted in 360 for reporting to the Congress, 124 against.

A none too generous working fund was provided for the Committee by an annual levy on each affiliated society of ten shillings for every thousand members or fraction thereof. Trades Councils or Co-operatives, if they joined, were to pay £5 for every 25,000 members or fraction thereof. Expenses of candidates and their maintenance if elected, however, were to be met locally, a proposal for a parliamentary fund meeting with almost unanimous disapproval. Socialists like Hardie and MacDonald were not overly anxious, for the time being, about this absence of a central war chest. On the contrary, they felt that financial autonomy for each organization was desirable: separate finances discouraged any recrimination about socialists coquetting with trade unionists only to dip into trade union coffers.

The Committee was instructed to keep in touch with trade unions and other bodies, local and national, running Labour candidates and to convene a Labour Representation Conference each year in the month of February. As elections approached, it was to prepare a list of L.R.C. candidates and to publish the same as the official candidates of the United Labour Party, recommending them to the support of working-class electors. With no further definition of the duties of the Committee, considerable leeway of interpretation fell to the Executive and Secretary. And the man chosen as Secretary, James Ramsay MacDonald, possessed both the courage and imagination to use his position to full advantage.

To those at all sympathetic with what it set out to accomplish the Memorial Hall Conference was regarded as a success. If the newly created L.R.C. was steeped in compromise, if, to some, it appeared over-prudent and vague in its stated objective, it had, nevertheless, imparted greater unity and coherence to Labour politics than had any similar effort. Socialists and trade unionists for the first time had met on common ground and agreed to run candidates under joint auspices. They had declared for independence without isolation, for a definite Labour group with latitude to negotiate and co-operate with other parties. There were drawbacks. They had formed only a federation composed of organizations, not a party to which individuals might directly adhere. The Executive in no sense commanded the prestige of a party headquarters. It was not only a Committee but, as MacDonald said, it had the limited mind of a Committee.[22] But as a first step, revealing a keen sense of the possible, the formation of the L.R.C. must be regarded as a master stroke.

Many old school trade unionists of course felt certain that the Committee would dissolve in the face of irreconcilable differences and that the problem of Labour representation would revert to a solution at a purely local level. The trade union response in general was anything but heartening. In the L.R.C.'s first year the number of trade union adherents was actually less than the number of trade unionists represented at the founding conference,[23] and when the Lancashire and Cheshire Miners, the only miners who attended the conference, decided not to join after all, their delegate who had been elected to the L.R.C. Executive was obliged to resign.

The atmosphere of conciliation which had pervaded the conference was reassuring to Fabian circles. Referring to the main resolution, their monthly journal remarked, 'The adhesion of the S.D.F. and the I.L.P. delegates to a resolution so typically Fabian in its Possibilist attitude towards politics, is a remarkable indication of the development of the opinions of those bodies. The policy advocated a few years ago, under the name of the Manchester Fourth Clause, seems at last to be formally abandoned. . . .'[24] Edward Pease, as the only Fabian delegate, appointed himself to the L.R.C. Executive, an action later confirmed by the Society. Shaw has written that the I.L.P. motion in favour of having one instead of the two Fabian representatives on the Committee was a Hardie device for keeping Pease who was considered 'harmless' and getting rid of Shaw. Hardie had learned, according to Shaw, 'that mixed committees of clever bureaucrats and journalists and of genuine Labour men will not work: their brains do not go at the same speed or in the same channels.'[25] Pease—thorough, hard-working, level-headed—was an asset to any committee. Born a Quaker, he had, in disgust, abandoned a career as a stockbroker and become a skilled carpenter. A founding member of the Fabian Society, he had served since 1889 as its able and energetic Secretary. 'The Socialist lions have lain down with the Trade Union lambs,' he wrote of the conference, 'and if either party be "inside," it is certainly not the lambs!'[26]

The conference had hardly ended when the S.D.F. was expressing its resentment at I.L.P. opposition to the 'class war' resolution. Although that opposition could hardly have come as a surprise, *Justice* chose to describe it as a display of 'treachery,'[27] and the I.L.P., by protesting to the S.D.F. Executive Council, virtually obliged it to openly endorse this sentiment. The I.L.P. then announced that it could have no further relations with the official heads of the S.D.F. until the charge of treachery was withdrawn.[28] In the preliminary committee, Hardie argued, the S.D.F. representative had accepted the agenda without raising the question which they afterward 'sprung' upon the conference.[29] *Justice* denied this, claiming that the S.D.F. representatives had not been present when the final draft agenda was drawn up.[30] Though inclined to sulk and to have little faith in the new body, the S.D.F. did appoint two members to its Executive. 'We can heartily and honestly co-operate with anyone for any immediate end which makes towards our goal,' wrote Quelch in explaining the S.D.F. position, 'but there can be no united party without unity of principle, and to pretend a unity which does not really exist in order to display a strength which we do not actually possess is only to make ourselves appear weaker than we really are.'[31]

The I.L.P. was almost lyrical in its response to the creation of the new body. 'The long hoped for Labour Conference has come and gone, and has left nothing but pleasant memories and great expectations behind it. . . ,' said the *I.L.P. News*. 'The national combination for which we worked and prayed [has been] brought about. How long have we dreamt of the "United Democracy!" It has come. It is a tender life. . . . "Poor little child of danger, nursling of the storm." May it be blessed.'[32] The I.L.P. had placed one of its own, MacDonald, in the L.R.C. Secretaryship, an excellent vantage point for such a skilled tactician and administrator. It was said at the time and has been repeated in numerous places since, that MacDonald owed his election to a case of mistaken identity, that many of the delegates thought they were voting for James MacDonald, the West End tailor, Secretary of the London Trades Council, and one of the S.D.F. delegates. The story apparently is of S.D.F. origin. Will Thorne has supported it[33] and Hyndman repeats it in his *Further Reminiscences*. 'I was told,' he writes, 'that most of those who voted for this smart middle-class manipulator as Secretary thought that they were voting for the James MacDonald who had introduced the Socialist resolution, and that, the two Social-Democratic delegates being absent during this important vote, there was no one present to put the matter right.'[34]

There are good reasons for doubting this. Hyndman was not present at the Conference and is not reliable about it even in matters clearly determinable. Another S.D.F. writer who recounts the mistaken identity story has claimed that 'Mac-

Donald was in no sense responsible for the inception or the establishment of the L.R.C.,'[35] a statement demonstrably false in view of MacDonald's pre-conference activities described earlier. Also cited as proof of his election by a freak chance is MacDonald's comparative anonymity among trade unionists at this time. He was not, it is true, a popular figure as yet, but as a member of the National Administrative Council of the I.L.P. and the Fabian Executive who cultivated connections with the London Trades council, and who had run for Parliament in 1895, he could hardly have been a stranger to a goodly number of the trade unionists present. And if he were unknown, there were many I.L.P.'ers among the trade union delegations who could set their colleagues straight, unless, of course, there was a deliberate attempt to mislead, as Hyndman implies.

More likely than not, few delegates thought much of the post of Secretary anyway, and as Snowden points out, it went 'a-begging,'[36] Fred Brocklehurst of the I.L.P. having turned it down before recommending MacDonald in his place. Hardie, however, did not belittle the post, and he knew whom he wanted as Secretary. 'I remember,' he said in 1912, 'the anxious hours spent before the first Conference was called, trying to find someone who had the necessary qualities and abilities to undertake the most responsible of all tasks at that period— to act as Secretary to the Party. Those who had known Mac-Donald's work in the I.L.P. felt that he was the one man above all others who, if he could be induced to take the position, would give our then nascent movement its best chance of coming to fruition.'[37] This was no strictly hindsight observation. To Hardie's credit he recognized the young Scot's endowments from the outset and was determined to see them effectively employed. He was soon calling MacDonald the party's 'greatest intellectual asset'[38] and 'the best all-round man the movement ha[d] yet produced.'[39] In 1903 when there were rumours of MacDonald's quitting the Secretaryship, so highly did Hardie estimate his worth that he wrote to Glasier, 'If it should come that he has to give up the L.R.C. job that of itself will be no reason for our withdrawing and may be the making of our own movement. If Mac became secretary of the I.L.P. the party would soon rise to a position of influence and strength such as it has never yet reached.'[40]

MacDonald in 1900 was thirty-four. Born in Lossiemouth in the Scottish lowlands, the illegitimate son of Anne Ramsay and a Highland farm-hand named MacDonald, he was brought up by his mother and maternal grandmother, given a first-rate elementary schooling and for a time was employed as a pupil teacher. Ambition led him South before he was twenty, first to Bristol, then to London. In London he led a rather grim existence which combined a Spartan diet, low wages as a clerk, long hours of intensive study, especially in science, and, finally, physical breakdown. In 1888 his luck changed. He was hired as private secretary to a Liberal politician named Thomas Lough. He passed four years with Lough enlarging his knowledge of politics and making numerous acquaintances among London newspaper men and politicians. When he quit this position in 1891, he was able to earn his livelihood as a journalist. He joined the I.L.P. in 1894 and within two years was a member of its National Administrative Council. In the late eighties he had become a member of the Fabian Society, and from 1894 to 1900, when he resigned over the Society's refusal to condemn the South African War, he served on its Executive. The S.D.F., which he had joined when he first came South to Bristol in 1885, he soon abandoned.[41]

MacDonald later defined in numerous writings his philosophy of government and what he meant by socialism. 'Socialism marks the growth of society, not the uprising of a class,'[42] he wrote. To him it was not so much a revealed doctrine as a general tendency. As for a socialist party, this was to be the last, not the first, form of the socialist movement,[43] for in Britain, Socialism could not create a party founded on its dogmas. It could only hope 'to become the spirit of a party which . . . [would] take the Socialist outlook and use Socialist constructive ideas as guides in practical legislation.'[44] The evolution of socialist propaganda he described as follows:

It begins with street corner work which is necessary to make people familiar with the Socialist position. Thereby it gains its first adherents. This propaganda drifts nearer and nearer to the actual conditions of the day, and in our country, the work of the old Fabian Society stands conspicuously as the type of this. Then, our general ideas are expressed in municipal work as an increasing number of Socialists are elected to public administrative bodies. Finally comes Parliament and legislation, and Socialism has to be adapted to the organization of the State. But from the moment when Socialism leaves the market-place and the study, to invade the Council and the Senate . . . it has to return from its Edens of perfection to the point to which Society has at present reached. . . .[45]

MacDonald was by nature both a visionary and a practical planner, an idealist and a prudent manipulator. In politics this dualism of character took the form of desiring 'a sane laborious policy of reconstruction having for a background an active platform idealism.'[46] In both the Fabian Society and the I.L.P. he could find elements which appealed to him, the one scientific and full of hard common sense, the other more dependent on faith and sentiment. That he sought to combine the advantages of both meant inevitably that he could be fully satisfied with neither, and, in the nineties at least, he did not hide his criticisms. The Fabians he considered too ingrown, too willing to ignore a vast untapped source of socialist energy that would come from the creation of a new political force, and he said that he had been glad to leave them 'when they took up an equivocal position in the Boer War and continued their opposition to the formation of an Independent Labour Party.'[47] Of the I.L.P. he was at first even more harshly critical, fearing that its sectarianism in the nineties might deteriorate into impotence. With Hardie's unrestrained attacks on the Liberals in the General Election of 1895 he was completely at odds and spoke to a friend of Hardie's 'incapacity' and I.L.P. 'excesses.'[48] The more lenient attitude which characterized the I.L.P. after its 1895 defeats reassured him, and he observed in 1896 that the elimination of the I.L.P. oath requiring the severance of all connections with other parties put the movement in fine fighting trim by allowing for greater liberty of action.[49] Hardly a week after joining the I.L.P. he had criticized its stress on propaganda and had argued that the creation of sentiment on street corners was not enough since foes as well as friends might capture that sentiment and that the time had come to stress electoral organization and the construction of an effective election machine.[50]

In many ways MacDonald's selection as L.R.C. Secretary in 1900 was the ideal choice. Patient, hardworking and shrewd, a gentleman whom the trade unionists would treat with a deference they denied their fellows, no man in the movement seemed better suited to the particular task at hand. Hardie's role was that of the pioneer, the propagandist, in the period when independent Labour had fought tenaciously for the slightest recognition. Now the tactician, the architect of a political machine, the man who loved the subtleties of politics and could manage disparate elements was needed. Hardie might chafe at the intrigue and restraint that this task entailed, but as impatient as MacDonald to see Labour battalions marching to the polls, he loyally backed the younger man even after some elements in his party had begun to condemn Mac-Donald as a self-seeker and lukewarm reformist. In the first years Hardie could feel confident that he had judged correctly. No man would do more than MacDonald to insure the Labour Party's initial electoral success.

\* \* \*

The L.R.C. left each member organization free to maintain and propagate its own theory and to bring forward as it saw fit its own independent 'Labour' candidates. The I.L.P., however, impoverished financially and plagued by a declining membership, was in a poor condition to do either. It had other problems. Proposals for abolishing the I.L.P. Chairmanship had again been introduced, and although they were not accepted,[51] Hardie in 1899 had felt obliged to announce that he would not stand for the office the following year. Low in spirits, he had written to Glasier, 'I have seriously and sanely discussed with myself the wisdom of getting out of the position into which circumstances not of my choosing have driven me, by taking a plunge into the void as the best possible service I could now render the movement.'[52]

Glasier, convinced that Hardie was to go, allowed his own name to be put forward for the Chairmanship 'for fear,' as he put it, 'that the office might fall, by others withdrawing their names, to some unsuitable person.'[53] When, with no other contestants for the position, Glasier took over from Hardie in April 1900, Robert Blatchford made no secret of his satisfaction. 'I think [Hardie] has been vain, greedy, crooked and bumptious. . . .' he wrote to the new chairman, 'I think he has nearly ruined the I.L.P. which would have done well but for him. I think by his jealousy and vanity he has made many thousands think *we* were jealous of him. Whereas God knows I have always regarded him as too small to be jealous of. . . . And I am very, very glad that at last the I.L.P. is quit of him. . . .'[54]

Hardie remained on the N.A.C. and the party was not 'quit of him' by any means. He was anxious at this time for any new ideas or methods which might again set the party on its feet and revive a flagging interest. The I.L.P. branches continued to show a lack of enthusiasm, and, as the year progressed, Hardie grew more and more pessimistic and impatient. Late in June he wrote to Glasier, 'A note from J. R. M[acDonald] says the work at [the I.L.P. office] is getting further into arrears. In the parlous state of our movement this may easily be fatal. . . . There is lethargy where there shd. be energy & a spirit of heaviness where an inspiration is needed.'[55]

Financially the party was in a very sad plight. Ordinary fees were insufficient to meet the expenses of the head office. There was talk of a crusade to the branches, but even the means for this were, for the time being, lacking.[56] With the party on the verge of bankruptcy, Snowden in August 1900 was asking France Littlewood, the party Treasurer, to meet accounts from his own purse, and Hardie was so distressed that he wanted to take over the secretarial work if John Penny resigned. 'I feel a terrible sense of helplessness as things are,' he wrote to Glasier.[57] Glasier, meanwhile, aside from soliciting aid from individuals within the party like T. D. Benson and outside sympathizers like the Cadburys, was suggesting some retrenchments in expenditure: the N.A.C. should perhaps go into commission with three or four members acting as a deputy N.A.C. He himself might undertake a circuit of the branches provided the N.A.C. could pay his expenses of £1 for Sundays, and five shillings a night afterwards with fare, all the collections made at his meetings to be returned to the N.A.C.[58] The first encouraging break in this otherwise gloomy picture was the success of an appeal for contributions to the I.L.P. Election Fund. Then with Hardie's return to Parliament in the General Election in October, a new burst of confidence swept the party. The really bad days were over.

J. Bruce Glasier, the new I.L.P. chairman, had been born in Glasgow in 1859. His father was an Ayrshire farmer and his mother the daughter of a Highland crofter. In the summer, while a schoolboy, he herded sheep. Later he was an architect but was drawn from this work by the enticements of platform agitation. He joined the Irish Land League in Glasgow, along with Shaw Maxwell and others, and helped to inaugurate the Henry George campaign in 1883. The next year he assisted in forming a Glasgow branch of the S.D.F. Later he abandoned the S.D.F. for the Socialist League from whose leader, Morris, he drew much inspiration and about whose role and work in the early movement he later wrote a most admirable study. In 1893 he married Katherine Conway, a student of Newnham College, Cambridge, then a member of the National Council of the I.L.P. Together they dedicated their lives to the movement and, as Hardie said, added to it a touch of romance. One of the most indefatigable of itinerant propagandists, Glasier also served on the N.A.C. almost continuously after 1896, was chairman of the I.L.P. from 1900 to 1903, and just after the 1906 Election, took over the editorship of the *Labour Leader* for some four and a half years.[59] Like Morris, he approached socialism largely through art and morals. His philosophy was humanist and in many respects Utopian. 'It is on this better nature, this higher self, that the only true hopes of human progress and civilization depend,' he wrote, just before his death in 1920.[60] To Snowden,

'Bruce Glasier was more than any man the embodiment of the spirit, the idealism and the hope of Socialism.'[61] It is doubtful if anyone in the I.L.P. leadership was less self-seeking than he. His suspicion of the psychology and outlook of doctrinaires of the S.D.F. stamp was intense. 'Perhaps the greatest thing that the I.L.P. has achieved for Socialism,' he wrote to Hardie in 1903, 'is the rescuing of the cause of Socialism from these men.'[62] For a time he was close to the *Clarion*, wrote for it, and spoke from the *Clarion* vans, but his loyalty to Hardie finally made him turn against Blatchford and dismiss him as an 'egomaniac.'[63] Happiest when on the road, Glasier, though he ran for Parliament, seems never to have had any strong desire for office. In a letter addressed to his wife in July 1900 there is a description of a *Clarion* van tour, revealing something of both the man and the movement at the turn of the century. He writes from Painswick in Gloucestershire.

The sun is warm and bright again today, and inside the Van is all alight with its glow. Mrs. Macpherson sits opposite me on the locker shelling peas for the dinner, while Fenton has gone off on his cycle to post notices of our meeting tonight in a village six miles away.

Our meeting last night was one of the most interesting that I have ever seen. The people stood round us for two hours and the murmurs of approval especially from the older men were quite touching.

At the close of the speaking a vote of thanks was proposed and seconded to us, and all hands save those of a few angry and ill-mannered local villa dwellers were held up. Thereafter the crowd broke up into groups and we could hear them discussing till nearly eleven o'clock (a very late hour here) as we sat in the Van. . . .

The night being very mild I felt quite comfortable in the tent and did not waken save once till morning. Not an animal, bird or insect of any kind has intruded under our shelter either of the nights. I looked dilligently [*sic*] for earwigs but could find none! It must be that there are certain soils which they particularly favour: for at Winterbourne Down when

Grady was in the tent, they crawled in hundreds and thousands up the canvas, and every now and then a careless-footed one would fall down upon the unfortunate *Clarionette*!

Here as in Stroud we have found several people who have been anxious to extend hospitality to us. It is very encouraging to note how in some curious way Socialism has penetrated into every part especially among better-to-do folk.

Not the least active hostility has been exhibited towards the Van either in Stroud or here save by a rather rich lady who lives opposite the road and who last night shook her hand at us while I was speaking—but she was under the influence of brandy.

At several places—Wotton-under-Edge and Westbury-on-Trym—there were I am told some turbulent people who used violent language and one or two who threatened violence to the Van, but no real assault or battery actually took place. Since I have been in the Van, its progress has been pleasant and triumphant.[59]

## NOTES

1. MacDonald, *A Policy for the Labour Party*, 23.
2. *I.L.P. News*, Nov. 1899.
3. MacDonald to Pease, card, Nov. 29, 1899.
4. *ibid.*, letter, Nov. 29, 1899.
5. No specific instructions were given to Pease and Shaw. Fabian Executive Minutes, Dec. 1, 1899.
6. MacDonald to Pease, Dec. 5, 1899.
7. Hardie in *Labour Leader*, Jan. 13, 1900.
8. N.A.C. Minutes, Jan. 8, 1900.
9. Cole, *Working Class Politics*, 154–155; *Labour Leader*, Jan. 13, 1900.
10. *Labour Leader*, Jan. 13, 1900.
11. *Justice*, Jan. 13, 1900.
12. *I.L.P. News*, Jan. 1900.
13. Where a newspaper source is not cited all references to the proceedings at the Memorial Hall meeting are from the official report, and will not be cited separately.
14. For Pickard's long statement on the conference in the Miners' Federation Annual Report see Arnot, *The Miners*, 353–357; see also *Labour Leader*, Nov. 11 and 25, 1899.
15. Before the conference Barnes had urged moderation and the avoidance of programmes and of the raising of those 'isms' which had been the death knell

of united action in the past, thus aptly expressing the Hardie-MacDonald approach to the problem at hand. From the *Ethical World* as quoted in The *Echo*, London, Feb. 24, 1900.

16. John Hodge, *Workman's Cottage to Windsor Castle*, London, 1931, 138; *Labour Leader*, Nov. 25, 1899.

17. As early as the spring of 1897 Hardie and Burns had appeared on the same platform in Battersea Park, and on Burns' bid for an end to mutual censure, they had shaken hands. Lowe, *From Pit*, 114.

18. Burns' diary: Entry of Sept. 30, 1899.

19. Hyndman, *Further Reminiscences*, 269.

20. *Manchester Guardian*, Feb. 28, 1900.

21. When a Trades Council Member was later added there were 13 on the Executive.

22. MacDonald, *A Policy in the Labour Party*, 27.

23. There were 545,316 trade unionists represented at Memorial Hall; in the first annual report of the L.R.C. the number of trade unionist adherents given as 339,577 and from Trades Councils 94,000.

24. *Fabian News*, April 1900.

25. Fabian Exec. Minutes, Mar. 9, 1900; Shaw in *Webbs and their Work*, 9; Elton, *MacDonald*, 103.

26. The *Economic Review*, London, April 17, 1900, 236.

27. *Justice*, Mar. 3, 1900.

28. *S.D.F. Ann. Report*, 1900, 14-15; Fred Brocklehurst in *Clarion*, April 21, 1900; *I.L.P. Ann. Report*, 1900, 6-7, 22-23.

29. *Labour Leader*, Mar. 10, 1900.

30. *Justice*, April 28, 1900.

31. *Reynolds's Newspaper*, April 29, 1900.

32. *I.L.P. News*, Mar. 1900.

33. Lee and Archbold, *Social Democracy*, 85.

34. Hyndman, *Further Reminiscences*, 269.

35. Lee in *Social Democracy*, 161.

36. Snowden, *Autobiography*, vol. i, 92.

37. *Labour Party Ann. Report*, 1912, 67; quoted in Elton, *MacDonald*, 104.

38. Hamilton, *MacDonald*, 30.

39. Hardie in *Labour Leader*, Aug. 9, 1902.

40. Hardie to Glasier, Nov. 10, 1903.

41. Lord Elton, *The Life of James Ramsay MacDonald, 1866-1919*, London, 1939; H. Hessell Tiltman, *J. Ramsay MacDonald: Labor's Man of Destiny*, New York, 1929; Mary Agnes Hamilton, *J. Ramsay MacDonald*, London, 1929; Herbert Tracey, *From Doughty Street to Downing Street: The Rt. Hon. J. Ramsay MacDonald, M.P.*, London, 1924; L. Macneil Weir, *The Tragedy of Ramsay MacDonald*, London, 1938.

42. J. Ramsay MacDonald, *Socialism and Society*, London, 1905, 127.

43. MacDonald, *The Socialist Movement*, London, 1911, 195, and 235.

44. *Socialism and Society*, 142.

45. MacDonald, 'Socialism and the Labour Party,' *The Socialist Review*, vol. i, Aug. 1918, 21-22.

46. MacDonald to J. Bruce Glasier, May 31, 1907.

47. Foreword by MacDonald to Arthur Compton-Rickett, *I Look Back: Memories of Fifty Years*, London, 1933.

48. MacDonald to Herbert Samuel, Aug. 16, 1895, quoted in Samuel, *Memoirs*, London, 1945, 26-27.
49. MacDonald to Edward Pease, April 8, 1896.
50. In the *Labour Leader*, July 28, 1894.
51. *I.L.P. Ann. Report*, 1899, 31.
52. Hardie to Glasier, Dec. 28, 1899.
53. Glasier to his sister, Lizzie, Mar. 23, 1900.
54. Quoted in Thompson, *Blatchford*, 139.
55. Hardie to Glasier, June 27, 1900.
56. Glasier to Hardie, Aug. 2, 1900.
57. Hardie to Glasier, Aug. 8, 1900.
58. Glasier to Hardie, Aug. 31, 1900.
59. *Labour Leader*, June 8, 1906 and June 10, 1920; *Labour Annual*, 1895, 171; *I.L.P. Jubilee Souvenir*, 1943, 37.
60. J. Bruce Glasier, *The Meaning of Socialism*, London, 1919, 10.
61. *Labour Leader*, June 10, 1920.
62. Glasier to Hardie, Mar. 2, 1903.
63. Glasier to his sister Lizzie, Oct. 12, 1906.
64. Glasier to his wife, July 8, 1900.

# CHAPTER VI

# The Liberal and Labour Reaction
# to the South African War

IN the later nineties the political Labour movement had appeared to be standing still; no one realized that it was on the eve of a new resurgence. Shaw thought that this period showed 'an utter slump in Socialism and everything else intellectual.'[1] Although some interest was raised by the meeting in London of the International Socialist and Trades Union Congress in 1896, British trade unionists were as much alarmed as enlightened by the impassioned orations of the foreign delegates.[2] In the House of Commons debate often languished for want of an effective opposition, and it seemed as if nothing in domestic politics could arouse popular enthusiasm. Many socialists and a large section of the Liberals were reduced to futile protest as they disassociated themselves from the growing sentiment of Empire which occupied the nation.

The war with the Boer Republics brought these political doldrums to an end. There was an eruption of blatant Jingoism. Party conflict was intensified, and public discussion invigorated. So bitter were critics and defenders of the war in denunciatory exchange that moderate counsels went largely unheard. Ties of party were put to the severest test, even prominent Unionists joining in upbraiding the Government. The Liberal party was nearly rent in twain on the war issue. In the slender ranks of the socialists there was a marked disagreement. While most socialists, including those in the I.L.P. and S.D.F., attacked Chamberlain's war as a wicked aggression, prominent Fabians pointed to the backwardness and inefficiency of the Boer farm communities as a very good argument for their having to be defeated, and Blatchford of the *Clarion* spoke strongly against those socialists who seemed to be praying for British failure.

In October 1899, when hostilities began, there were high hopes of an early triumph for the Empire forces. They would, many assumed, celebrate their Christmas in Pretoria. But by late December such light-hearted optimism had all but disappeared. A series of setbacks at the hands of the Dutch farmer had proved him a shrewd and stubborn adversary and a master of veldt terrain and guerilla warfare. The war, dragging on until the summer of 1902, cost the home island its greatest military effort up to that time—the Crimean War not excluded—and petered out rather ignominiously in a campaign of attrition in which gigantic webs of barbed wire were thrown across the open country and Boer women and children were herded into concentration camps, there in huge numbers to fall victims to disease and epidemics.

Before the outbreak of war the I.L.P. had accused the Government of revealing by its actions an intention 'to promote a war of conquest . . . in the interest of unscrupulous exploiters.'[3] This official party view was in no way altered when President Kruger of the Transvaal anticipated the British in issuing an ultimatum and sent Boer cavalry sweeping into Natal. On I.L.P. platforms the Dutch were portrayed as heroic defenders of national rights and liberties, a viewpoint which the more cynical Fabian dismissed as overly romantic, if not a bit stupid. Men like Hardie did, in fact, display a certain naïveté where that tight-lipped old Boer patriarch, Paul Kruger, was concerned. Steeped in the Old Testament lessons of just revenge, Kruger since the Jameson raid had been arming his country to the teeth, and any objective observer might well have concluded that his preparations were not wholly defensive. Moreover, the Old Radical notion strong among I.L.P.'ers that England must champion weaker freedom-loving governments was at least questionable when applied to Oom Paul's régime, a virtual dictatorship which was not only obscurantist, a relic of another century, but in many instances clearly oppressive. Hardie's statement that 'the opposition to the Transvaal Government was due to the fact that that Government had set itself to watch the interests of the working classes and the very poor'[4] was indeed close to nonsense. I.L.P. orators, however, did not rally the faithful by close reasoning as much as by appeals to righteous resentment and by playing on heart strings attuned to the emotional pitch of the great Gladstone's Midlothian campaigns. The style at its best is revealed in a speech made by Snowden in Blackburn during the 'Khaki' Election of 1900. He denies that he is a 'Little Englander.' 'I wish to see a great England,' he declaimed, 'whose courageous sons shall leave her shores, not to the beating of martial drums, but like David Livingstone who never shed a drop of human blood. I wish to see the adventurous sons of a great England go forth to win, by love and example, all the victories of Peace which are more renowned than War.'[5]

That this war was not a war for the civil rights of British subjects in the Transvaal but an imperialist capitalist war for territory and for dividends was a favourite argument of spokesmen for the S.D.F. and the I.L.P. as they worked in the 'Stop-the-War' movement and shared with pro-Boer Liberals the obloquies of the Yellow Press and the threats and jostlings of the mob. Hyndman aimed his most choice invective at the 'scoundrelly adventurers who had got hold of the mining country of the Rand,' and though aware that the old world religious and economic methods of the Boer Republics could not endure, he still stressed that it was the motive of exploitation which determined England's policy,[6] a motive which naturally seemed paramount to anyone interpreting the war in terms of the class struggle. The prime motive of the war, proclaimed Hardie, was the 'enslavement of black labour and the pauperization of white labour.'[7]

Into the anti-war campaign John Burns threw himself wholeheartedly, and among anti-war Liberals his stock rose appreciably, thus paving the way for his eventual appointment to a Liberal Cabinet. To him Kruger seemed 'infinitely better than the horde of Jews and greedy gentiles who ha[d] corralled the old fellow in,'[8] and two months after the war had begun he drew in his diary this dreary prognosis: 'This war means the abdication of the aristocracy, the collapse of the government classes.

The honest are incompetent; the competent, corrupt. The Jew has exploited the impecunious amongst them while the able and honest have allowed a charlatan at the Colonial Office to drive them to the meanest war ever waged.'⁹ In the House of Commons Burns condemned the war in telling phrases and fearlessly bearded Chamberlain. '. . . this war [he said] is for territory, for gold, for capitalist domination masquerading in the guise of freedom and franchise. . . . I protest against the incompetency displayed in the arrangements for the war, the hollowness of its object, the immorality of its aims, the stupidity with which the negotiations were conducted, and above all the want of taste, tact and temper too frequently shown by the Colonial Secretary. . . .'¹⁰

Many, perhaps most, trade union officials shared these sentiments, and the non-socialists among them were often in the forefront among pro-Boer Liberals. In 1900 the Trades Union Congress, on the motion of John Ward of the Navvies Union, adopted an anti-war resolution protesting against the 'suppression of these two independent states [the Transvaal and the Orange Free State] at the dictation of cosmopolitan capitalists.'¹¹ Yet patriotic sentiment and the fact that war production usually meant increased pay and more jobs could not be ignored, and the resolution passed by only a small majority. The following year the Congress refused to suspend the Standing Orders so that another of Ward's resolutions—this time in favour of a cessation of hostilities—might be submitted for consideration.¹²

If trade union officials tended to waver on the war issue, their following from the outset was less indecisive. The British working man had already exulted in Kitchener's revenge for Khartoum and in the humiliation of the French at Fashoda. Now he could strut vicariously in the shoes of the Colonial Secretary and express indignation at a new threat to the Empire. In such circumstances the chief architects of the newly formed Labour Representation Committee might well have despaired of seeing their brain-child survive its first year.

The attitude of the more prominent Fabians toward the war helped to undermine both their interest and their influence in the larger political Labour movement. In the quarrels which disturbed the Society late in 1899 the Transvaal crisis was the determining but not the sole factor. Rather, the question of whether there should be an official Fabian pronouncement on the war served to dramatize once again the earlier query posed by MacDonald and others as to whether the Society was too narrow in interpreting its functions and too out of touch with the broader socialist currents. The old guard argued that the Society was under no obligation to take sides on the war, which had nothing to do with their particular mission as socialists. In any case, such a step might prove suicidal. 'Don't let us, after all these years, split the Society by declaring ourselves on a non-Socialist point of policy,' wrote Shaw to Pease. 'To wreck ourselves on the Transvaal after weathering Home Rule would be too silly.'[13]

Probably not over a handful of Fabians would have advocated force as a solution in South Africa, but once hostilities had begun most of them apparently felt that final settlement could come only through the arbitrament of arms and that the British Empire had to win. The minority opposing this stand included those members connected with the I.L.P.—MacDonald, S. G. Hobson, G. N. Barnes—and some who were attached to the anti-Rosebery section of the Liberal party. From this group on October 13, 1899, two days after the war began, came notice of a motion for a vote of urgency to express sympathy with the Boers. The Executive Committee, in control of the older Fabians, including Webb, Shaw, Frederick Whelen and Hubert Bland, urged the Society to reject such a motion, and urgency was refused.[14]

There was one voice in the older section sharply condemnatory of the Executive's action. This was Sidney Olivier who was soon to become the Governor of Jamaica and who in 1924 would be the Secretary for India in the first Labour Government. Olivier insisted that it was incumbent on the Society to declare itself. If it did not, this would mean 'that the dry rot which had collared the Liberal party . . . had also got hold of the Fabian Society' and left no reason for its continued separate existence.[15] The opposing view was expressed by Hubert Bland, a Tory Democrat and a founder member and honorary

Treasurer of the Society. 'It looks,' he wrote to Pease, 'as though you and I and the remnant of the old gang (of which Olivier has never been at heart a member) would have to make one more big fight to secure the Society's usefulness in the future, a usefulness which will be entirely crippled if we throw ourselves dead athwart the Imperialist, or any other, strong stream or tendency. As we cannot break up those streams but only be broken up by them, we should try in our humble, but sometimes quite effective, way, to direct them. We may possibly be able to do for "sane" imperialism what we have already done for "sane" socialism. More we cannot do; we may, if we are unwise, do infinitely less.'[16]

The pro-Boer Fabians remained strong in their determination to thrash out the question with the 'conservative section.' There was a 'disease' in the Society, in Hobson's view, which went deeper than a mere refusal to discuss the Transvaal question. 'We are losing all our strenuousness—over *diablerie*,' he wrote to Olivier, 'we have ceased to be feared and are only respected as amiable and harmless students of certain restricted phenomena. I can quite understand a keen man like Webb denying that our activities are to be limited to discuss (say) the Transvaal iniquity. But in point of practice do we not persistently refuse to tackle various outside problems?'[17]

At a members' meeting in December both sides had their say. When Hobson moved a resolution calling for the Society to disassociate itself from 'the Imperialism of Capitalism and vainglorious Nationalism,' Shaw, for the Executive, countered with an amendment belittling the idea of a vote of the members on the war and stressing rather the problem of the peace settlement and the need of some practical scheme for securing public ownership of the Transvaal mines. This amendment simply by-passed the question at hand and was defeated by a large majority. Nevertheless a showdown on Hobson's resolution was avoided, a motion for the previous question being carried by 58 to 50. Thus nothing was settled, and, on the insistence of MacDonald[18] and others, the Executive finally decided on a postal referendum of all members to determine whether there should be some official pronouncement. Each side issued circulars presenting its case. In the final tally 217 members were in favour of a statement, 259 against. About 15 Fabians then resigned in protest, including George Barnes and Pete Curran, both I.L.P. members and future Labour M.P.s. Two members of the Executive, J. Frederick Green and J. Ramsay MacDonald, also resigned,[19] the latter's departure being regarded by the Webbs and some others as a case of good riddance. The members of the pro-Boer section who remained did their best to gain control of the Executive in order, so they said, 'to bring the Society into closer touch with the General Socialist Movement' and because they felt that 'a majority of the Fabian Executive should be pledged opponents of an aggressive national policy.'[20] In the elections of officers in April, however, the old members were all re-elected, only the two seats vacated by resignation being filled by pro-Boers. The composition of the Executive remained, therefore, essentially unaltered.

By refusing to commit itself the Fabian Society had not, as some of its critics asserted, thrown its support behind militarism and imperialist expansion. Yet those who supported the views of Shaw and the Webbs in this matter certainly left themselves open to such suspicions. Was it little wonder that men like Hardie and Glasier, imbued as they were with a strong evangelicalism and with notions of international brotherly love, reacted unfavourably to Webb when he dealt with the problem in South Africa largely in terms of tidying up the Empire.[21] Not that the Webbs were uncritical of what was being done. They hated Jingoism—or, for that matter, any extreme display of emotion—and Beatrice, on the eve of the war, had felt that whatever may have been the rights and wrongs of Chamberlain's policy in its broader issues, his methods had been 'vulgar and tricky.'[22] The main point, however, was that both she and Sidney failed signally to appreciate the tremendous import and emotional value still attaching to words like 'liberty' and 'freedom,' words which were the stock-in-trade of every I.L.P. spell-binder and every unreformed Gladstonian Liberal. Already the Webbs, and Shaw too, were displaying that myopic infatuation with measurement by results which left little room for small independent states of backward farmers and which accounts in part for their later rather sudden and uncritical acceptance of a gigantic bureaucratic dictatorship. 'What in the name of common sense have we to do with obsolete hypocrisies about peoples "rightly struggling to be free",'[23] wrote Sidney Webb of South Africa. By sponsoring such views the I.L.P. and socialists of like persuasion had only proven themselves hopeless. 'When the war came, the secret was out,' he wrote in 1901. 'Outside the two spheres of labour and local government, the majority of the Socialist leaders proved to be, with regard to the British Empire, mere administrative Nihilists— that is to say, ultra-Nationalists, ultra-Gladstonian, Old-Liberal to the fingertips. They out-Morleyed Morley on the burning topic of the day, and now the Independent Labour Party is as hopelessly out of the running as the Gladstonian Party.'[24]

Even before Webb wrote this reproof the Society had made an official pronouncement on Imperialism. It took the form of a Manifesto for the General Election in October 1900. Entitled *Fabianism and the Empire* and drafted by Shaw, the Manifesto was submitted to the members and opportunity given for wide criticism and alterations before its publication. Regarding the South African War it whitewashed neither major party but insisted that aside from the rights and wrongs of the situation 'the notion that a nation had the right to do what it pleases with its own territory, without reference to the interests of the rest of the world' could no longer be held tenable. '. . . a Great Power, consciously or unconsciously, must govern in the interests of civilization as a whole; and it [was] not to those interests that such mighty forces as gold fields and the formidable armaments that [could] be built upon them, should be wielded irresponsibly by small communities of frontiersmen. . . .'[25] In February, in a speech to the Fabian Society, Shaw had expressed this even more strongly: 'The world is to the big and powerful states by necessity: and the little ones must come within their borders or be crushed out of existence.'[26]

From his retirement Lord Rosebery had assumed the role of mouthpiece for those Liberals who agreed that no government could repeat the policy pursued by Gladstone after the British reversal at Majuba. Sharing most of Rosebery's views in imperial matters were Grey, Haldane, Asquith and Fowler, all of whom found it increasingly difficult to support the official Liberal leader in the House, Sir Henry Campbell-Bannerman. Rosebery, however, proved a poor chief for a section which neither controlled the party machinery nor enjoyed a commanding support of the Liberal rank and file. Irresolute, unpredictable, and apparently not avid for a return to the premiership, he emerged from seclusion only periodically. The speeches he then delivered, though brilliant and enhancing to his own reputation, served largely to spread consternation and division in the party so long as he himself remained outside its inner councils.

Campbell-Bannerman tried hard to maintain a middle position between these so-called Liberal Imperialists and the pro-Boer wing of the party and was closely supported by Lord Spencer, Bryce, and by Herbert Gladstone, the Chief Liberal Whip. While admitting the necessity of successfully prosecuting the war once it had begun, 'C.B.' would not forgo criticism of what he deemed the Government's earlier policy of bluff and provocation. By a speech late in 1901 attacking the British concentration camps and the burning of Boer farms as 'methods of barbarism' he finally abandoned his on-the-fence proclivities. Thereafter he was regarded with much warmer feelings by the party's anti-war section. Its leaders included, among others, Harcourt, Morley, Sir Robert Reid, and a fiery young Welsh M.P., David Lloyd George.[27]

It so happened that the Liberal leaders whom the Webbs thought most promising and progressive—including Grey, Haldane and Asquith—were almost all in the Liberal Imperialist camp. If these men were not convinced collectivists they were, it appeared to the Webbs, at least not fearful of cutting new paths either in domestic or foreign policy and were not guilty, at any rate, of the almost axiomatic Gladstonian hostility to state action. Sidney Webb had hopes that Lord Rosebery, their ostensible chief, might 'escape from Houndsditch' and give expression to a new Liberalism in touch with the progressive instinct of the twentieth century. As President of the L.C.C. Rosebery had been friendly to the Progressives and, no longer hampered by any considerations for the Liberal Front Bench, he spoke of the need for a new party and a new programme. The Fabians also stressed this need. In 1898 Shaw had written that the old parliamentary lines of division were 'boneless and dead.' Another 'To Your Tents, O Israel!' might be desirable, he suggested, to give the Tory Government a scolding similar to that inflicted on the Liberals five years earlier, but a programme, if one were drafted, should not be offered to the Liberals but to whomever would take it up. 'It seems to me,' he wrote, 'that the only chance of securing notice of such a thing is to make a pretence of organizing a populist party to consist, not of Socialists or of I.L.P.'ers but of disgusted Radicals and Progressive Liberals.'[28]

Apparently this idea was never considered seriously, and, in any case, divisions in the radical and progressive ranks as a result of the war would have made any feigned attempt to organize a new party around some Fabian programme not altogether feasible. Still the Webbs were intrigued by the possibility that the anti-Gladstonians and non-Morleyites in the Liberal party might rally to Rosebery. Though they were puzzled by the former Prime Minister and had grave doubts about his conversion to their measure of collectivism, they felt that he held no stubborn views inconsistent with their own. Admittedly, his speeches on domestic problems were largely a series of negative injunctions—he called for a policy of the 'clean slate' and as a substitute for the old Liberal programme had almost nothing to offer beyond suggesting that the main stress be on 'efficiency.'[29] The Webbs, however, were not altogether dismayed by this. A good sweeping of the dusty Gladstonian attic was in order and a considerable gain by itself. Yet, in cultivating connections with the Rosebery section of the Liberal party to the neglect of Campbell-Bannerman and the emerging leaders of the radical wing, they displayed a formidable lack of political foresight. They were not over-sanguine of Rosebery and his lieutenants, it is true, and by 1904 had little faith in the leaders of either Liberal section, but it is doubtful if they ever dreamed that 'C.B.' would prove a successful premier of a cabinet pursuing a programme of social reform while Rosebery, their former 'leader,' would within a few years publicly avow that to him 'socialism was the end of all, the negation of faith, of family, of property, of the monarchy, of the Empire.'[30]

In their likes and dislikes for individual Liberal leaders the 'old guard' Fabians often ran directly counter to the I.L.P. and the officials of the trade unions. Asquith and Haldane were extremely suspect to some of the builders of the Labour Party.[31] Asquith was a particularly vulnerable target. As Home Secretary he has been labelled, quite unjustly, as the 'murderer' of two miners killed in 1893 when troops fired on strikers in Featherstone, West Riding, and the label stuck to him for years.[32] If the I.L.P.er shared with the trade unionist admiration for anyone in the Liberal limelight it was for Morley whom Glasier thought stood 'for much that [was] essential to a socialist state and international peace'[33] but whom many Fabians regarded as a mere receptacle for outworn Gladstonian prejudices. Then, too, there was Lloyd George who in a few years would be stealing much of the socialists' thunder with his new budgets and workmen's insurance but whom the Webbs, as late as 1904, according to one acquaintance, considered 'absolutely apathetic'[34] in this direction. Also there was Campbell-Bannerman whom socialists and trade unionists came to admire and respect for his dogged courage and for his insistence on a magnanimous peace but whom the Webbs appear to have completely misjudged. Beatrice after meeting him at a dinner in December 1900 described him as 'a quite stupid person for a leader—well suited to a position of wealthy squire or a sleeping partner in an inherited business.'[35]

These Fabian judgments, on the surface, may seem to have been decidedly well taken, especially in the case of Morley, a quite unregenerate individualist by socialist standards. Had Glasier's own socialism not contained a strong admixture of old-style Radicalism he would never have regarded Morley as he did. One might also admit that Lloyd George should perhaps be regarded only as a fair-weather friend of socialism, an astute general fighting a Liberal rear-guard action through timely concessions; Shaw later referred to his reform efforts as 'the blundering attempts of this disastrous ignoramus to regurgitate what he had swallowed of Socialism.'[36] As for 'C.B.' he was to move much further to the left than seemed likely on the basis of his previous record, and few men, even in his own party, would have predicted his development into an effective parliamentarian. The point, however, is that those socialists who were moved more by sentiment than by cold logic, and who were far less clever than the Fabians, were better able to identify themselves with men in the Liberal party who later did yeoman service in the cause of social reform. Many Fabians denied that there could ever be any latent constructive power in indignant Nonconformism, whether middle- or working-class, or in 'Labour candidates officially run by the great trade unions and backed by pro-Boer capitalists.'[37] They underestimated the genuineness not only of anti-imperialist feeling but later of Nonconformist resentment to the Education Bill. As a result they alienated many a Liberal and Labour politician of influence. The I.L.P. and the main elements of the Labour Representation Committee became more and more identified with Liberalism on the major issues of the day, and thus rode to victory on the great Liberal wave of 1906. The Fabians on the morrow of that victory found their suggestions ignored by many of the rising young lights of the Liberal and Labour parties. The Fabian imprint was therefore lacking on many of the great social measures which these men helped to bring forward.

The war period may be presented as a time of discouragement for the political Labour movement when the price of championing an unpopular cause was the boycotting of Labour candidates by a vast section of the electorate. Contrariwise it may be recalled as an exhilarating episode, a fine, fighting time, when to risk the buffetings of the mob was to feel oneself in an heroic and select company. With emotions so centred on a single issue, long-held political antagonisms, if there was common agreement against the war, were bound to temporarily weaken or dissolve, and a mutual sympathy and respect and even a camaraderie grew up between those socialists and Liberals who fought at each other's side.

With the Liberal forces torn by inner strife many Liberals found it difficult to know for just what principles their party stood. A. H. D. Acland, Vice-President of the Education Board in Gladstone's Fourth Cabinet and of that younger group, including Asquith and Grey, in whom the Fabians put so much store,[38] inquired of Asquith in 1901 whether, if he returned to politics he would be obliged to choose between two parties, one of which contained Thomas Burt and John Burns whose sympathies he now shared, or the other party containing men like Grey? Was he to be ostracized by the party he did not join?[39] Younger men in the party often had grave doubts about embarking upon a political career, feeling that their own leaders were using the war as a plaything of politics and were as much interested in personal vindication as in a just peace settlement. Some of these young Liberals were attracted to socialism. George Unwin partly expressed their feelings when he wrote to the wife of Leonard Courtney in September 1900, describing how in certain Liberal circles the view was growing that the only hope of the party lay in adopting whatever was practical in the socialist programme. 'What is really needed in my opinion,' he wrote, 'is not a half sincere adoption of Socialist principles for the sake of re-invigorating party life (Asquith and Chamberlain have already followed that line) but a vigorous lead by a man who is in real touch and real sympathy with the needs and aspirations of the intelligent part of the working class. I wish John Burns were capable of it. The "we are all Socialists now" attitude is too cheap and ineffectual, and it does not remove the root evil which lies in classes and which leaves us at the mercy of the demagogue and the mob.'[40]

In the Radical section of the Liberal party were some of the most extreme pro-Boers, H. J. Wilson, C. P. Scott, F. A. Channing, Duncan Pirie and Lloyd George among others, whose sympathy with working-class demands and aspirations was widely recognized. Since 1870 there had been a distinct Radical group in Parliament with Sir Charles Dilke as its first secretary and with Campbell-Bannerman and Harcourt among its first members. It remained loosely organized, sometimes having a secretary but never a chairman. Labour members were generally regarded as belonging to this section. 'It was always understood,' according to Dilke, 'that the whole of the section were favourable to the Miners' Eight Hours Bill and were favourable to every drastic action with regard to the House of Lords and the payment of members. Most of them were supporters of adult suffrage and Home Rule. All of them took part in balloting for Labour measures.'[41] Dilke himself, in close touch with the trade union leaders, regularly arranged with them for the introduction of certain measures in the House. Also, he commanded the respect of Hardie and of most I.L.P. socialists. In his diary he makes the claim that the Labour Party as realized in 1906 was his original scheme for the I.L.P. developed in talks with Henry Hyde Champion and Ben Tillett before the Bradford conference of 1893.[42]

The question of the proper socialist attitude toward these Liberal Radicals was a recurrent one, the Manchester Fourth Clause having been the most drastic suggestion for dealing with the problem. In large part the I.L.P. had studiously avoided any co-operation with Radicals for electoral purposes or otherwise, but the venomous denunciation of all Liberals, no matter what their stamp, had been toned down considerably. Even before the South African War, proposals for a more sympathetic attitude toward certain Radicals were being seriously mooted among socialists. From *Clarion* and S.D.F. sources in 1898 came suggestions for a closer collaboration with 'democratic' members of Parliament,[43] and from A. M. Thompson, 'Dangle' of the *Clarion*, the argument that exceptions should be made where candidates professed principles leading in a socialist direction.[44] In the *Labour Leader*, however, this 'worship of the Radical Democrat' had been derided, and Hardie had vowed that he would have no part in 'betraying the Socialist movement into the hands of its enemies.'[45]

It was Hyndman's boast, early in 1899, that socialists had it in their power, either by voting Tory or by abstaining, to prevent the Liberal leaders from ever taking office again. If ever Radicals broke from the older parties, he argued, it would be possible for socialists to make political arrangements with them without compromise of principle. For the present, however, though

Radical leaders had been urging him to throw in his lot with theirs,[46] Hyndman wanted socialists to vote Tory so long as Liberals refused to give place to socialist candidates. At the S.D.F. annual conference in August 1899, a resolution was passed, despite strong opposition, calling for S.D.F. members to work for the extinction of Liberal candidates by voting steadily on the Tory side up to and through the General Election.[47]

The I.L.P., by this time, was pursuing a different line. In January 1899, an article by Hardie and MacDonald entitled *The I.L.P. Programme*, authorized for publication by the N.A.C., had appeared in the *Nineteenth Century*. Already the party had decided against undertaking unlimited propaganda candidatures, and Hardie in the summer of 1898 had admitted that a repetition of 1895 might be disastrous and that if no seats could be won, Parliamentary contests might best be left alone.[48] The policy finally adopted called for concentrating I.L.P. energies on no more than twenty-five seats in the coming General Election—actually it fought only ten—and one of the purposes of the article in the *Nineteenth Century* was to forewarn the Liberals of I.L.P. plans. 'If there is any serious intention to let us alone in a certain number of constituencies,' wrote Hardie and MacDonald, 'an early announcement of what these constituencies are may lead to that harmony which, we are constantly assured, some of our opponents desire. If, however, the lesson of the last election has not been assimilated, and candidates are run indiscriminately against us, the result may be another Liberal smash—but the blame will not be ours. . . .' More important than this were the suggestions of a more tolerant attitude toward Liberal Radicals. 'The party as a propagandist and educating body,' the article stated, 'must remain as heretofore Socialist. But we can now afford to identify ourselves with those questions of immediate reform upon which Radicals and Socialists are alike agreed, with less fear of allowing our aims to be obscured and the party swallowed up in the ranks of the shiftless opportunist . . . independence is not isolation, and in so far as co-operation with kindred sections is possible, whilst retaining our freedom, there is no barrier to it in our methods or tradition. We have always been aware that a policy of wrecking for its own sake would not commend itself to the thinking portion of the electorate.'[49]

The sympathetic middle-class voter and the Liberal trade unionist were reassured by such remarks. They were written by men whose interests and energies were centred, as at the Memorial Hall Conference, not so much on uncompromisingly preaching socialism as on removing obstacles to political success.

## NOTES

1. Shaw annotation to the manuscript of Pease's *History*.
2. The Parliamentary Committee wondered 'if it would be wise and prudent policy for the Trades Union Congress in the future to identify itself with Congresses of this character.' Herbert Tracy, editor. *Book of the Labour Party*, 3 vols., London, 1925, vol. i, 115.
3. *I.L.P. Ann. Report*, 1900, 3.
4. *ibid.*, 1901, 35.
5. Carl Roberts, *Philip Snowden*, London, 1929, 74.
6. Frederick J. Gould, *Hyndman Prophet of Socialism*, London, 1928, 129-130.
7. *I.L.P. Ann. Report*, 1900, 21.
8. Burns diary: Entry of Oct. 10, 1899.
9. *ibid.*, Entry of Dec. 13, 1899.
10. Parliamentary Debates, Commons, Burns, Feb. 6, 1900, cols. 795 and 797.
11. *T.U.C. Ann. Report*, 1900, 54-55.
12. *ibid.*, 1901, 37 and 80.
13. Shaw to Pease, Oct. 30, 1899.
14. *Fabian Ann. Report*, 1900, 8; Pease, *History*, 129-130.
15. Olivier letter of Oct. 14, 1899, considered by a meeting of the Fabian Executive on Oct. 20.
16. Bland to Pease, Oct. 17, 1899.
17. Hobson to Olivier, Oct. 24, 1899.
18. MacDonald to Pease, Dec. 28, 1899.
19. *Fabian Ann. Report*, 1900, 8; Pease, *History*, 133.
20. Circular letter sent out by S. G. Hobson and J. Lawson Dodd soliciting votes for their list of candidates for the Executive, March 1900.
21. '. . . so to organize it as to promote the maximum development of each individual state within its bounds.' Sidney Webb, 'Lord Rosebery's Escape from Houndsditch,' *Nineteenth Century*, Sept. 1901, 372.
22. Beatrice Webb diaries: Entry of October 10, 1899.
23. Sidney Webb, 'Lord Rosebery's Escape, etc.,' 371.
24. *ibid.*, 374.
25. Bernard Shaw, ed., *Fabianism and the Empire*, London, 1900, 23 and 24.
26. Speech to Fabian Society, Feb. 23, 1900.
27. In late February, 1900, about a week before the conference which founded the Labour Representation Committee, Beatrice Webb recorded the following remarks on the feuds and dissensions among the Liberals:

# The Advent of the Labour Party

'From all accounts matters are going from bad to worse with the Liberal Party. Rosebery, Haldane says, has decided that the Liberal Party is no good as an instrument for him, and the bulk of the Liberals are angry at his aloofness and upsetting interventions. Campbell-Bannerman, nominally a "sane" Imperialist, is at heart a "Peace man," with all the old Liberal principles and prejudices writ large on his mind—retrenchment in public expenditure and no compulsion either at home or abroad. The little clique of Imperialists . . . have been forced to sit tight on the fence, openly condemning the methods whilst they secretly approve of the policy of the Government. The small knot of thoroughgoing opponents of the war have not made themselves felt in the Liberal Party, the limelight of creed, of Peace at any price, being taken by Leonard Courtney and Sir Edward Clark, two Unionists. Wherever two or three Liberals are gathered together there is a wrangle which ends in a black ball or a motion for expulsion in a Liberal Club. And this friction is made more distracting by the fact that the cleavage about the war runs right across the cleavage on economic affairs: the old "Illingworth set" being again on the left of the Liberal Party whilst some of the most progressive reformers are flirting with Imperialism and even talk well of Milner. The result is that Liberal M.P.s no longer press their young friends to try to get into the House of Commons.' Beatrice Webb diaries: Entry of Feb. 20, 1900.

28. Two letters of Shaw to Pease, July 21, 1898.

29. Sir William Harcourt, whose dislike for Rosebery was undisguised, wrote to Herbert Gladstone of one of Rosebery's speeches, 'Perhaps if we have "divested ourselves of the impulses of party", "annihilated faction", "discarded obsolete shibboleths" and obtained "freedom from formula" we may be able to do without any contest at all and unanimously elect a purely Tory House of Commons. . . .' Harcourt to Gladstone, June 4, 1900. Herbert Gladstone Papers, vol. xxii, 22.

30. Rosebery speech in early Sept. 1909, quoted in E. T. Raymond, *The Man of Promise: Lord Rosebery*, London, 1923, 228.

31. See Chapter XIV, p. 244, for Hardie s views of Asquith and Haldane.

32. J. A. Spender and Cyril Asquith, *Life of Asquith*, London, 1932, 2 vols., vol. i, 83.

33. Glasier to Hardie, Feb. 26, 1903.

34. 'At the same time they developed, on the Radical side, a similar repugnance to Lloyd George! The present writer had notes of a conversation as late as 8 June, 1904, in which they described him as "absolutely apathetic" towards social reform.' (R. C. K. Ensor, 'Permeation', in *The Webbs and Their Work*, 67). Yet on this very same date, when the Webbs had Lloyd George to dinner, Beatrice's reaction to him was not unsympathetic and certainly not one of repugnance. 'Lloyd George is altogether superior both in character and in intellect to Winston Churchill or Herbert Gladstone. He is a worthy little person with intense personal ambition, but with assiduous industry and honest convictions and brilliant Parliamentary talents. But he, also, has no notion of national administration or the problems that it involves.' Beatrice Webb diaries: Entry of June 8, 1904.

35. *ibid.*: Entry of Dec. 15, 1900.

36. Shaw's annotation to manuscript of Pease's *History*.

37. Webb, *Our Partnership*, 232.

38. This group had in the early nineties hoped to see Acland become the

party's Chief Whip. H. H. Asquith, *Memories and Reflections*, Boston, 1928, 2 vols., vol. i, 185.

39. A. H. D. Acland to J. A. Spender, July 17, 1901. Spender papers.
40. George Unwin to Kate Courtney, Sept. 23, 1900, Courtney papers, vol. vii, 231-234.
41. Dilke memorandum of Jan. 31, 1906. Dilke papers.
42. Stephen Gwynn and Gertrude M. Tuckwell, *Life of Sir Charles Dilke*, London, 1917, 2 vols., vol. ii, 356 and 467.
43. Lowe, *From Pit*, 152.
44. *Clarion*, Oct. 15, 1898.
45. Lowe, *From Pit*, 152 and 155.
46. Hyndman to Dilke, Feb. 9, 1899, Dilke Papers; Hyndman in *Clarion*, Jan. 21, 1899.
47. *S.D.F. Ann. Report*, 1899, 22-25; 1900, 12.
48. *Labour Leader*, May 14, 1898.
49. J. Ramsay MacDonald and J. Keir Hardie, 'The I.L.P. Programme,' *Nineteenth Century*, Jan. 1899.

# CHAPTER VII

# 1900—*Labour and Liberalism in the 'Khaki' Election*

THE first L.R.C. Executive chose as its Chairman Frederick Rogers of the Vellum Bookbinders and as Treasurer Richard Bell. The other trade union representatives were Pete Curran (Gasworkers), Alan Gee (Yorkshire Textile Workers), Alexander Wilkie (Shipwrights), John Hodge (Steel Smelters), and Thomas Greenall (Lancashire Miners). When Greenall's society chose not to affiliate, he was replaced by H. Brill of the Coal Porters' Union. For the I.L.P. sat Hardie and James Parker, President of the Halifax Trades Council; for the S.D.F. Harry Quelch and A. A. Watts (James MacDonald having resigned soon after appointment); and for the Fabian Society, Edward Pease.

In the lean first years the Committee used the Ramsay MacDonald home in London for its headquarters. This was a simply furnished flat at 3 Lincoln's Inn Fields. In one of the rooms, rather dark, none too spacious, and looking out upon the rear of the Holborn Music Hall, an office was set up. The atmosphere at the MacDonalds' was hectic. Mrs. MacDonald, like her husband, pursued an active public life—in the Women's Industrial Union among other organizations. Journalists, social workers, politicians and other acquaintances crowded to frequent 'open house.' There were the MacDonald children to care for, and the apartment as both home and office was often strewn with blue books, committee reports and playthings while an office assistant, both parents being absent, added baby sitting to his other tasks. Physical arrangements were at times rather makeshift, and Jim Middleton, who became MacDonald's assistant, recalls the burly John Hodge at one meeting of the Executive seated firmly on a coal scuttle. A meeting ended, the Committee members would sometimes gather round the fireplace to chat before going their separate ways; on these occasions, Pease noticed, the usually reserved MacDonald was at his most affable.[1]

The meetings were business-like, sticking closely to the point at issue. As a rule deliberations were marked by a spirit of compromise and caution, but the socialist-trade union cleavage sometimes revealed itself in sharp exchanges as was the case when the Committee had to decide between Wilkie and Curran as rival claimants to a Labour candidature at Jarrow. Hardie, steering a wary course aimed at avoiding such factional outbursts, was usually the dominant figure and a good committee man, according to Pease. Some of those close to the L.R.C. came to suspect that MacDonald envied Hardie this ascendancy. Withdrawn, somewhat superior in manner, respected but not loved for his intellectual attainments, MacDonald could never win the warm affection bestowed upon the older man. Moreover, beneath the surface of an apparent imperturbability, he was deeply sensitive to contradiction and to criticism, and later, though not so much in these first years when he was still feeling his way, he would quarrel with many of the members of the Executive and reveal to intimates a burning irritation with Hardie's propensity for taking action without consulting colleagues. No matter what was said of MacDonald, however, no one denied his ability, his tremendous capacity for work, and the admiration which he inspired in the rank and file. He looked and acted like a leader, and he towered above most of his associates in education and in all-round capability.

As Secretary, MacDonald was obliged to maintain an air of impartiality. He was not officially a member of the Executive, had no vote, and in committee was inclined to refrain from expressing his opinion even when asked to do so. Yet, whenever he felt it necessary he could make suggestions with frankness and with force, as some of his letters to Executive members show. Also if he would not speak himself, others could speak for him, and given Hardie and Glasier's respect for his judgment, he must have exerted a considerable influence in determining I.L.P. decisions. As the L.R.C. expanded and its task grew more complex, the Executive, meeting infrequently, found it impossible to cope with many questions demanding swift solution, especially whenever elections approached. It was left therefore to MacDonald to exercise an increasing control and initiative in improvising and organizing for electoral success. As Secretary he travelled a great deal, urging affiliations to the L.R.C., campaigning on behalf of its candidates, and smoothing over all sorts of difficulties at local levels. Deputations to trade unions and trades councils had to be arranged, information on electoral prospects amassed, L.R.C. pamphlets written and a stream of reports and replies to queries sent out to member societies. In addition to his L.R.C. work MacDonald contributed to periodicals and newspapers, bore his share of the load as a leader in the I.L.P. and even found time to write at length on a trip to South Africa in 1902, and to produce a book on his philosophy of evolutionary socialism.

By mid-July 1900, close to five months after its creation, the Committee was getting its bearings, but it was doing little more. Ignored by the vast body of trade unionists it needed above all to advertise itself. To all unions with a membership of over 500 and to several with a smaller membership the official report of the founding conference had been sent out—over 4,000 copies being distributed. Affiliations were coming in slowly. There were only 232,000 members, not counting two or three trades councils. Several of the larger societies, including the Engineers and the Boot and Shoe Operatives, were taking a vote on the question of joining. A large trade union meeting at Leeds had been attended by members of the Executive. Hardie and Wilkie had addressed the North Yorkshire and Cleveland Miners. Speakers had been sent out to a number of trades councils, including those at Manchester and Sheffield. In a few instances affiliated organizations ready to sponsor candidates—the Sunderland Trades Council, for example— had asked the Committee to recommend a list of eligible aspirants, but just what the Committee should do in regard to assisting candidates was still uncertain. Though information was being accumulated from all over the country, effective electoral work was extremely difficult for a new body too weak and too wrapped up with its own growing pains to possess much prestige or authority. The General Election, less than three months away, found the L.R.C., therefore, quite ill-prepared. There were by then 312,000 members. The Committee issued 330,000 election manifestos but left most of the work to the individual societies, its total expenditure during the whole fight being no more than £33. The I.L.P. fighting ten of the fifteen contests in which the L.R.C. engaged, bore the main burden.[2]

As the Boer War was widely regarded as 'Chamberlain's War' so was the Election of 1900 considered to be his election. Around him the storm of campaign oratory centred, and Liberals were at least in agreement in their hearty dislike of the Colonial Secretary. For the Liberal Imperialists Chamberlain had little respect, and with the feeling reciprocated, this constituted a major barrier to any widespread Liberal defections. At first Chamberlain wanted an election in June just after Johannesburg and Pretoria had been occupied, but he was unable to convince others in the Cabinet. In July when they were convinced, the problems arising from the Boxer Rebellion in China made for delay.[3] The dissolution of Parliament finally came on September 25. The polling began in less than a week and extended over more than a fortnight. It was clearly an appeal to 'Khaki,' an attempt to exploit patriotic sentiment and war success in terms of votes for the Government, and it was regretted as not quite 'cricket' even by many Tories. Chamberlain maintained the offensive, lumping all Liberals together and heaping ridicule on those who voted supplies for a war which they publicly condemned. The leaders of political Labour he hardly noted, and when he did, it was with undisguised contempt. Even in 1893 he had argued that anyone with sympathy for the working classes and a political programme might ignore such leaders.[4] The 'so-called champions of Labour' in Parliament, he said in 1900, were like fish out of water blindly following the lead of the Liberal and Home Rule Party. The working classes had gained most from the Conservatives, he asserted, two of the main contributions being Free Education and Workmen's

Compensation; yet the latter measure had been pushed through only in the teeth of certain Labour M.P.s.[5] At this studied insult to Labour's worthy representatives Liberal speakers were quick to express their indignation.[6]

The Liberal position in the Election of 1900 appeared no more enviable than that of Labour—in fact, less so; there was so much more to lose. With war the main issue, with the Liberal coat of mail plainly splotched with 'Khaki,' and with some of the Liberal leaders hardly on speaking terms, any effective opposition seemed impossible, and Herbert Gladstone, the Liberal Chief Whip, soon despaired of his responsibility for organizing a national campaign. As the Election approached, Campbell-Bannerman displayed little of the drive and firmness which characterized his later leadership. In attempting to maintain a centre position, he annoyed the party's two extremes and, at the same time, was unable to spark any emotional reponse among the Liberal middle-grounders. With only a semblance of unity in the party and with some Roseberyites unwilling even to concede him as their leader, he naturally laboured under terrible handicaps in pretending to speak the party's mind. He had been encouraged to avoid any strong stand by Gladstone who feared that an outright condemnation of the Government's war policy might split the Liberal Front Bench.[7] In late July, however, the Liberal pro-Boers had forced the issue, and a division on the conduct of the war had been taken in the House. Thirty-one Liberals voted against the Government, forty voted with it, and 'C.B.' and thirty-five others abstained.[8] This spectacle of party disintegration was in no way mitigated by 'C.B.'s' inaction and his disbelief in the imminence of an Autumn Election. The dissolution, as has been stated, came on September 25. In August and up to September 22 he remained in Europe with his ailing wife, despite Gladstone's entreaties that he return early to England. He was at Marienbad in mid-August, when Gladstone wrote to Robert Hudson, Secretary of the National Liberal Federation, that the whole party waited 'for the smallest of inspiration, but it is all smothered in a Marienbad mud bath. . . . Our efforts to find a leader are about as successful as Tommy Atkins' efforts to shoot a Boer.'[9] At the end of the month Hudson informed Gladstone, who was neglecting work at headquarters, that very little was being done there to advance preparations for the Election, since only Gladstone and his chief lieutenant, Jesse Herbert, had handled the negotiations with candidates, and both were away. 'If [the Election] is coming in four weeks' time,' wrote Hudson, 'I'm afraid there will be an awful scramble here in the office to get things into shape!'[10] Gladstone's reply was pessimistic: 'If I thought I could advance matters I would come up at once. But what profit is there in urging lagging constituencies to expose their mostly unsaleable articles to people who don't want to buy? It really comes to this, that if the election comes in October & our leaders won't lead we must scramble through as best we can.'[11] Writing to 'C.B.', Gladstone told him that headquarters, only able to dig and coerce, had suffered 'some disgusting rebuffs' over appeals for money. 'Of course,' he added, 'everyone asks what the policy of the party will be. . . . They say that the election may and probably will be on us in a fortnight and not a single front bench man has spoken or written anything.'[12]

Later Gladstone had to defend himself against accusations that Liberal headquarters failed to advise and remonstrate properly with the associations, so that many seats were left uncontested, and that unsuitable candidates had been sent down who discouraged Liberals in the constituencies. 'I undertake to say,' he wrote to one of his critics, 'that no Whip ever ransacked the country for candidates as I did. I interviewed hundreds of men. It was a hopeless business. I wrote to the best local men in every district of England for possible names and ran dry every organization like the N.L.F. and the 80 Club. A number of constituencies absolutely *refused* to fight, in some cases where capable candidates were available.'[13],

From all this and the fact that over 160 seats went to the Government without opposition, it can be seen that the old arguments about Labour endangering Liberal prospects at the polls could have little force in 1900. It was not only from a sense of expediency that the Liberals left a number of L.R.C. candidates free to fight the Tory but also out of necessity and partly out of sheer apathy. At the Memorial Hall Conference

Will Thorne had spoken of the L.R.C. as a possible intrument for reaching some agreement with the Liberals in regard to seats, and Hardie had given assurances that nothing in his past record would prevent him from supporting such a proposal though he doubted that much could be gained. Two weeks after Thorne and Hardie had made these remarks, Sam Woods, Chairman of the Parliamentary Committee, was writing to MacDonald urging that the L.R.C. approach the Liberal Chief Whip who, he thought, might be disposed 'to set apart a reasonable number of fairly hopeful constituencies.'[14] In May, however, at a meeting of the L.R.C., Pete Curran and Harry Quelch spoke against the Woods proposal, and a motion by John Hodge, seconded by Alan Gee, that all parties be approached also failed to carry, the Committee dividing evenly in a four to four vote. The proposal again came up for consideration—in early June and on the first of September—but the Committee remained divided, deferred discussion, and appears never to have sought positive assurances from Liberal or any other party headquarters.[15] That MacDonald or some other member of the Committee was able informally to let Herbert Gladstone know the L.R.C.'s intentions is not at all unlikely, but that any formal top-level understanding was ever arrived at seems highly doubtful.

Related to this question of seeking clear runs was the much debated problem of whether socialists should cast their votes for certain non-socialists. When at a by-election in May the Manchester and Salford I.L.P. resolved to support the anti-war Liberal, Leif Jones, the N.A.C. was disturbed lest this constitute a dangerous precedent.[16] Early in the same month Glasier had dealt with the question in the *Clarion*. 'I have ventured to raise the question of an "Exemption List" for a few *Pro Labour* and *Pro Peace* M.P.s,' he wrote Hardie. 'I don't know that we have ever discussed the matter—except that you once mentioned the name of Dilke. However if the point will raise any discussion from the outside it may liven interest in our party a little. Several folk like Lloyd George *et al* are, I understand, to be asked to write, and I thought it might be "politic" not to bang the door in their faces if we wished to draw any statement from them. I really hope I am not becoming a politician at a day's notice!'[17]

As men clearly dissentient from their own parties on Labour and social questions Glasier mentioned Dilke, Lloyd George, F. A. Channing, Henry Labouchere, C. P. Scott and Sir John Gorst, a Tory Democrat. He recalled as a precedent for supporting these men that the Irish when deciding to cast the whole Nationalist vote against the Liberals in 1885, exempted a few Liberals who had consistently opposed coercion in Ireland. 'The difficulty of deciding upon such a list would, however, be great,' Glasier concluded, 'and the temptations toward a political latitudinarianism not a few.'[18] Hardie in backing the idea suggested John Morley and Leonard Courtney as worthy of support, revealing, in doing so, how much he put the anti-war attitude foremost.[19] At one point he called on Morley to lead disgruntled Liberals and the new working-class political movement in a new combination,[20] but this may have been largely a rhetorical flourish; at any rate Morley did not respond. Richard Bell expressed the view that, 'Men who ha[d] dared to stand out against this Chamberlain-Rhodes war should be supported whatever their opinion [might] be with regard to other matters,'[21] but there were warnings against this readiness to make the war the sole test. G. N. Barnes pointed out that a candidate's attitude on pensions, housing, and factory regulation was also worth considering and that from what he had seen of some of the anti-war men, little could be expected from them in these directions.[22] Shaw, having just finished *Fabianism and the Empire*, wrote to a colleague, 'The Labour Leader "White List" is the final stroke—the white flag held up to Liberalism at the moment when we are on the verge of victory over it.'[23]

Yet no formal list was ever drawn up, and when the I.L.P. held its General Election Conference on September 29 a proposal that the branches be strongly recommended 'to vote in favour of those candidates with a good anti-imperialist and Labour recommendation' was defeated, though by a close vote, forty-two to thirty-nine. Such a declaration would have been of small importance anyway. That there was no stigma attached to voting for certain non-socialists was clearly understood, and when it was decided that each branch should be left to itself to decide 'what action to take, if any, so as to best promote the interests of Labour and Socialism at the polls'[24] it was obvious that many I.L.P. votes would be cast for Liberals unless, of course, they were regarded as imperialist or anti-Labour.

Hardie, while favouring this support of certain pro-Boers, continued sceptical of asking the Liberals for any promises of abstentions, and cited the situation in West Fife in Scotland as proof of the worthlessness of such overtures.[25] Here, with no Liberal taking the field, the miners agreed to run one of their own men, a non-socialist, and the Scottish Miners Federation gave its approval; but instead of allowing the miner a clear run, as might have been expected, the Liberal Association decided finally to put forward its own candidate, a Mr. J. D. Hope.[26] Feeling it unwise to pursue the fight the miners had withdrawn, but with much ill-feeling.

John Burns, hard pressed by a Conservative for his Battersea seat, continued to urge the closest Liberal-Labour co-operation, but he was not sanguine of its being achieved. 'I had hoped that Labour and Liberalism might at this Election have united on a common action against this Government, if only over this dreadful war,' he wrote Gladstone on September 12, 'but it seems only to have increased the cross currents and added a ground swell of faction difficult to override, guide or direct. . . . If there had been a strong clear cut lead either against the war as a whole, or even critical of its main defects, this Government could have been turned out.'[27]

Regardless of local difficulties and the apparent absence of any formal Liberal-Labour agreement the Liberals deliberately left certain Labour and Socialist candidates a free field. And in a number of places, this, together with the widespread feeling in socialist and trade union ranks in favour of backing anti-war candidates, brought the electoral forces of the L.R.C. and the Liberal party into a temporary juxtaposition.

In running only fifteen candidates, the L.R.C. was not necessarily making a maximum effort. True, if the Election had not come unexpectedly and at a time when the Committee's very survival was still in doubt, there would have been more candidates. But given the discouraging conditions under which the Election took place, there seemed little possibility of any sweeping success, no matter how many seats were contested, and the Committee was by no means anxious to urge candidatures regardless of the chances of winning. In June, in fact, it had approved a resolution 'That, as there [would] be little interest taken in domestic affairs, owing to the war, the time [was] not favourable for a long list of Labour candidates, and we recommend that the affiliated organizations should concentrate their strength and be responsible for no more candidatures than they think necessary to maintain their political position in the country.'[28] Ten of the L.R.C. candidates were put forward by the I.L.P., one of these running under joint S.D.F.-I.L.P. sponsorship; one was sponsored by the S.D.F. alone; and four candidates were run by the trade unions. W. B. Byles ran in East Leeds as an L.R.C. candidate on the mistaken assumption that he was sponsored by an affiliated trades council, and since this error was only recognized after the Election,[29] Byles' vote may be included as part of the L.R.C. poll.

The I.L.P. contests were largely financed out of the I.L.P. Election Fund which reached £1,888. A contribution of £500 came from George Cadbury, the Quaker Liberal, and was specifically earmarked to assist Hardie, Snowden, Fred Brocklehurst and A. E. Fletcher.[30] 'I hope that any influence I may have acquired will be used to prevent the I.L.P. from opposing Liberals,' wrote Cadbury to Gladstone, who had apparently raised some objection; 'if this is not the case they will get no more from me.'[31] As it turned out, only three of the seats sought by the I.L.P., Leicester, Halifax, and Merthyr, all double member constituencies, had one or more Liberals in Parliament. In two places, at Rochdale and Ashton-under-Lyne, the Socialist contended with a Liberal for a Conservative seat. In five contests the I.L.P. had a clear run against the Conservative, but two of these contests were in Tory strongholds, namely, Preston and Blackburn, where Liberal opposition would seemingly have been hopeless to begin with.

The I.L.P. put five men into Lancashire—at Rochdale, Ashton-under-Lyne, South-West Manchester, Blackburn and

Preston. All were unsuccessful. In Rochdale the party ran Allan Clarke jointly with the S.D.F. in a three-cornered fight. The Liberal emerged only nineteen votes behind the Conservative so that Clarke's poll of 901 votes had obviously cost the Liberals the seat. At Ashton the Tory was 1,148 votes ahead of the Liberal while the I.L.P. candidate received only 739 votes. In South-West Manchester the Liberal Executive, though it put no one forward to oppose Fred Brocklehurst, decided against asking Liberals to support him.[32] To this unfriendliness the defeated Brocklehurst attributed the poor Liberal showing in South Lancashire generally,[33] but in a letter published just before the polling he urged voters in other Manchester divisions not to abstain from voting Liberal on account of the 'ungenerous treatment' given him. It was 'of supreme moment that the solid Socialist and Labour vote should be cast against militarism and an aggressive foreign policy,' he wrote.[34]

In Tory Blackburn Snowden faced two Conservative members of Parliament who retained their seats with a total poll of over 20,000, Snowden getting 7,096. He was backed by the local Liberal paper, and the Liberals, in the main, supported him though not officially. On the eve of the polling the Tories introduced a handbill, 'Down with Atheism, Socialism, and Anarchy!' There were 5,335 plumpers for Snowden and 1,700 who split their votes between him and the most popular Conservative. His vote was the largest for a Socialist candidate in Great Britain up to this time.[35] In another two-member Tory citadel, Preston, Hardie also fought two sitting Conservative members. The local Conservative organization was reputedly in excellent condition, and most of the workers in textiles and other local industries were traditionally its staunch supporters, but Hardie, though personally drawn toward Merthyr in South Wales, thought that Preston offered the better chance of success.[36] Glasier shared this misjudgment. On polling day the two Conservatives won easily, each with over 8,000 votes. Hardie had 4,834 supporters of whom 3,453 were plumpers and the remaining 1,381 splits between Hardie and one of the Tories.[37]

Glasier in July, at Hardie's request, had put out feelers in

Merthyr in Wales through a local trade union leader as to the possibility of Hardie's being sponsored by the local Trades Council. He had given assurances that if elected Hardie would require no financial support but would depend, as before, on his own pen and lecturing.[38] By the time a group of miners had met and decided to push Hardie's candidature, however, he had committed himself to Preston. Glasier earlier had seen obstacles in Merthyr: 'the war ha[d] *apparently* brought great prosperity to the South Wales Miners,' and the Liberal candidates for the two seats were 'playing cunningly their parts.'[39] For these and other reasons Hardie thought it best to devote all of his time to Preston, and only on the announcement of his defeat there did Hardie rush south to Wales with but one day to campaign before the polling. Fortunately for Hardie the Liberals in Merthyr were divided. One candidate, D. A. Thomas (later Lord Rhondda) was a pro-Boer; the other, Pritchard Morgan, was an outspoken Liberal Imperialist whom Hardie described as 'one of the most dangerous types'[40] in the House of Commons. Thomas, even before Hardie was chosen, had let it be known that he was bound by a former pledge to support any Labour man with the general backing of the miners.[41] Attacked by Morgan, Thomas took little notice, but when nominations were closed and it was certain that no Conservative could enter the lists, he delivered a series of anti-Morgan speeches. When Morgan made the mistake of issuing a poster 'Vote for Hardie and D. A. Thomas, both pro-Boers!'[42] the majority of the electors followed his advice. Hardie became the junior member for Merthyr with 5,745 votes to 8,508 for Thomas. Of the votes for Hardie 4,874 were split with the Liberal candidates and of these no fewer than 4,437 with Thomas. There were only 867 Hardie plumpers.[43] In no sense could this contest be regarded as a clear fight between Liberalism and Labour.

The I.L.P. fought two campaigns in Yorkshire, at Halifax and West Bradford. In Halifax two Liberals, a Conservative, and Councillor James Parker of the I.L.P. fought for two seats, the Conservative coming in at the top of the poll and a Liberal, second. The defeated Liberal, who had represented Halifax in

I

the last Parliament, came close to victory, however, making Halifax the only place other than Rochdale where an I.L.P. entry appears to have cost the Liberals a seat. Parker claimed that he had lost hundreds of votes due to the Liberal insistence that his chances were hopeless and that he could only split the Liberals.[44] In West Bradford, in a clear fight with a Tory, Alderman Fred Jowett came within only forty-two votes of victory. In 1895 the Tories had taken East, West and Central Bradford, all formerly Liberal seats, and Liberals generally had attributed this severe set-back to I.L.P. opposition. This opposition had resulted from the Liberal refusal to let alone West Bradford where Ben Tillett of the I.L.P. was running and where he had in 1892 opposed a pillar of Northern Non-conformity and Liberalism named Alfred Illingworth. In 1900 many Liberals with long memories argued that as a means of insuring a kindlier I.L.P. attitude toward the Liberals the West Division might best be left open to the I.L.P. Although Liberal headquarters apparently supported some such compromise, Illingworth threw his powerful influence against it. Bradford Liberals could not work with nor place any confidence in the I.L.P. he told Gladstone and warned him that they would 'not be bartered and disposed of in attempting to square circles elsewhere.'[45] As the Election approached he assured Campbell-Bannerman that the I.L.P. was growing weaker in Bradford[46] and continued to insist on a Liberal candidate for Bradford West. When just prior to the dissolution of Parliament, however, a member of the Bradford City Council presented himself before the Western Division Liberal Executive as a possible candidate, only thirteen of its members favoured putting him forward, eight voting against. He refused, in such circumstances, to stand, and in protest against the Executive's conduct, Illingworth resigned as President of the Bradford Liberal Association.[47] The *I.L.P. News* acknowledged that the understanding with the Liberals had given Jowett a considerable number of votes.[48] Finally, in all of the Midlands there was only one I.L.P. candidate, Ramsay MacDonald, in the double-member constituency of Leicester. MacDonald received 4,164 votes, while Henry Broadhurst, the 'Lib-Lab,' topped this poll with 10,385. A Conservative took the second seat and another Liberal ran a fair third.

All of the I.L.P. candidates except Hardie, had been at the bottom of the poll, but there had been a total I.L.P. vote of 37,209 for ten candidates or an average of 3,720, as contrasted with 44,594 votes for twenty-eight candidates in 1895, an average of only 1,592. Given the Jingo atmosphere in which the Election was conducted this was a notable achievement revealing an I.L.P. solidarity, vitality and appeal which a year earlier some of its dejected leaders would hardly have suspected existed. The improved average poll owed much, however, to a more judicious distribution of effort and to a lesser number of three-cornered fights than was the case in 1895. If there were only ten candidates, this was not solely because of an inability to fight but because there was now a greater insistence on fighting well. Interest in mere propaganda candidatures had declined, and except for Ashton, and possibly Rochdale, there were none of those pathetically low I.L.P. polls so numerous in 1895. Glasier was jubilant about the results. 'Hardie's election is a great event,' he wrote to his sister. 'It will quite revive the party, though indeed the big polls for the other candidates and the fine election fund shows that the party was in any case on the point of leaping up into new life. However, Hardie's return quite crowns our hopes for the present.'[49]

Reflecting the prevailing mood among socialists the S.D.F. at its annual conference in August had rescinded its 'vote Tory' decision of the previous year and in spite of Hyndman's disapproval had passed a resolution in favour of voting for those anti-war candidates who also favoured free maintenance of children in Board Schools, adequate housing and railway nationalization.[50] Then in Burnley, where Hyndman might have stood, the pro-Boer Philip Stanhope was left free to fight the Tory, and the local S.D.F. advised its members to support him.[51] Aside from running Clarke at Rochdale with the I.L.P., and seeing a member of the S.D.F., Will Thorne, run as a trade union candidate, the S.D.F. contested Bow and Bromley with George Lansbury, who came in 1,845 votes behind the Conservative victor. Lansbury had no Liberal opposition. In a by-election in Bow and Bromley in October 1899 he had retired from the contest, ostensibly due to illness, after the Liberal pro-Boer candidate had urged a common front on the war issue and had held out the promise of Liberal abstention later on.[52] But the S.D.F. would never admit that socialists had received any Liberal favours. When Gladstone, once the Election had begun, argued that the Liberals had left Labour and socialist candidates clear runs,[53] *Justice* answered that the Liberals had nowhere left socialists a clear field except where their own chances were quite hopeless.[54]

There were four L.R.C. trade union candidates, many others, being considered, having to be dropped when the Election came so unexpectedly. Richard Bell of the Railway Servants, the only victorious L.R.C. candidate other than Hardie, ran against two Conservatives in the double-constituency of Derby. He worked in very close co-operation with a Liberal, who also won, Labour and Liberalism splitting their votes fairly evenly.[55] In the North-East at Sunderland, another double-constituency, where the Conservatives took both seats, Alexander Wilkie of the Shipwrights likewise worked closely and split votes with the Liberal, though, like Bell, maintaining a separate platform.[56] In London, Will Thorne of the S.D.F. ran in Hardie's old seat, South West Ham, as candidate of the Gasworkers, against a Conservative who polled 5,615 to Thorne's 4,419.

The fourth L.R.C. trade unionist, John Hodge of the Steel Smelters, engaged in the only clear fight between a Labour and a Liberal candidate. This was at Gower (Glamorganshire) in South Wales. Hodge consented to go forward only after John Williams, a miners' agent, mentioned as the possible Liberal candidate, had declined to run. When the Liberals then introduced another candidate, Williams spoke at the pit-heads on the Liberal's behalf.[57] Liberal headquarters was disturbed by the presence of the Labour man and wanted William Abraham ('Mabon'), the Welsh miners' leader and M.P., to use his influence to prevent a split nomination.[58] With little organization, only a fortnight in which to campaign and aided by Ben Tillet and by Hardie (after Merthyr had been won) Hodge got 3,853 votes to his opponent's 4,276.

In sum, the L.R.C. in a total of fifteen contests had polled 62,698 out of some 177,000 votes, that is about thirty-five per cent of the total poll. In five constituencies it had fought both parties, in two the Liberals alone, and in eight the Conservatives alone. One L.R.C. socialist and one L.R.C. trade unionist had won, both with strong Liberal backing. As for the 'Lib-Labs,' all of the miners, except Sam Woods, who did not represent a miners' constituency, held their seats. Ben Pickard, secure in Normanton, was the only Labour representative returned for the whole of Yorkshire. The 'Lib-Lab' group in the House was largely now a miners' group. There was also Broadhurst from Leicester and from the London area, William Cremer of Haggerstown and Burns of Battersea, but these men no longer had formal trade union ties. There were too some Irish and Radical members who worked closely with the Labour group, but, over all, 'Lib-Lab' representation in the House had been reduced by five, having suffered four important losses and Joseph Arch of the Agricultural Workers having retired.

In the new Parliament the Government had a majority of 134, only eighteen less than the anti-Home Rule majority of 1895. Scotland for the first time since the Reform Bill of 1832 had returned a minority of Liberals, but in Wales, thanks largely to Lloyd George, the Liberals gained four out of eight seats formerly held by the Tories and lost no seats. In spite of the large Conservative majority, moreover, the total popular votes for each side showed that the Liberals had far more supporters in the country than their number in Parliament would indicate. Many Conservatives realized that their victory had resulted as much from an ineffectual and disorganized opposition as from any love felt for the Government. Finishing the war, the electorate felt, might best be left to those heretofore responsible for its prosecution. Indeed many Liberals were relieved that this task had not fallen to them.[59]

Liberal differences, nevertheless, were only accentuated by the defeat for which the Liberal Imperialists were inclined to blame the anti-war section of the party. The Liberal Imperial Council which had vouched for fifty-six candidates passed a resolution after the election which stated 'that the time had arrived when it was necessary to clearly and permanently distinguish Liberals on whose policy with regard to Imperial questions patriotic voters might justly repose confidence from those whose opinions naturally disqualified them from controlling the actions of the Imperial Parliament of a world-wide community of nations.'[60] The 'pro-Boers' however, were not ready to admit that their attitude had been costly at the polls. Quite the reverse, in fact. 'Observe that very few of us who voted against the Government that afternoon in July have gone down . . ,' wrote John Morley to Frederic Harrison. 'If C. B. had only shown one half the buoyancy and verve a year ago that he shows now, the party would not be in the wretched condition it is today.'[61] Asquith, who was closer to 'C.B.' and those in his camp than most of the Liberal Imperialists, commented on the Liberal losses in a letter to Gladstone: 'The explanation of the whole thing is very simple. Where we have had a man of any real personality . . . he has held his own. But elsewhere the man in the street, who has little love for this weak and noisy Government, has failed to discern any possible alternative, and has voted, or abstained from voting accordingly.' Chamberlain was the true culprit, thought Asquith, and was contrasted unfavourably with Disraeli: 'Meanwhile, we have seen the worst fit of vulgar political debauch since 1877-78, with the difference that the orgy was then presided over by a genius, whereas now the master of the part has the manner of a cad and the tongue of a bargee.'[62]

To those socialists who were apprehensive of any collusion between the I.L.P. and the Liberal Party, the Election had not been reassuring, but the *I.L.P. News* pointed out that the fear of pro-Liberalism in 1900 was merely the counterpart of the fear of Pro-Toryism incidental to the General Election of 1895.

A neutrality or abstention policy [the *News* reminded its readers] is no more a condition of independence in politics than isolation is a condition of independence in ordinary life. It is a policy which will become more and more difficult and impolitic as our party grows and our power becomes more determinative on the political issues before the nation.

Common action with one or other of the political forces in the field must inevitably become one of our resources at elections. . . . Failure is not always a proof of honesty, nor unpopularity of wisdom.[62]

## NOTES

1. Some of the information in this and the following two paragraphs is based on talks of the author with the late Mr. Edward Pease, and with Mr. James Middleton, Assistant Secretary of the Labour party from 1903-1935 and General Secretary from 1935-1945.

2. MacDonald to Sam Woods, July 19, 1900; MacDonald to Pease, June 27, 1900; L.R.C. Minutes, June 8, 1900; L.R.C. Circular Letter on 'Labour Representation and the Election,' Nov. 1900, L.R.C. Annual Report, 1901, 11.

3. J. L. Garvin, *Life of Joseph Chamberlain*, 3 vols., London, 1932-3-4, vol. iii, 583.

4. As he stated in a letter to Dilke. See Gwynn and Tuckwell, *Dilke*, vol. ii, 347.

5. Speech at Birmingham, Sept. 29, 1900, *Manchester Guardian*, Oct. 1, 1900.

6. Including Sir William Harcourt who in Monmouthshire, on October 1, called the Chamberlain attack 'unjust and malignant' and 'a burning shame.' *The Times*, Oct. 2, 1900, and Herbert Gladstone at Walthamstow, Oct. 10, *Man. Guardian*, Oct. 11, 1900.

7. As Gladstone confided to a friend of Dilke. See Dilke papers, vol. xxix, 119.

8. R. H. Gretton, *A Modern History of the English People, 1880-1922*, London, 1930, 536.

9. Herbert Gladstone (afterward H. G.), vol. xxiii, 52.

10. Hudson to Gladstone, Aug. 29, 1900, H. G., vol. xxiii, 58.

11. H. G., vol. xxiii, 62-63.

12. Gladstone to Campbell-Bannerman, Sept. 9, 1900. C. B. papers, vol. xi.

13. J. M. Paulton to Gladstone, Jan. 30 and Feb. 5, 1903; Gladstone to Paulton, Jan. 31, 1903. H. G., vol. lxvii, 169, 187, and 172.

14. Sam Woods to MacDonald, Mar. 14, 1900.

15. After the L.R.C.'s negative decision in May, the N.A.C. decided that if the question again arose the I.L.P. would be against approaching the Whips (L.R.C. Minutes, May 10, 1900; N.A.C. Minutes, May 28, 1900). In June an L.R.C. sub-committee consisting of Frederick Rogers, Bell, Pease and MacDonald, submitted a report containing this suggestion:
We think that it would be advisable to write to the Liberal and Conservative Whips, stating that we are supporting certain Labour candidates in certain constituencies, with a view of forming a Labour Group: that we have no power to initiate or withdraw such candidatures: that as a Committee we have no hostility to the political parties, and that so far as it is possible under the conditions of our constitution, we shall be glad of their co-operation in getting these candidates elected. (L.R.C. Sub-Committee Report —June, 1900).
The S.D.F. representatives, Quelch and Watts, wanted this part of the report deleted, but Hardie's motion that consideration of it be deferred was accepted by four votes to two. (L.R.C. Minutes, June 8, 1900). Then on September 1,

Wilkie, seconded by Gee, moved that deputations be sent to the Whips of the Unionist, Liberal and Nationalist parties, but Curran, seconded by Hodge, moved that the matter be deferred and this was carried by five to four. (L.R.C. Minutes, Sept. 1, 1900).

16. N.A.C. Minutes, May 28, 1900.
17. Glasier to Hardie, May 2, 1900.
18. *Clarion*, May 5, 1900.
19. *Labour Leader*, Aug. 4, 1900.
20. Stewart, *Hardie*, 169.
21. *Labour Leader*, Aug. 11, 1900.
22. *ibid*.
23. Letter to H. T. Muggeridge, Aug. 31, 1900, quoted in Hesketh Pearson, *G.B.S.: A Full Length Portrait*, London, 1942, 217.
24. N.A.C. Parliamentary Committee Report, Oct. 11, 1900.
25. *Labour Leader*, Aug. 11, 1900.
26. Hope stressed his sympathy with working class demands and later threatened to quit the Liberal party and join Labour in the House. On December 9, 1902, he wrote to Charles Geake, who was closely associated with Liberal headquarters, 'It seems to me that the Liberal party is done. Rosebery, Haldane, Asquith and Co. have destroyed it, and unless the party can re-assert itself and put itself forward as a *Democratic* party meaning business I mean to refuse all whips and as representing a working class constituency will join the Labour men. The present state of shame cannot last long.' H. G., vol. lxvii, 137.
27. H. G., vol. lxiii, 99. Gladstone's letter to Burns in this exchange is not available.
28. L.R.C. Minutes, June 8, 1900.
29. *ibid.*, Nov. 2, 1900.
30. *Reynolds's Newspaper*, Sept. 30, 1900.
31. Cadbury to Gladstone, Oct. 2 and 8, 1900. H. G., vol. lxiv, 4 and 18.
32. One of the reasons given by the Liberals for withholding support was the aggressive tone towards the Liberal party in which Brocklehurst's candidature had been announced early in the previous year. *The Times*, Oct. 3, and *Man. Guardian*, Oct. 1, 1900.
33. *Man. Guardian*, Oct. 3, 1900.
34. *ibid.*, Oct. 2, 1900.
35. Snowden, *Autobiography*, vol. i, 96–102.
36. Hardie to Glasier, July 21, 1900.
37. *Labour Leader*, May 23, 1903.
38. Hardie to Glasier, Aug. 12, 1900.
39. Glasier to Hardie, Aug. 8, 1900.
40. Stewart, *Hardie*, 174.
41. *Man. Guardian*, Sept. 22, 1900.
42. *Labour Leader*, Oct. 20, 1900.
43. *The Times*, Oct. 5, 1900.
44. *Labour Leader*, Nov. 17, 1900.
45. Illingworth to Gladstone, Sept. 27, 1899. H.G., vol. lxii, 110.
46. Illingworth to Campbell-Bannerman, Aug. 17, 1900. H.G., vol. xi, 100–101.
47. *Man. Guardian*, Sept. 22, 1900.

48. *I.L.P. News*, Oct. 1900.
49. Glasier to Lizzie, no date.
50. *S.D.F. Ann. Report*, 1900, 7-10.
51. *The Times*, Oct. 2, 1900.
52. See letters of the Liberal candidate in 1899, Harold Spender, to George Lansbury, Oct. 18 and Nov. 14, 1899. Lansbury correspondence.
53. Speech at Accrington reported in *Daily News*, Oct. 6, 1900.
54. *Justice*, Oct. 13, 1900.
55. *Man. Guardian*, Oct. 5, 1900.
56. See Wilkie in *Labour Leader*, Nov. 10, 1900.
57. Hodge, *Workshop to War Cabinet*, 140-141.
58. Telegram Jesse Herbert to Gladstone, Oct. 1, 1900. H.G., vol. xxviii, 54.
59. Even before the Election Herbert Gladstone had *publicly* admitted that the Liberals were in no position to furnish a strong Government and that there was no chance of their winning enough seats to justify their taking office. Speech at Leeds, Sept. 18, 1900. *Liberal Magazine*, Nov. 1900, vol. viii, 492.
60. *The Times*, Oct. 20, 1900.
61. Morley to Harrison, Oct. 11, 1900. Harrison correspondence.
62. Asquith to Gladstone, Oct. 7, 1900. H.G., vol. x, 29-30.
63. *I.L.P. News*, Nov. 1900.

# CHAPTER VIII

# Taff Vale and Clitheroe

FOR more than a year after the General Election the L.R.C. was beset by grave doubts that it could survive, much less prosper. No nation-wide organizing work was yet deemed feasible, and MacDonald and his associates gave their main attention to constituencies fought in 1900.[1] At the first annual conference in February 1901 an air of despondency prevailed;[2] only forty-one of some 1,200 existing trade unions had seen fit to join. The Committee continued to advance at a snail's pace. Many trade unionists were unaware of its existence, and it was feared by no one. Since the public, still preoccupied with the war, displayed a singular indifference to socialist propaganda, the I.L.P. section found the Committee's anonymity doubly irritating. Engaging in two by-elections, at North-East Lanark (Scotland) in August 1901, and at Wakefield (Yorkshire) in March 1902, the I.L.P., though unsuccessful, made an impressive showing due in no small part to Liberal support. This growing rapprochement with the Liberals caused Hardie some concern. 'Would to God the Liberals were again in office,' he wrote to Glasier. 'Then we could make things hum once more.'[3]

In the House of Commons the creation of a distinct Labour group seemed as remote as ever. To Hardie, the Labour members were scarcely distinguishable from the ordinary Liberals,[4] while Bell, his L.R.C. colleague, was primarily concerned with purely trade union matters. Conceding that if a Labour bloc were possible John Burns was in the best position to organize and lead it, Hardie vainly sought his co-operation.[5] Others in the I.L.P. laid even greater stress on Burns' importance, 'Marxian' of the *Labour Leader* maintaining in 1902 that the movement would be set back ten years if Burns were lost to the Liberals[6] and in private urging Burns to join and to lead the I.L.P.[7] 'The Colossus of Battersea' listened but was unmoved. On numerous occasions he supported Hardie in the Commons but skirted any suggestion that he work in close harness with his old-time adversary.[8]

Hardie, addressing many questions to the House, felt no constraint to limit himself to what were regarded as traditional Labour demands. On the accession of Edward VII he found opportunity to express his strong republicanism and to oppose increases in the civil list.[9] In April 1901, he enjoyed a personal triumph, introducing on a private member's motion a resolution for the creation of a Socialist Commonwealth. 'The last has not been heard of the Socialist movement either in the country or in this House . . .' he said, 'just as sure as Radicalism democratised the system of government politically in the last century so will Socialism democratise the country industrially during the century upon which we have just entered.'[10]

No doubt Hardie at times felt terribly alone, and looked with envy upon the united and disciplined ranks of the Irish Nationalists, now under John Redmond. If the I.L.P. had only half a dozen men in Parliament everything would be changed he thought. As the sole I.L.P. member his burdens were heavy. Any socialist follower visiting London who wished to be shown through the House could hardly be refused. Tea on the terrace was part of this formality and cut deeply into Hardie's meagre income.[11] Then there was the *Labour Leader* to be brought out each week and the work at I.L.P. and L.R.C. headquarters. Hardie worked at a feverish pace. In July 1902 he suffered a temporary physical collapse.[12]

At the beginning of 1901, the total membership of the forty-one trade unions affiliated to the Committee was 353,070. In all of Great Britain there were 1,272 unions with a membership of 1,905,116. Practically all of the new unions, those founded after 1889, had joined the Committee at the outset. The older unions that had joined were among those that had suffered seriously from the effects of unemployment and trade depression and so had looked more favourably to political action, such unions in heavy industry as the Blastfurnacemen, the Shipwrights, the Ironfounders and the Steel Smelters. The Amalgamated Society of Railway Servants had turned to the L.R.C. after repeated failure to gain recognition from the railway employers. Even among those unions affiliated to the Committee, the rank and file response to joining had been rather discouraging. One large union, the Boot and Shoe Operatives, had affiliated without consulting its members[13] while the Typographical Association, with some 16,000 members had done so though only one-fourth of the membership took the trouble to vote on the question, 3,097 in favour and 1,077 against.[14] In the powerful Amalgamated Society of Engineers with some 500 branches, only twenty-seven had responded to a poll on attending the Memorial Hall conference, eighteen for and nine against, and though there were 93,000 members, the vote on joining the L.R.C. was so small in 1900—2,897 for and 700 against—that the Engineers' Council decided for the moment to take no action.[15] The Carpenters, the Boilermakers, the Cotton Operatives, had all remained aloof.

It was obvious that despite legal uncertainties and industrial setbacks the unions were not sufficiently aroused in 1900 to turn *en masse* to the L.R.C. A new impetus was needed, and luckily for the Committee it came in 1901 with a decision of the Law Lords in the Taff Vale Case. Arising out of a strike on the Taff Vale Railway in South Wales this judgment surprised not only the trade union world but almost the entire legal profession as well.[16] In effect it held a trade union liable for damages or injury caused by any person considered to be an agent or official of that union. For thirty years it had been assumed that under the laws of 1871-1876 a trade union's corporate funds were immune from such action. Now this favourable legal status was destroyed. Moreover, in August 1901, in the case of Quinn vs. Leathem, a decision was handed down which filled up many of the loopholes left open by Taff Vale and made the acts of any strike organizer more easily declared tortious.[17] Thus at a period of growing strain in industrial relations and of an ominous increase in the number of employers' associations, a trade union's chances of effectively conducting a strike were sharply curtailed. While the Taff

Vale Case was still *sub judice*, *The Times* in a series of articles on 'The Crisis in British Industry' lent its support to the employers' arguments, attacking the unions for their restrictive practices and urging legislation to limit their scope and effectiveness.[18] Throughout the country, trade unions both large and small awakened to the realization that organized employers could deal them crippling blows through litigation in the courts and at the same time obstruct their efforts to secure remedial legislation in Parliament.

The L.R.C. was quick to exploit the new situation. It sent out thousands of circulars almost immediately after the Taff Vale announcement urging trade unions to work for increased labour representation through the L.R.C. Attacked in workshop, court of law and the press, it was pointed out, trade unionism had no refuge but the ballot box. The trade unionists agreed. By the beginning of 1902 the number of affiliated unions had risen from forty-one to sixty-five and trade union membership from 353,070 to 455,450. At the beginning of 1903 there were 127 unions with 847,315 members.[19] Among the new affiliates were the Engineers. Barred from the Trades Union Congress since 1899, when they were charged with supplanting members of a small local society on the Tyne while they were on strike, the Engineers for a time had looked to the newly formed General Federation of Trade Unions as their main hope,[20] but the Federation had not attracted the majority of the unions and its functions had developed little beyond the administration of a strike fund. According to the Engineers' Secretary, George Barnes, 'the need for increased Labour representation' was the chief lesson to be drawn from Taff Vale,[21] and in February 1902, the Engineers decided to affiliate with the L.R.C. by a vote of 5,626 to 1,070.[22] The members of the Amalgamated Association of Operative Cotton Spinners, over 100,000 in number, were told in their annual report in 1902 that 'many people think that the foundations on which our trade unions have been built are now undermined.' They voted heavily in favour of joining.[23] 'It was left to the judges and the law courts to unconsciously be the instruments in converting the organized British worker to the present view of political action,' commented the General

141

Secretary of the Furnishing Trades Association when it affiliated with the Committee early in 1903.[24] No large group except the Miners still remained outside.

It has often been said that Taff Vale made the British Labour Party, that without it the L.R.C. would have foundered. Certainly Taff Vale powerfully stimulated the party's growth, and no one would deny that without it the extent of the 1906 victory would have been inconceivable. Yet that victory owed much to other than purely trade union issues and much also to the organizing and tactical skill of the L.R.C. Secretary and his I.L.P. supporters. It should not be forgotten that what firmness the L.R.C. possessed on the principle of independence came mainly from the I.L.P. and that if the I.L.P. leadership had not remained steadfast in its loyalty to the Labour Alliance, most of the L.R.C. trade unionists returned in 1906 would not only have been ready to co-operate with the Liberal party but might very well have been absorbed by it. Taff Vale laid a large part of the groundwork for the triumph of 1906. But it required much hard work and no little skill to marshal the discontent which Taff Vale helped create and then to translate that discontent into a political victory which was at least ostensibly independent.

Most of the decisions which the L.R.C. reached in these first years were I.L.P. inspired. Nearly all of the resolutions introduced at the 1901 conference were of I.L.P. origin. Even after the number of trade union affiliates neared the million mark, the I.L.P. continued to exercise an influence out of all proportion to its size, which is not surprising, since any army is ready to allow its shock troops a special position and extra privileges. With some uneasiness, however, Hardie and his associates came to realize that, as a result of their emphasis on the L.R.C. connection, the I.L.P. was losing some of the spark and vitality of former years as it became increasingly involved with political exigencies. No longer was it primarily a socialist propagandist organization, for in working to organize trade unionists for political action it had to forgo socialist exhortations and concentrate on appeals to a narrower trade union interest. So long as the policy of 'Independence' was not flouted openly,

Hardie, Glasier and MacDonald, all suspicious of rigidity of creed, could with no great difficulty adapt themselves to this need for encompassing those outside the faith. Yet there was the danger that too great a flexibility over too long a period might make their own socialism seem largely decorous. From the S.D.F., from Blatchford, from men in their own ranks came constant warnings that in laying so much emphasis on political success they were making weaklings of their following and risking capture by the enemy.

The S.D.F., after unsuccessfully proposing for a second time that there be a socialist test for all L.R.C. candidates, voted at its own conference in August 1901 to withdraw from the Committee.[25] This decision caused less excitement in socialist circles than Hyndman's announcement at the same time that he was resigning from the S.D.F. Executive, because he had failed to detect sufficient class antagonism among the English workers and because the members of the S.D.F. seemed to him to be wholly destitute of political aptitude.[26] The officials of the I.L.P., still smarting under the S.D.F. charge of betrayal, exulted in Hyndman's resignation. According to MacDonald it constituted 'a frank acknowledgment of the complete failure of the Marxian movement' in England.[27] Hardie's comment was equally terse. 'The propaganda of the class hatred is not one which can ever take root in this country. . . .' he wrote. 'Mankind in the mass is not moved by hatred but by love of what is right. If we could have Socialism on the S.D.F. lines nothing would be changed —save for the worse.'[28]

Despite its mortification, the S.D.F. was quick to strike back. Its journal accused I.L.P. candidates in by-elections of 'trimming' to win Liberal favour, and it treated the running of I.L.P. candidates as 'Progressives' for the London County Council in a like vein.[29] To those in the I.L.P. who belittled the teachings of the S.D.F., 'Tatler' of *Justice* retorted that 'Socialism based on the economics of the Fabian Society and the ethics of the New Testament [was] not Socialism at all, but glorified bureaucracy tempered by Christian charity.'[30]

A less opportune time for reviving the question of fusion would be difficult to imagine, but the S.D.F. Executive did exactly this, no doubt aware that it could thus cause considerable discomfiture to its I.L.P. critics. What made these fusion overtures particularly difficult for the I.L.P. leaders to counter and disproved their impression that Hyndman's resignation had dealt his organization a death blow, was the S.D.F.'s fine showing in a three-cornered by-election in Dewsbury (Yorkshire) in January 1902. Previously the Dewsbury Trades Council and the I.L.P. had met with the local S.D.F. to choose a joint candidate only to find that the latter body, acting hastily and unilaterally, had put forward Harry Quelch. There were protests. Two deputations came before the L.R.C., one from the Dewsbury S.D.F. and Clarion Fellowship, the other from the Dewsbury Trades Council and I.L.P., the latter group favouring the candidature of E. R. Hartley who had contested Dewsbury in 1895. To adjudicate in the dispute the L.R.C. appointed a sub-committee of three of its members. After hearing both sides it decided against the S.D.F.[31] 'I suppose this should be expected from people who are our political opponents and supporters of the Liberal party which it is our business to fight,' wrote an S.D.F. member to MacDonald.[32] No longer connected with the L.R.C. and having accused the I.L.P. of intriguing at Dewsbury to secure the selection of a 'Lib-Lab' candidate,[33] the S.D.F. felt no qualms in flouting the Committee's authority, while the I.L.P. Executive for the moment confuted, advised its followers against supporting Quelch.[34] Both Hardie and Glasier insisted publicly that he had no chance of attaining a respectable poll,[35] but Quelch's drawing strength was greater than almost anyone had anticipated.

Liberal headquarters had cautioned the Dewsbury Liberals against precipitous action in opposing Quelch,[36] and their choice for candidate, Walter Runciman, though not pleasing to Campbell-Bannerman,[37] did have working-class appeal and won local Irish support. Yet Runciman was regarded as an Imperialist, and some anti-war Liberals backed Quelch. Moreover, several I.L.P. branches, ignoring the N.A.C.'s advice, urged their Dewsbury colleagues to do likewise.[38] Most embarrassing of all to the N.A.C., its choice for the seat, Hartley, not only came out openly for Quelch but attacked the I.L.P. leadership and its advocacy of abstention. 'The great work of the official section of the I.L.P. at the present,' he wrote to Thompson of the *Clarion*, 'seems not so much to push Socialism as to try to intrigue some half a dozen persons into Parliament. There is probably not more than one place in Britain (if there is one) where we can get a Socialist into Parliament without some arrangement with Liberalism, and for such an arrangement Liberalism will demand a terribly heavy price—more than we can possibly afford.'[39]

Even before the polling the signs were clear. Hardie was disconsolate. 'Dewsbury promises to be the best bit of luck the S.D.F. has ever had . . .' he wrote Glasier, 'If they have the gumption to follow it up properly it will rehabilitate them all round.'[40] With the results in, Runciman had won with 5,669 to the Conservative's 4,512. Quelch, in spite of the disunity in socialist and trade union ranks, had a poll of 1,597, greater than Hartley's in 1895, 'a sign of the times,' said the *Manchester Guardian*, 'which thoughtful men will not ignore.'[41] 'Quelch's vote is twice as high as I believed it would be,' Glasier confided to Hardie. 'We can take general encouragement from it, but it will help the fusion feeling. The S.D.F. will regard it as a triumph, though indeed he [Quelch] had to assume the role of a Trade Union candidate and use the I.L.P. branch resolutions and I.L.P. speakers for all they were worth.'[42]

Blatchford in the *Clarion*, meanwhile, was adding fuel to the S.D.F. fusion agitation by indulging in one of his periodic outbursts against Hardie and the I.L.P. Though Blatchford's influence in the movement had lessened, because of his war stand and apparent agnosticism, he still aimed telling barbs. Hardie, he wrote, was neither a wise nor successful leader and was the major obstacle in the way of socialist unity. As for the alliances with Radicals or Irish then being mooted in I.L.P. circles, Blatchford wanted neither. Home Rule, he reminded his readers, was not socialism. The I.L.P. was undemocratic; it was cursed by leaders;[43] accordingly, when the *Clarion* came out strongly for a unity convention of all socialists, it demanded that all leaders—Hyndman, Blatchford and Hardie among them —absent themselves from this convention. The demand was ridiculed by George Bernard Shaw, by *Justice*, and by George Barnes, the Engineers' Secretary, who, nevertheless, admitted that the I.L.P. was perhaps concentrating too much 'on getting there.'[44]

The I.L.P. chieftains might not have been deeply concerned with such a meeting had not incidents like Dewsbury revealed a tendency of an S.D.F. fringe to grow up in the party.[45] 'I have spoken out and told Dangle [Thompson of the *Clarion*] plainly what I think of his S.D.F. alliance and this attempt to wreck the I.L.P. . . .' wrote Glasier to Hardie. 'This threat of a rival convention has undoubtedly a dangerous ring in it, and it must be prevented—if it takes place at all—from assuming to speak for the I.L.P.'[46] At the I.L.P. Conference which came, as usual, in April, Glasier in his address ridiculed 'clamour for unity' that sounded more like the 'clamour for war' and again defended what he considered the unique mission of the I.L.P. 'Already they had made the terms Labour and Socialism almost synonymous. Give them time and the two terms would be wedded together and the cause of Labour and Socialism would be one and indivisible. The securing of a great united Labour Party in Parliament constituted the greatest political hope of their time. He saw no salvation of the people without it.'[47]

After two hours of discussion the conference refused even to consider the fusion proposals by a vote of sixty-nine to forty, twenty of these forty voting against, according to Glasier, not because they were in favour of fusion but because they wanted a clear issue. When the conference returned the old N.A.C. on the first ballot, a thing that had never happened before, Glasier was jubilant, regarding this as a 'Splendid reply to the *Clarion* and the S.D.F.'[48] A most effective polemicist when the occasion demanded, Glasier suggested that if Blatchford were so avid of unity, the *Clarion* and the Clarion Fellowship should take the first step by fusing with the S.D.F.[49] The Clarion Fellowship was not a political party, Blatchford retorted, and could no more unite with the S.D.F. than a violet could unite with a steam engine.[50] How then, asked Glasier, did the Clarion Fellowship in Dewsbury unite with the S.D.F. to promote Quelch?[51] There the matter stood for a while, Glasier by this time having lost much of his respect for Blatchford and being determined that the I.L.P. must rid itself of 'the *Clarion*'s dictatorship.'[52] MacDonald, writing under a pseudonym, called the socialist unity proposal a 'foolish hunt after a will o' the wisp. . . . A paper unity would be disastrous to the Socialist movement in England. The I.L.P. and the S.D.F. will not mix and that [is] the end of the matter.'[53]

Loyalty to the bargain with the trade unions remained the bedrock of I.L.P. policy despite all these criticisms and though socialism was sometimes submerged to such an extent that the political basis of the L.R.C. could be described in a Committee broadsheet as 'Trade Unionism and the Principles of Trade Unionism applied to national affairs.'[54] Still the I.L.P. would lean backward only so far, and at the L.R.C. Conference of 1901 it introduced a collectivist resolution, though insisting that it not be required as a pledge of L.R.C. candidates.[55] The year following it unsuccessfully recommended that the name 'Socialist and Trade Union candidate' be substituted for 'Labour candidate' in order better to express the Committee's comprehensiveness.[56] Beyond this, the I.L.P. on occasion took a rigidly uncompromising stand against the more conservative members of the Committee. Wilkie of the Shipwrights, for example, was regarded by Hardie and his colleagues as lukewarm on 'Independence'; he had expressed what they regarded as a 'Lib-Lab' position at Memorial Hall, and at Sunderland in the 1900 Election he had kowtowed too much to the Liberals. When in 1902 he and the Pete Curran of the I.L.P., who represented the Gasworkers' Union on the Committee, were both anxious to be selected to run for the Jarrow Division of Durham, the I.L.P. stood firm in insisting on Curran, the Committee split pretty much on socialist-trade union lines, and, finally, Curran was chosen.[57]

Serving as an offset to Dewsbury and as a considerable boost to L.R.C. morale was the L.R.C.'s first by-election victory, at Clitheroe in Lancashire in July 1902. When the Liberal member for Clitheroe, Kay Shuttleworth, was elevated to the peerage, his party had looked about for a replacement. Strong anti-war sentiment in Lancashire made a Liberal Imperialist undesirable, and since the constituency probably had more cotton weavers than any other in the kingdom, a man with a good record on Labour questions was required. Shuttleworth thought that A. H. D. Acland would be a most admirable choice, but Acland was too ill to accept.[58] The son of John Bright seemed a possibility, especially with free trade as a prominent issue, but the Irish Question was coming to the front again, and his opposition to Home Rule made him a risk. Besides, on Trade Union questions, Shuttleworth noted, the Brights had always proved 'rather unbending.'[59]

While the Liberals procrastinated, the L.R.C. acted. As early as the previous March it had held a meeting in Clitheroe, and when the vacancy occurred, MacDonald, to make the Liberals hold their hand, had hastily penned a letter to the press stating that the Committee would assuredly contest the seat and had, in fact, already called a meeting to choose a candidate.[60] The I.L.P. had long considered putting Snowden forward here. He had frequently lectured in the district and had local trade union support including that of a small group of textile workers that had joined the L.R.C.[61] The I.L.P. now had a magnificent opportunity. By withdrawing in favour of a textile candidate, not only could it demonstrate its sympathy with political trade unionism; it could also pave the way for the entry of thousands of textile workers into the Labour Alliance. Apparently on MacDonald's plea, Snowden, with N.A.C. approval, stepped aside, and on July 5, Sexton and MacDonald for the Committee met with trade union deputations and chose David Shackleton, Secretary of the Darwen Weavers, as the L.R.C. candidate.[62] 'We must not seem to act as if we were either disappointed at Shackleton's selection, or were disposed to allow ourselves to be reckoned outsiders,' wrote Glasier to Hardie. 'It must be our campaign as well as that of the Trade Unionists.'[63]

A wealthy anti-war Liberal named Philip Stanhope had emerged by this time as the Liberals' best hope, but he was unwilling to go forward once Shackleton was chosen. Kay Shuttleworth wanted the Chief Whip to try for some arrangement with Labour through Burns or some other Labour M.P., but the Clitheroe Weavers' Unions proved intractable.[64] The

Liberals did not retire gracefully, however. Until the time of nomination they continued to look about for a candidate, even though Shackleton had been a firm Liberal and it was clear that his sympathies were with the Liberal party. In fact Shackleton met with a group of Clitheroe Liberals at Manchester and in the *Manchester Guardian*,[65] was reported to have satisfied them as to his Liberalism. The I.L.P. quite naturally took exception to the report. 'It would be a great misfortune to prejudice the independent attitude,' Glasier wrote Hardie, 'and I am wondering if we cannot in some perfectly frank and courteous way indicate that any Liberal compact business will alienate the I.L.P. and the resolute Labour vote. Snowden I presume only retired on the assumption that Shackleton would run true.'[66] Had an I.L.P. man been on Shackleton's committee, Glasier felt certain, the Manchester meeting would never have occurred. He went to Manchester to talk with Snowden, who expressed the opinion that the meeting with the Liberals had resulted from a natural desire to avoid the expenses and uncertainty of a three-way fight. Not fully reassured, Glasier wrote out an interview with himself as I.L.P. Chairman, which Snowden approved. He then took it to the *Manchester Guardian*, where a member of the staff agreed to print it as an interview by a special correspondent. It praised Shackleton but repeated the points made in the letter to Hardie and added that if Shackleton gave way to the Liberals in any fashion this would involve the probability of an I.L.P. fight.[67]

The warning was perhaps unneccessary. Shackleton had had few connections with the political Labour movement; he was a Liberal, but he was perfectly willing to forgo any open declaration of Liberalism and to run as an 'Independent' in keeping with the L.R.C. Constitution. This being the case and no Liberal standing, the Tories decided not to oppose him, and he was returned for Clitheroe without opposition. On August 6, he was introduced in the House by Bell and Hardie. Many Clitheroe Liberals, feeling that the Labour people had acted high-handedly, were bitter about the outcome and wrote abusive letters to Stanhope for his part in the affair.[68] The L.R.C. Executive sent Stanhope its official thanks.[69] An early result of

Shackleton's victory was the affiliation of the Lancashire Textile Operatives to the Committee, 103,000 strong. 'The triumph at Clitheroe,' said the L.R.C. Quarterly Circular, 'illustrates the advantages (1) of being ready for emergencies, (2) of swiftly seizing the opportunity, and (3) of allowing "sweet reasonableness" to govern all the actions of the different sections of the Labour Party.'[70]

The Committee did not always act with such dispatch nor show such effectiveness in harmonizing the various sections. When a vacancy occurred in Cleveland (in the West Riding of Yorkshire) in the following September the Executive called a meeting with the local Miners' Council to discuss putting forward a candidate. MacDonald was away in South Africa, the arrangements were poorly handled, and no decision was reached.[71] Cleveland was a large constituency, much of it agricultural and moor land. It was costly to fight with around 12,000 electors, some 3,000 of whom were miners. Hardie and Glasier visited the area, found many of the miners' leaders closely identified with the Liberal party and doubted whether an I.L.P. man could be put forward, unless his only intention was to 'throw the Liberal.' When Wilkie was mentioned as a possible L.R.C. candidate, the feeling of the N.A.C. was that the election of Philip Stanhope, one of the Liberal aspirants, was preferable. If Stanhope won, this would remove him from Lancashire where his strong hold on the working-class vote made the I.L.P. anxious to have him out of the way. The mere threat of running a Labour man it was believed, might force the Liberals to choose Stanhope.[72] Contrary to these expectations the Liberals chose Herbert Samuel, who, styling himself a 'Labour' as well as a Liberal candidate, received the support of Bell, Sam Woods, Ben Tillett and other prominent trade unionists. Glasier, infuriated by this outcome, contemplated advising a 'vote Tory' policy but feared that this would prejudice the chances of the I.L.P. men in the coming General Election.[73] He did, however, address a letter to the press condemning the Liberals for thwarting the nomination of a Labour man and for 'the spectacle of a Liberal Imperialist masquerading in the role of a Labour candidate.' The Tories tried to cash in on this by printing it as an election leaflet,[74] but Samuel, with the staunch backing of most of the miners' leaders, was elected.

Then in October in Devonport where the L.R.C. had hopes of running someone in the General Election a sudden vacancy again caught the Committee unprepared. MacDonald was still away. There were some expectations that the Liberals would nominate a trade unionist, but instead they ran a wealthy adherent of the Rosebery section of the party who was defeated by the Tory. The L.R.C. had vacillated and put no one forward though there were possible candidates including Wilkie. A lack of local preparation was given as the official explanation for inaction,[75] but as far as any I.L.P. candidate was concerned the feeling that Devonport was not too hopeful a seat was probably the deciding consideration. Glasier had written to Hardie, 'A *Labourer's* candidate would in my opinion have no chance whatever in Devonport—a town filled with skilled government artisans who are more middle-class than the middle-class themselves; as well as pensioners, officers and officials. If Wilkie cares to run let him. It would not be wise on the eve of a General Election (as may happen) for us to have another scuffle with Wilkie or deplete our funds in a "fizzle out" candidature.'[76]

As 1902 drew to a close the L.R.C., with its membership expanding and with three men in Parliament, was confident that it would henceforth command increasing attention and respect. For this the L.R.C. Secretary deserved a great deal of the credit. In late 1901 MacDonald had told the Executive that he was considering retiring as Secretary,[77] for the work at headquarters continued to grow heavier while his own duties elsewhere were increasing. In November 1901, he had been returned without contest to the London County Council to fill the Finsbury vacancy created by the retirement of Hardie's old friend, Frank Smith.[78] The Committee, anxious to retain his services, voted MacDonald thirty shillings a week for clerical assistance.[79] His newspaper work now included a weekly column in the London *Echo* entitled 'Work and Workers' and written under a pseudonym, 'Spectator.' Very few people knew his identity, and 'Spectator's' comments on current issues and the affairs of the Committee are therefore often candid and revealing.[80] In August 1902 Macdonald and his wife went to South Africa, returning to England the following January. Their observations were published in a booklet which came to be regarded as an important statement of the pro-Boer case.

By December 1902, the L.R.C. had eight approved candidates with constituencies chosen. Three were I.L.P.—Jowett for West Bradford, Snowden for Blackburn and James Parker for Halifax. The trade unionists were W. Clery of the Fawcett Association for Deptford, Pete Curran of the Gasworkers for Jarrow, Will Thorne of the Gasworkers and the West Ham Town Council for West Ham, John Ward of the Navvies for Stoke, and John Hodge of the Steel Smelters for Gower (Glamorganshire), the latter candidature being still somewhat in doubt. There were nine trade union nominees without constituencies, and five of them were from the Engineers, including George Barnes. During the year major L.R.C. conferences had been held in at least fifteen cities. The total income of the Committee for the year was £716 of which £549 had been spent.[81] The I.L.P. also closed its books in December 1902, with renewed confidence and hope. Its chairman wrote in a letter, 'The movement is really in an excellent state just now—indeed I do not think it has ever been in better trim. All the *Clarion* worry and dissension have melted away, and the party is more self-reliant and capable than ever it has been.'[82]

The end of the war in South Africa in March 1902 had given the movement a needed boost. Public interest had turned again to home affairs with agitation for social reform all the more intense for having been so long cooped up. Yet the Balfour Government continued to show a remarkable lack of concern for such agitation and with working-class demands in general. Chamberlain still gave lip service to his promise of old age pensions, but he distinguished between the deserving and undeserving poor and insisted that, in any case, the time was not yet ripe.[83] There was no serious attempt to satisfy the growing demand for an eight-hour day, no sign of any genuine effort to remove the trade union grievances arising from Taff Vale. This was grave political shortsightedness. Whatever sections of organized Labour were still pro-Government were almost certain to be driven into the arms of the Liberal party or into independent action, especially since real wages went down in the next two years and unemployment increased.[84]

## NOTES

1. Report of MacDonald and Edward Pease to the Committee. L.R.C. Minutes, Jan. 10, 1901.
2. Snowden, *Autobiography*, vol. i, 94.
3. Hardie to Glasier, Jan. 24, 1902.
4. *I.L.P. News*, Sept. 1901.
5. Through Burns' friend and confidant, the journalist H. W. Massingham. Hardie to Glasier, Oct. 15, 1900.
6. *Labour Leader*, Nov. 29, 1902.
7. Burns' Diary: Entry of Mar. 21, 1902.
8. Bell was largely responsible for blocking in the Commons in 1901 an attempt of the Great Eastern Railway to inaugurate a compulsory pension scheme over which the railway workers would have no control. Hardie wrote to a friend that Burns was grumpy about fighting the bill and would thwart the efforts of Bell and Hardie if he could and if they were not backed by the Irish. Hardie to David Lowe, Mar. 13, 1901, as quoted in Lowe, *From Pit to Parliament*, 193. But on the day after Hardie made these observations, Burns, spoke forcefully and at length against the bill in the Commons. Parl. Debates, Commons, 4th series, vol. 90, Mar. 14, 1901, cols. 1527-1530.
9. Stewart, *Hardie*, 188.
10. Bell seconded the Socialist resolution. Parl. Debates, Commons, 4th series, vol. 92, Apr. 23, 1901, cols. 1175-1180.
11. Hardie to Glasier, Aug. 23, 1901.
12. Stewart, 195.
13. *Boot and Shoe Operatives, Monthly Report*, Mar. 1900.
14. *Typographical Circular*, Sept. 1900, 11.
15. *Monthly Journal, Amalgamated Society of Engineers'*, Feb. 1900, 55; Mar. 1900, 53-5, April 1900, 56.
16. Webbs, *Trade Unionism*, 600-604.
17. Frederic Harrison, 'The End of Trade Unionism,' *The Review of Reviews*, vol. xxiv, Sept. 14, 1901, 203.
18. Written for *The Times* between November 1901 and January 1902 by its industrial correspondent, E. A. Pratt, the articles were published as a book, *Trade Unionism and British Industry*, London, 1904.
19. While in the year 1901 the membership had increased by some 93,000, the increase for only the first six months of 1902 was not less than 238,120. *L.R.C. Quarterly Circular*, Dec. 1902, 11.
20. See Tom Proctor in Engineers' *Monthly Journal*. Nov. 1901, 13. Isaac Mitchell of the Engineers was Secretary of the Federation.
21. *Annual Report A.S.E.*, 1901, xiii.
22. *Monthly Journal*, Feb. 1902, 65.
23. *Annual Report Operative Cotton Spinners,* 1902, 10 and 15.

24. *Annual Report Furnishing Trades Association*, 1903, 11.
25. *S.D.F. Ann.*, 1901, 6.
26. *Reynolds's News*, Aug. 11, 1901.
27. *Echo*, Aug. 15, 1901.
28. *Labour Leader*, Aug. 17, 1901.
29. *Justice*, Sept. 28, 1901; Mar, 22, 1902; Mar. 23, 1901.
30. *ibid.*, Aug. 24, 1901.
31. Report of the L.R.C. Sub-Committee—Alan Gee, Textile Workers; John Hodge, Steel Smelters; and O. Connellan, Leeds Trades Council—on the Dewsbury controversy, Nov. 12, 1901.
32. L. E. Quelch to MacDonald, Dec. 5, 1901. L.R.C. correspondence.
33. *Justice*, Nov. 30, 1901.
34. N.A.C. Minutes, Nov. 30, 1901.
35. *I.L.P. News*, Nov. 1901.
36. See Charles Trevelyan to Herbert Gladstone, Sept. 28, 1901, H.G., vol. lxv, 111, and Herbert Gladstone to William Beadsley of the Dewsbury Liberal Ass., Oct. 31, 1901, H.G., vol. lxv, 127.
37. '. . . a pugnacious sectional partisan who will be, as in the past, a mutineer whenever mutiny is possible, cannot expect my full, open, hearty support,' wrote C.B. to Gladstone, Oct. 30, 1901. H.G., vol. xi, 191-192.
38. On the Huddersfield, I.L.P. branch taking such action, see N.A.C. Minutes, Nov. 22, and 23, 1901.
39. *Clarion*, Dec. 13, 1901. Glasier answered these accusations in the *Clarion* of Dec. 20, 1901.
40. Hardie to Glasier, Jan. 24, 1902.
41. Quoted in *Clarion*, Jan. 31, 1902.
42. Glasier to Hardie, Jan. 29, 1902.
43. Blatchford in the *Clarion*, Jan. 10 and 24, Mar. 14, 1902.
44. *Clarion*, Feb. 14, 1902; *Justice*, Feb. 15, 1902.
45. Glasier to Hardie, Jan. 20, 1902.
46. Glasier to Hardie, Jan. 10, 1902.
47. *I.L.P. Ann.*, 1902, 21.
48. *ibid.*, 22 and 23; Glasier to Lizzie, April 3, 1902.
49. *I.L.P. News*, June 1902.
50. *Clarion*, July 4, 1902.
51. *I.L.P. News*, July, 1902.
52. Glasier to Lizzie, Aug. 16, 1902.
53. In the *Echo*, June 26, 1902.
54. L.R.C. broadsheet, Nov. 1901.
55. *L.R.C. Ann.*, 1901, 20-21.
56. *ibid.*, 1902, 23.
57. A sub-committee of three appointed to inquire into the Jarrow controversy had divided, Richard Bell and Frederick Rogers supporting Wilkie's claims, James Parker of the I.L.P., Curran's. See report of sub-committee, May 17 1902 and also L.R.C. Minutes, Sept. 1, 1902.
58. Kay Shuttleworth to C.B., June 6, 1902. C.B., vol. xvi.
59. Kay Shuttleworth to H.G., June 16, 1902. H.G., vol. lxvi, 169.
60. The letter appeared in the *Daily Chronicle*, June 27, 1902. It apparently had some effect. Lulu Harcourt wrote to Gladstone that he did not wish to be considered for the seat and pointed to the MacDonald letter as proof of

Labour's strength. L. Harcourt to H.G., June 27, 1902, H.G., vol. xxi, 28.
61. Snowden, *Auto.*, 104-5.
62. James Middleton has informed the present writer that MacDonald was largely responsible for this action. See N.A.C. Minutes, July 28 and 29, 1902, and the report on a special meeting at Colne, July 3, 1902, in the L.R.C. papers.
63. Glasier to Hardie, July 13, 1902.
64. Philip Stanhope to H.G., July 8, 1902. H.G., vol. lxvi, 97; Kay Shuttleworth to H.G., July 3, 1902. H.G., vol. lxvi, 188.
65. *Man. Guardian*, July 15, 1902.
66. Glasier to Hardie, July 15, 1902.
67. Glasier to Hardie, July 17, 1902; *Man. Guardian*, July 18, 1902.
68. Kay Shuttleworth to H.G., July 23, 1902. H.G., vol. lxvi, 205; Philip Stanhope to H.G., Aug. 7, 1902. H.G., vol. lxvii, 8.
69. L.R.C. Minutes, Sept. 6, 1902.
70. *L.R.C. Quarterly Circular*, Sept. 1902.
71. There was a general mix-up at headquarters when a young assistant acted without consulting Pease, whom MacDonald had hoped would watch over things while he was gone. . . . See letter of John McNeil, the assistant, to Pease, Oct. 23, 1902, in L.R.C. correspondence.
72. Glasier to Hardie, Sept. 18 and 19, Oct. 21 and Dec. 1, 1902; N.A.C. Minutes, Sept. 29 and 30, 1902.
73. Glasier to Hardie, Oct. 21, 1902.
74. *I.L.P. News*, Nov. 1902.
75. *L.R.C. Ann.*, 1903, 13.
76. Glasier to Hardie, Oct. 10, 1902.
77. L.R.C. Minutes, Nov. 15, 1901.
78. *Our Partnership*, 228; *Justice*, Nov. 30, 1901.
79. *L.R.C. Ann.*, 1902, 20-21.
80. Lord Pethick Lawrence, who at this period was editor of the *Echo*, has informed the present writer that, to the best of his recollection, 'Spectator's' identity was a very well-kept secret.
81. *L.R.C. Quarterly Circular*, Dec. 1902.
82. Glasier to Lizzie, Dec. 5, 1902.
83. See his speech at Birmingham on Jan. 6, 1902, as reported in *The Times* o the day following.
84. According to the Board of Trade, while prices rose, wages were almost stationary in the textile trades from 1900 to 1904 and in mining and engineering dropped considerably. Real Wages did not reach their 1900 level again until 1913. See appendix of *Labour Party Annual Conference Report*, 1909 and J. W. Clapham, *Economic History of Modern Britain*, 3 vols., Cambridge, 1926-1938, vol. iii, 29 and 468.

# CHAPTER IX

# Independence and Woolwich

THE cessation of hostilities ameliorated but did not end the dissension within the Liberal party. In February Rosebery had publicly repudiated the leadership of Campbell-Bannerman and had founded the Liberal League with himself as President and with other Liberal Imperialists, Fowler, Grey and Asquith, as Vice-Presidents. Campbell-Bannerman, remembering the 1886 secession over Home Rule, had been ready to make a desperate fight if a formal split were attempted, and though his worst fears in this regard proved unfounded, resentment and distrust remained. The large centre group in the party was expected to support Campbell-Bannerman if it came to a showdown, and his adherents controlled most of the party machinery, but the Liberal League, if weak in numbers, was strong in brains and money. It was accused by the Bannermanites of acting like a separate party, of sowing mischief in the constituencies, and of bidding against the Liberal Central in order to place League candidates.[1]

These divisions led many observers in 1902 to underestimate the Liberal party's recuperative powers. Hardie regarded it as a spent force, its squabbling factions as a warning against socialist fusion, and again and again he predicted that a Liberal majority was impossible and that the most likely eventuality on the political horizon was an alliance between Rosebery and Chamberlain.[2] On both counts he was wrong. There were many factors working in favour of a unified Liberal majority. Aside from Chamberlain's scorn for the Liberal Imperialist attitude, there were the mounting differences within the Government itself, a coalition of Liberal Unionists and Conservatives. More important, the Balfour Cabinet was to display an almost unfailing knack for raising questions which, regardless of their merits, were politically explosive and could only serve to reunite the opposition. This can be seen in the case of education reform and to an even greater extent in the case of tariff reform.

The Education Act was introduced on March 24, 1902, in the week the war ended. Perhaps the most important piece of reform legislation of this whole period, it has since come to be regarded as a far-sighted and salutary measure. Pushed by Balfour, despite warnings from Chamberlain that his Liberal Unionist following might prove rebellious, it abolished school boards and handed over control in both secondary and technical education to county councils and county borough councils. Not only board schools but voluntary (i.e. denominational) schools were put on the local rates. The Act was greeted by a whirlwind of Nonconformist indignation that swept through the Liberal party and through the ranks of Labour. The Rev. John Clifford and Lloyd George led in decrying the act as 'undemocratic' and as 'putting Rome on the rates.' Virtually all Liberals opposed it. So did the I.L.P. and the Trades Union Congress.

The difficulties in the way of a federation like the L.R.C. having any clear and definite programme were revealed when MacDonald wanted the Committee to protest the Education Bill and the Fabian Society objected. Sidney Webb had been an advocate of many of its provisions and with the Fabian Tract, 'The Education Muddle and the Way Out' had helped pave the way for its introduction. The Bill was no concern of the L.R.C., the Fabians asserted,[3] and when the Committee adopted a resolution against it, the Fabian Executive agreed to have Pease point out to the L.R.C. 'that its action on the Education Bill [was] *ultra vires* and that the Committee's practice of travelling beyond the purpose for which it was appointed by passing and publishing general political resolutions [was] likely to lead to the withdrawal of constituent bodies and the disruption of the Committee.'[4] In spite of this Fabian threat, the L.R.C. Conference of 1902 adopted a resolution, sponsored by the I.L.P., favouring a continuance of the school boards. All in all, however, the Labour movement generally was not as greatly stirred as the Liberal party by the education controversy and was inclined to stress that free meals for school children were as important as any other aspect of the question. The President of the Trades Union Congress in 1902 cogently expressed this viewpoint when he stated, 'Under our present system an attempt is made to feed the brain while the body is starved.'[5]

Labour was much more aroused by and involved in the controversy over tariff reform. A series of by-election victories was already reviving Liberal hopes when Chamberlain by a speech at Birmingham on May 15, 1903, transformed the whole political picture. Already as Colonial Secretary he had urged an Imperial Zollverein. Now he came down squarely on the side of protection—with food taxes, preference and retaliation against foreign tariffs—as a means of consolidating the Empire. Though certain Liberal Imperialists at first seemed more attracted than repelled by the proposal,[6] this attack on Free Trade, a Liberal idol, united that party as nothing else could.

The Balfour Government, on the other hand, seemed about to disintegrate. Most of the older members of the Cabinet opposed Chamberlain. There were resignations, Chamberlain himself resigning in order to carry his fight to the country. In the House Unionist Free Traders were befuddled, then disgruntled, and in a few cases openly mutinous. Some of the leaders in the Liberal party, including the Chief Whip and Lord Tweedmouth, were anxious to secure the co-operation of these Free Trade Unionists, in part by guaranteeing their seats if they opposed the Government or resigned.[7] Campbell-Bannerman, however, had doubts about hampering himself by such concessions. Of about fifty-three Free Traders on the Government side only twenty were vigorous in their belief and fewer still were willing, like Winston Churchill, to make an open break.[8] 'Tweedmouth is full of a scheme for half a dozen voting with us on the Address resigning their seats and standing as Liberals,' wrote Campbell-Bannerman to James Bryce in December 1903. 'A little melodramatic for John Bull's taste! And after all Winston is hardly worth any increase in complications.'[9]

Over a two-year period nine Unionists, including 'Winston,' did in fact secede to the Liberals, who were willing in certain instances to make electoral arrangements, but as signs pointed more and more to a Liberal victory, the selling power of Free Trade Unionists who were still on the fence went rapidly down. If they were safe on Tariff Reform could they be trusted on Education, and was it worth the risk of alienating the Non-conformist vote? Moreover, many Free Trade Unionists came to prefer Protection to what they feared might be a Radical victory under a Free Trade cloak. They therefore maintained a lukewarm loyalty to the coalition. It was this support and not only Balfour's dialectical skill and masterful political juggling that kept the Government in office for over two years while its imminent collapse was almost hourly expected. Fear of Home Rule and radical reform undoubtedly motivated Hicks Beach and his following in supporting the Government,[10] and a like fear must have been shared by the Tory Free Fooder Hugh Cecil when he informed the House that he was against Protection because it would help to make the Labour party stronger and hinted that the same spirit that was behind Protection would be behind future demands to fix wages by law.[11] Such a man could hardly be expected to seek or to find favour from a Radical leader like Bannerman, who was becoming increasingly sympathetic to Labour's demands, and well might Sir Charles Dilke warn that for the Liberals to take on a great number of Free Trade Unionists would be to hopelessly handicap the party and make its destruction by the Labour party only a question of time. Other questions were not to be forgotten while unregenerate Tories were welcomed in a blaze of anti-Chamberlainism.[12]

Barnstorming the country to convert Conservative Associations and British manufacturers to his views, Chamberlain at the outset was probably confident of commanding a wide working-class support. Protection, he could argue, would not only bring increased trade and wages; it would provide additional revenue with which the Government could treat for old age pensions and other social reforms.[13] Yet no matter how sincere may have been his early suggestions for linking Imperial Preference to social legislation, Chamberlain made no commitments in this direction.[14] Perhaps he could not do so for the same reason that the Unionist Government was in a poor position to woo the support of Labour by undoing Taff Vale. The men who paid, the rich industrialists in the party, including those who had abandoned the Liberals over Home Rule, would not have it. And so anxious was Chamberlain to gain their support that his scheme of Protection to strengthen the bonds of Empire soon deteriorated into a scheme whose chief aim was to strengthen British industry against foreign competition. Still, if the bait of social legislation was lacking, could not the working classes be told that the increased unemployment of these years was due largely to Free Trade? Unfortunately for Chamberlain this argument could not convince even the Tory Lancashire cotton operatives, and it lost all its potency when trade suddenly improved in 1905.

In any case, most socialists and trade unionists were anti-Chamberlain from the start. They regarded the Government with which he was associated as anti-Labour in spirit and so suspected any proposition he might make. Especially feared and resented was the proposed tax on food, and the image of the 'little loaf' and bitter attacks on 'stomach taxing Chamberlainites' were a prominent feature in the Labour party's campaign. The I.L.P. threw itself into anti-tariff propaganda with enthusiasm, and its speakers pursued Chamberlain throughout the country. Often giant meetings were held, many of them addressed by Snowden and MacDonald. As L.R.C. Secretary, MacDonald wrote a Free Trade Manifesto which was signed by the Parliamentary Committee of the T.U.C., the General Federation of Trade Unions and the L.R.C. Executive and distributed as L.R.C. Pamphlet No. 10.[15] He also wrote a shilling booklet, *The Zollverein and British Industry*, which unfortunately for its title and bias appeared after the question of a Zollverein no longer figured prominently in the dispute.[16]

Were the Liberals crying 'dear loaf' merely to distract attention from their own shortcomings? Robert Blatchford thought so and saw nothing unworthy in Chamberlain's demands. 'Under Free Trade the consumer gets his goods cheap,' he wrote in the *Clarion*, 'and the British producer gets short work and low wages.'[17] A. M. Thompson, 'Dangle,' joined his chief and ridiculed the Trades Union Congress for opposing Chamberlain while defending the notions of John Bright, the consistent opponent of factory legislation, and Cobden, the enemy of trade unions.[18] Nor could the Fabians be happy about the stand taken by Labour. When the question of a tract on Tariff Reform was being considered by the Fabian Executive in September 1903, Shaw wrote to Pease '. . . a Socialist society cannot take the Free Trade point of view. We are necessarily anti-Free Trade, anti-Manchester, anti-laissez-faire, anti-Cobden and Bright, anti all the Liberal Gods. Twice already within a few years the Socialists and Labour men have bolted into the Liberal camp: first, on the war, second, on the Education Bill. In both cases there was room for difference of opinion. But now it seems that there is going to be a third bolt over Free Trade, about which no difference of opinion should be possible, unless any of us is prepared to advocate the importation of Chinese Labour—which is the real test of a thoroughgoing Free-trader.'[19]

This latter argument—a favourite of Chamberlain's—that free trade in commodities was inseparable from free trade in labour was never effectively countered by the Labour party. Shaw felt that the best reply to Chamberlain was to surrender the Cobdenite fortifications unconditionally and then argue that Chamberlain must accompany his scheme with a national minimum wage and a guarantee that any extra revenue would be used for public purposes and not just to reduce 'the existing shamefully inadequate taxation of unearned income.'[20] Beatrice Webb was sure that Chamberlain would romp into power after a few years' propaganda if he took up the policy of a national minimum. In such a case the import duties could be thrown in as 'a silly and expensive ornament to attract the employing class to the policy of state regulation.'[21] When the Fabian tract on the fiscal question appeared in February 1904, it was not surprising that the strongest criticism was reserved for the Free Traders.

Of course no socialist worth his salt could mouth Cobdenite arguments, long grown stale, and pretend that Free Trade was the answer to unemployment and low wages. Under Free Trade as under Protection, said a resolution of the L.R.C. in

1904, the condition of the working classes remained deplorable. Free Trade had to be supplemented with socialist measures, with nationalization of the railways and of land, or even with a national minimum, and though MacDonald opposed this latter idea, a resolution favouring a national minimum was carried by the I.L.P. conference in 1904.[22]

One of MacDonald's main concerns as L.R.C. Secretary was to make sure that Labour's arguments did not become simply an echo of Liberal propaganda. With some concern he noted that prominent trade unionists and Labour M.P.s signed a Free Trade Manifesto of the Cobden Club,[23] and when the Liberals pirated the L.R.C. Manifesto (Leaflet No. 10) and issued it in areas where L.R.C. candidates were running, the independent position was undoubtedly becoming compromised,[24] and MacDonald protested and hastened to repair the damage. But it was impossible to take an entirely different line, and L.R.C. men appeared on the platform of the Free Food League, even in Liberal company. By 1905 the I.L.P. could argue, however, that Chamberlain's proposals were now discredited and that the Liberals were only trying to beat the issue into life in order to avoid pronouncement on important social questions. As the *Woolwich Pioneer* put it, 'Is the country to have no choice between standing still and going back to the old, exploded fallacies of sixty years ago? Unemployment is no less real because it is not due to dumping; poverty is no less grinding because so-called Tariff Reform would make it still more bitter; it is not because the nation does not want its ailments cured that it repudiates Birmingham quack remedies.'[25]

The Labour party was meanwhile becoming more and more indistinguishable from other elements in the opposition as it shared their stand on these major questions of the day. If independence was to be of any value, it was asked, must it not include independence of programme and not merely of organization?[26] Yet, for the L.R.C., programme making would create as many problems as it would solve. The socialists and trade unionists, some Tory, some Liberal, would argue endlessly over such a project while to limit the programme to the issues on which there was a wide agreement such as the recent war, education and tariff reform, would be to invite the accusation, already common in S.D.F. circles, that the L.R.C. had become a mere appendage of the Liberal party. Had not an arch-critic of class representation, James Bryce, said in March 1902, that the I.L.P. stood for the primary principles of Liberalism?[27] And did not C. P. Scott's *Manchester Guardian* find in the I.L.P. programme, of all places, the old traditional policies of Gladstone and Bright—Peace, Retrenchment and Reform?[28] If outright socialist resolutions were still to be voted down by the trade unions at L.R.C. conferences,[29] MacDonald and his colleagues thought it best to leave the party's object vague. Much education work had yet to be done before the movement could be as unified on principles and object as it was on method.[30] Let critics say that to vote for an L.R.C. nominee was to vote in the dark or opposition to a programme be carried to a ridiculous extreme when an affiliated society called on all L.R.C. candidates to 'abstain from reference to vexed matters that might alienate votes.'[32] The main thing was to get a Labour party into the House and keep it there. Then there would be time enough for official programmes.[33]

\* \* \*

When the L.R.C. Conference convened at Newcastle in February 1903, membership had risen to 852,000. On the Executive of thirteen, only three represented socialist societies (Hardie and James Parker for the I.L.P. and Pease for the Fabians), but in the trade union sections Pete Curran of the Gasworkers, J. N. Bell of the National Union of Labourers and John Hodge of the Steel Smelters were all close to the I.L.P. in point of view. With no large group except the miners still unaffiliated, MacDonald was of the opinion that the L.R.C. could be left to grow of itself, that the main task was consolidation. Trade unions had to be brought into closer contact with headquarters in choosing and placing candidates. The decks had to be cleared for the coming General Election and MacDonald himself given authority to act in emergencies during the absence of the Executive.[24] Also, the time had arrived to inaugurate a Parliamentary Fund and to enforce a stricter discipline upon those members who too openly coquetted with the Liberals.

When S. G. Hobson, speaking for the Fabian Society, had urged a Parliamentary Fund in 1900, the I.L.P. had thought the time inopportune; it might discourage affiliations and revive the old objection that the socialists were seeking a free ride on trade union coat tails.[35] The voting of a parliamentary levy of a shilling a year by the Miners Federation in 1901 had helped stifle such objections and the year following, the L.R.C. Conference instructed the Executive to seek some method of raising funds for election expenses and for maintenance in the House. By September 1902 a scheme was ready for circulation among the member societies. At the Conference in February 1903 it was adopted. Contributions from affiliated bodies were to be based on a voluntary levy of one penny per member per year. The L.R.C. was to pay twenty-five per cent of the net fees of the Returning Officer in elections and if a candidate were elected, £200 a year toward his maintenance. Arthur Henderson of the Ironfounders favoured a levy of 4d. a year, but this was defeated. MacDonald felt that a good deal of jealousy and suspicion had yet to be overcome and stressed that the main thing was not the amount but getting the fund under way.[36]

Through the administration of this fund the L.R.C. would increase its control over its members in Parliament and over its affiliated bodies. General secretaries of the larger unions would no longer have an overwhelming advantage; smaller societies would now be able to run candidates and non-trade unionists would also have a better opportunity. Richard Bell might feel that trade union secretaries made the best Labour M.P.s,[37] but MacDonald wondered if the two jobs at the same time were compatible and if such men should not resign their trade union posts if elected to Parliament.[38] Like Hardie he was disturbed by the tendency to run men to represent trades rather than Labour as a whole.[39] How could the trade union officer alone, so involved in union matters and often imbued with a purely sectional approach, constitute a broad enough base for the kind of Labour party the I.L.P. wanted? There were only two million trade unionists. What of the other fourteen million voters?[40]

What was even more important than the Parliamentary Fund in strengthening the movement in 1903 was a firmer declaration of independence. This was encouraged by the affiliation of the Lancashire cotton operatives in the wake of the Clitheroe victory and by rising resentment against members of the L.R.C. who too closely identified themselves with the Liberal Party. In most parts of Lancashire the cotton operatives were still as strongly Tory as they had been in the days of Mawdsley; and Chamberlain's attack on Free Trade had not yet come to weaken this allegiance. Like the miners they were not only strong numerically but so heavily concentrated in some constituencies that they could well elect any man they chose. Hence their affiliation to the L.R.C. was highly prized and was not to be endangered by any over-zealous displays of friendship to official Liberalism.[41]

Yet difficulties in this regard were almost bound to arise. Though it had been generally understood that Labour was to be quite independent of Conservative and Liberal organizations, the L.R.C. Constitution in its definition of independence was not hard and fast, and even I.L.P. stalwarts were displaying a perhaps unnecessary affinity for Liberal causes. Such was the state of confusion that in late 1902 W. E. Clery, the L.R.C. candidate for Deptford, saw nothing incongruous in accepting an invitation from the Deptford Liberal Association to run under its auspices. The L.R.C. Executive felt obliged to let Clery remain on its list, but it did so with reluctance, with the members nearly evenly divided, and pointed out that this should not constitute a precedent and that the entire question would have to be submitted for decision to the Newcastle Conference.[42] Hardie, working with Pease and Frederick Rogers on amendments to the L.R.C. constitution, was confident that the conference would decide overwhelmingly against such latitudinarianism.[43]

What really brought the question of independence to a head was the actions of Richard Bell who in the previous February had been chosen Chairman of the L.R.C. Not only had he

165

appeared on Liberal platforms; in the House he sat on the Liberal benches, and in his own constituency, Derby, he held joint meetings with the Liberal member, Sir Thomas Roe.[44] Time after time he supported Liberal candidates in by-elections. When he congratulated Samuel in Cleveland[45] and backed a Liberal at Newmarket, these were minor offences. But at West Derby[46] he again backed the Liberal even though the majority of the workers in this area were Tory and although the Tory was more friendly to revisions in the trade union law than his opponent.[47] 'Bell seems to be delivering himself into our hands,' wrote Hardie to Glasier at the time of this latter episode. 'It is really fortunate that he has raised the issue at this stage in the career of the new movement. Had he waited till he had a half a dozen fellow delinquents with him the position might have been critical.'[48]

With strongly-worded resolutions censuring Bell on the agenda, the conference at Newcastle might easily have ended in disorder and disruption. Fortunately personal allusions to Bell were suppressed by clever management, and in not offering himself for re-election to the executive, Bell himself facilitated calmer deliberation. The constitution was amended by the adoption of a strong resolution in favour of independence. It required L.R.C. members on the Executive, in Parliament, and standing for election to 'abstain strictly from identifying themselves with or promoting the interests of any section of the Liberal or Conservative parties.' All candidates were to abide by the constitution, and by the decisions of the L.R.C. group in Parliament, or resign.

One way to have dealt with Bell would have been to form the L.R.C. group in the House into the nucleus of a Labour party acting together not only in Parliament but in elections. This is what MacDonald and Hardie desired and what the Newcastle conference recommended. But Bell thought the idea preposterous and said that neglecting the nine 'Lib-Labs' in the House to form a Labour group of Hardie, Shackleton and himself would cover the party with ridicule.[49] Bell continued to go his own way, seeking close co-operation between Liberal and Labour M.P.s, despite Hardie's protests,[50] and noting that for all the talk of Independence, Hardie himself had been returned for Merthyr in 1900 because of Liberal aid and that more recent L.R.C. candidates had not turned down Liberal assistance.[51] By December 1903, Snowden was provoked to write that 'for Bell to continue his association with the L.R.C. while conspiring to destroy it, [was] both dishonourable to himself and injurious to the prospects of other L.R.C. candidates.'[52]

Bell was not alone. Clery of Deptford found the Newcastle resolution impossible of acceptance.[53] So did John Ward of the Navvies' Union, L.R.C. candidate for Stoke, who openly encouraged negotiations with the Liberals. They and 'Lib-Labs' in general blamed the socialists for the Newcastle resolution even though it had passed by 659 to 154, that is by a vote of over four to one. At the Trades Union Congress in September unsuccessful proposals were made to get rid of socialist representation in the L.R.C. by making its membership the same as that of the Congress, and an abortive attempt in the same direction was made at the Newcastle Conference itself.[54] In some circles there was still a tendency to regard the L.R.C. as a creature of the Congress. Certainly this was John Burns' line of thinking when he spoke of the I.L.P. socialists at Newcastle as an 'outside' body with disproportionate power. The trade unions were not going 'to provide the money, the votes, the organization, and the prestige, while Socialists got all the candidates.' Their place was in 'the outworks of propaganda.' They made a mistake when they tried 'to garrison the citadel.' They had 'neither the men nor the money nor the measures to maintain a working-class party.' Such a party can exist for some years,' Burns wrote, 'in so far as it is tolerant and rational and adapts itself to the sympathetic aims of men who give up their time and are willing to go a very long way to help the Labour movement. . . . A policy of isolation spells impotence, a policy of exclusiveness rules out the best sympathies of other classes.'[55]

Of course, in a sense, the trade unionists were being 'used' by the socialists, but what men like Burns and Bell refused to admit was that they were often willingly so used. The suspicion that once attached to the I.L.P. had subsided, and its men were general secretaries of some of the most powerful unions. According to Beatrice Webb, the Trades Union Congress in 1902, as far as its formal expression of opinion was concerned, had been 'captured' by the I.L.P.[56] In any case, it was not a convincing argument to say that independence meant hostility to other progressives. Nor did it mean isolation. Essentially it was a means of preserving the integrity of the Committee and preventing its disruption, the only means, in fact, by which Tory, Liberal and socialist could be kept together under a single banner. Its purpose, in other words, stemmed as much from political expediency as from any firm adherence to principle. Harry Quelch of the S.D.F. might argue that to give support to a 'Labour' man who was a good Liberal while forbidding that man to give support to a fellow Liberal was merely a fictitious independence and a futile unity, for sooner or later the political leanings of such an adherent would prove stronger than his political independence.[57] Hardie and MacDonald were perfectly aware of this difficulty, but they were not willing to wait for full conversions. They felt that a Labour party victory was the *sine qua non* of the eventual realization of a socialist programme. Perhaps, from the socialist point of view, they thought too much of political victory, but they were almost certainly right in assuming that Independence was the most powerful weapon yet devised for attaining it.

Yet the Newcastle resolution was so strongly worded as to give more than one sympathizer a feeling that the whip was being cracked. Especially irritating was the clause on resigning. Isaac Mitchell, of the General Federation of Trade Unions, effectively criticized it. Glasier could give only a weak argument in its defence.[58] MacDonald early came to favour the removal of the 'resign' clause, said that it had been voted on hurriedly and in confusion at Newcastle, and predicted that it would be deleted. At Bradford in 1904 it was removed, but all attempts to further weaken the independent position were defeated.[59]

While the Newcastle Conference was still in session, an L.R.C. candidate named Will Crooks was campaigning against a Tory in a by-election in the arsenal town of Woolwich. A moderate, famed as a teller of Cockney stories, Crooks had been a member of the L.C.C. and mayor of Poplar. Ever since 1892 when he had left the workbench for the L.C.C., trade unionists, among whom he was extremely popular, had contributed to his wages fund. The I.L.P. socialist was less enthusiastic about Crooks, suspecting his Liberal connections, but in the interests of unity such uncertainties were kept hidden. Crooks had the backing of a local Labour organization at Woolwich and received wide Liberal support. The Liberal dailies, the *Morning Leader* and the *Daily News*, assisted him, Dr. John Clifford, the Nonconformist leader, worked in his campaign,[60] and the list of names in his subscription fund and for the carriages lent to him on polling day indicate that he united the Progressive vote.[61] With the working class of Woolwich engaged in war plant work, Crooks, though he had always been an ardent pro-Boer, avoided the South African question and concentrated on home politics—on unemployment, trade union wages, Taff Vale, better housing for the workers, and on the Education Bill. A Conservative majority of 2,805 he turned into a Labour and Progressive majority of 3,299. 'Almost incredible,' wrote John Burns in his diary.[62] 'The most astounding result of modern times,' said the *Yorkshire Observer*.[63] On March 16th, Crooks was introduced in the House by Burns and Shackleton. 'Chamberlain's face was a study and portent,' observed Burns, 'the Government of Raids and Capitalism is sinking.'[64] 'What it too clearly means,' the Conservative *Times* commented, 'is that the "Labour Movement" which has disturbed the balance of political parties on the Continent, has made itself manifest, in a practical form, here also, and that the nation at large, as well as both the political parties in the State, will have to reckon with it.'[65]

Two months later the movement looked hopefully for a Lancashire 'Woolwich' when a vacancy was created by the death of one of the Tory members for Preston, a seat that the I.L.P. had unsuccessfully contested in 1895 and again in 1900 when Hardie stood. Glasier strongly favoured MacDonald's running on the grounds that as Secretary of the L.R.C. he would get the full Labour support locally,[66] but Hardie wanted John Hodge, General Secretary of the Steel Smelters' Union, while MacDonald himself, though at first strongly drawn toward Preston, decided to concentrate on nursing Leicester.[67] When the Steel Smelters agreed to run Hodge, there was practically no danger of a three-way fight; nearly twenty years had passed since any Liberal had tried to win this Tory stronghold.

Hodge had become disillusioned with the Liberals when their party opposed him at Gower in Glamorganshire in the 1900 election. Having succeeded Bell as Chairman of the L.R.C., he was arrow-straight on independence, though not a member of the I.L.P., and, according to Glasier, he refused the proffered aid of both Herbert Samuel and Bell during the ensuing campaign.[68] Adopted late and with virtually no organization, Hodge faced one of the finest electoral machines in Lancashire. Moreover, the Mayor of Preston fixed the day of polling for as early a date as legally possible so that Hodge had less than a week to campaign. MacDonald, in a last minute rush to get out election posters and leaflets,[69] accused the Mayor of deliberately using his office in the Tory interest.[70] Hodge had one advantage, however—an experienced election agent, Arthur Henderson, Labour candidate for Barnard Castle, who had already been instrumental in Sam Woods' Walthamstow victory and that of Crooks at Woolwich. Henderson had been urged upon Hodge by MacDonald and had hastened to Preston where he soon made progress in creating an organization. By many I.L.P.'ers he was still regarded as a Liberal, and in his attitude toward Liberal support he differed markedly from Hodge. Preston could be the first real test of the independent stand taken at Newcastle, and Hodge felt that the Conservative cotton operatives far outnumbered the Liberals and that the main appeal should be to them.[71] Henderson, on the other hand, observed that Liberal assistance had not frightened Woolwich Conservatives away[72] and that attacks on the Liberal party would not only lose Liberal votes but also a £100 contribution promised by George Cadbury.[73] For whatever it was worth in Preston, Hodge did get Liberal blessing. A local body of representative Liberals issued a manifesto on his behalf,[74] the

Chief Whip congratulated them on their action,[75] and the Council of the National Liberal Federation wished him success.[76]

The defeat in the House at this time by only twenty votes of Shackleton's bill for relieving some of the disabilities of Taff Vale was felt to favour the Labour cause.[77] Also encouraging was the fact that in this strongly Roman Catholic area, many Catholics expressed displeasure with the Tory candidate's stand on removing offensive sentences from the Coronation Oath, while the Preston *Catholic News* in a special election issue urged Catholics not to vote Tory as of old but to take up an independent position.[78] The Tory, John Kerr, had the advantage of being a local employer; he was a member of a great electrical and tramway firm with a branch in Preston.[79] Nevertheless, in the Conservative Working Men's Clubs there were some defections among trade union leaders who went over to Hodge. For fear of antagonizing this Conservative support, Hodge, with some personal misgivings, decided that Keir Hardie should not share his platform. This tendency to keep socialism and socialists in the background at election time had been noted by the I.L.P. leaders at Woolwich. They, of course, resented it, but Glasier took solace in reflecting, '. . . what does it matter if we sow and they reap!—the harvest is ours, or rather our cause's, just the same.'[80]

The results showed 8,639 for Kerr and 6,490 for Hodge, 1,656 more votes than Hardie received in 1900. The principal reason for defeat, it was agreed, was lack of organization. The conservatism of the Preston textile operatives had been shaken, but few had followed their leaders in abandoning the old allegiance. Yet the election indicated, said Hodge, that this 'supposed impregnable fortress would fall at the next attack.'[81] In 1906 he was proven right.

## NOTES

1. In this connection see H.G. to Rosebery prior to the latter's Chesterfield speech, Dec. 13, 1901. H.G., vol. lxv, 170; H.G. to C.B., February 23, 1902, C.B., vol. xi; C.B. to H.G., Sept. 28, 1902, H.G., vol. xv, 25; and James Bryce to H.G., Sept. 29, 1902, H.G., vol. xv, 67-68.
2. Hardie in the *Labour Leader* (afterward the *L.L.*), March 8 and June 14, 1902; Hardie's open letter to Lloyd George, *L.L.*, March 7, 1903.

3. Fabian Society Executive Minutes, March 17, 1901.

4. *ibid.*, June 14, 1901.

5. *T.U.C. Annual*, 1902, 32. The Labour members in Parliament found a sponsor for a bill to provide free meals, but the Government refused to take the bill beyond a second reading. J. H. Stewart Reid, *The Origins of the British Labour Party*, Univ. of Minnesota, 1955, 102.

6. W. S. Hewins, *Apologia of an Imperialist*, 2 vols., London, 1929, vol. i, 65-67.

7. See Tweedmouth to C.B., November 28, 1903, C.B., vol. xxvi, 86-86.

8. On the size of the various groups among the Free Trade Unionists see H.G., vol. cxvi, 133.

9. C.B. to Bryce, December 7, 193, C.B., vol. vi, 250-251.

10. J. A. Spender, *Great Britain: Empire and Commonwealth, 1886-1935*, London, 1936, 214.

11. Parl. Debates, Commons, 4th series, vol. 139; August 1, 1904, cols. 339-340.

12. *Daily News*, July 11, 1904.

13. Parl. Debates, Commons, 4th series, vol. 123, May 28, 1903, cols. 186-187.

14. See Chamberlain's letter to Hugh Farren, President of the Coventry Trades and Labour Council, as printed in the *Leicester Pioneer*, Nov. 11, 1905.

15. L.R.C. Minutes, Feb. 3, 1904.

16. J. R. MacDonald, *The Zollverein and British Industry*, 1903.

17. *Clarion*, Sept. 25, 1903.

18. *ibid.*, Sept. 18, 1903.

19. Shaw to Pease, Sept. 30, 1903.

20. *ibid.*

21. Beatrice Webb's diaries: Entries of November 18, 1903, and Mar. 1, 1904.

22. *I.L.P. Ann. Rpt.*, 1904, 29; MacDonald's main argument was that the minimum would tend to become the maximum and actually depress living standards. See his article in the *L.L.*, April 23, 1904.

23. MacDonald in the *New Liberal Review*, Nov. 1903, as quoted in the *L.L.*, Nov. 21, 1903.

24. MacDonald to Pease, Jan. 22, 1904.

25. *Woolwich Pioneer*, Nov. 4, 1904.

26. On this point see Cecil Chesterton, *Gladstonian Ghosts*, London, 1905, and his speech to the Fabian Society on Nov. 11, 1904, as reported in the *Fabian News*, Dec. 1904.

27. *Daily News*, Mar. 22, 1902.

28. As reported in the *L.L.*, April 20, 1901.

29. A socialist resolution was only narrowly defeated in 1903 by a vote of 291,000 to 295,000 with about one-third the delegates abstaining. *L.R.C. Ann.*, 1903, 36.

30. See Snowden's article in the *L.L.*, Feb. 13, 1904.

31. *Reynolds's News*, Sept. 11, 1904.

32. Coachmakers' resolution to be presented to the Bradford L.R.C. Conference as reported in the *Postman's Gazette*, Dec. 9, 1905, 532.

33. At the L.R.C. Conference in 1905 Shackleton argued that in regard to an L.R.C. programme, the resolutions of the Trades' Union Congress could suffice for many years as the basis for its programme. *L.R.C. Annual*, 1905, 39.

34. MacDonald memorandum to members of the Committee, Feb. 24, 1903.
35. Fabian Executive Minutes, June 22, 1900; *L.R.C. Annual*, 1901, 17-18; L.R.C. Minutes, Sept. 1, 1900; and *I.L.P. Annual*, 1901, 30-31.
36. MacDonald as 'Spectator' in the *Echo*, Feb. 27, 1902; *L.R.C. Annual*, 1903, 34-35.
37. *Echo*, Nov. 8, 1901.
38. *ibid.*, Oct. 3, 1901.
39. *L.L.*, Dec. 27, 1902.
40. Penny article in the *Clarion*, Dec. 19, 1902.
41. MacDonald in the *Echo*, Feb. 11, 1903.
42. L.R.C. Minutes, May 8 and Sept. 6, 1902.
43. Hardie to Pease, Oct. 23, 1902.
44. Shackleton and MacDonald's report of an interview with Bell. L.R.C. Minutes, Dec. 17, 1903.
45. L.R.C. Minutes, Jan. 8, 1903, regarding several complaints on Bell's support of Samuel.
46. *L.L.*, Jan. 24, 1903.
47. See also MacDonald's letter to the Committee on the Bell case, Mar. 28, 1904, in the L.R.C. papers and a statement of the I.L.P. position in the *L.L.*, April 9, 1904.
48. Hardie to Glasier, Jan. 23, 1903.
49. Hardie in the *L.L.*, Jan. 31, 1903; Bell's statement, *Daily News*, Feb. 24, 1903.
50. *Reynolds's News*, April 5, 1903.
51. *ibid.*
52. *I.L.P. News*, Dec., 1903.
53. *Clarion*, Mar. 6, 1903.
54. *T.U.C. Annual*, 1903; *L.R.C. Ann.*, 1903, 26-27.
55. Interview in *Reynolds's News*, Mar. 8, 1903.
56. *Our Partnership*, 245.
57. *Reynolds's*, June 28, 1903.
58. Letters printed in the *L.L.*, Oct. 24, 1903.
59. MacDonald as 'Spectator' in the *Echo*, July 8 and Dec. 23, 1903, *L.R.C. Ann.*, 1904, 56.
60. *Westminster Gazette*, Mar. 7, 1902.
61. According to *Reynolds's News*, Mar. 22, 1902: 'A Liberal agent was engaged in every committee room during Crooks's campaign'. . . . 'Almost all the money for the last registration of the election was supplied by the London Liberal Federation.'
62. Burns' diary; Entry of Mar. 11, 1903.
63. *Yorkshire Observer*, Mar. 14, 1903.
64. Burns' diary; Entry of Mar. 16, 1903.
65. *The Times*, Mar. 12, 1903.
66. Glasier to Hardie, April 27, 1903.
67. Hardie to Glasier, April 28 and 30, 1903.
68. Glasier to Hardie, May 15, 1903.
69. MacDonald to Pease, May 12, 1903.
70. *Manchester Guardian*, May 9, 1903.
71. John Hodge, *Workman's Cottage to Windsor Castle* London, 1931, 144-146.

72. Interview with Henderson, *Westminster Gazette*, May 12, 1903.
73. Hodge, *Workman's Cottage*, 148.
74. *Daily News*, May 11, 1903.
75. *Newcastle Daily Chronicle*, May 12, 1903.
76. *N.L.F. Annual*, May, 1903, 52.
77. *Manchester Guardian*, May 9, 1903.
78. As reprinted in the *Newcastle Daily Chronicle*, May 14, 1903.
79. *Westminster Gazette*, May 7, 1903.
80. Glasier to Hardie, May 15, 1903; Hardie to Glasier, May 18, 1903.
81. *L.L.*, May 23, 1903.

# CHAPTER X

# The Deal with the Liberals

••••••••••••••••••••••••••••••••••••••••••••••••••••••••••••••••••••••••••••••••••••••

WHILE the Newcastle Conference was to all appearances pro-claiming a more rigid political separatism, MacDonald, the L.R.C. Secretary, was quietly discussing with Liberal head-quarters the first concrete proposal for an electoral pact. There was basis for such a pact not only in the common antagonism of political 'outs' to the party in power but also in the pro-Liberal sympathies of many L.R.C. trade unionists, in the co-operation of adherents of the Committee and pro-Boer Liberals on the war issue and in the essential agreement of the strongly Non-conformist L.R.C. majority and virtually the whole Liberal party on the education question. Already suggestions had been made for some sort of alliance of anti-war progressives, and Liberals in several constituencies had left L.R.C. candidates unchallenged and had frequently supported them at the polls. In the General Election of 1900 when the Committee had hardly begun to get its bearings and seemed in no position to threaten anyone, it had obtained a free field against the Unionist in eight of the fifteen contests in which it engaged. This was partly ex-plained by division and apathy among the Liberals and a dearth of suitable candidates; yet the victories of Bell and Hardie and the L.R.C.'s impressive showing in other constituencies had been due in no small part to open Liberal support. After 1900 in by-elections the two camps were again brought into concert, and though at Clitheroe and Woolwich this was to be expected, since Shackleton and Crooks were widely regarded as Liberals in all but name, a section of the Liberal party was equally ready to back I.L.P. socialists. This was strikingly demonstrated in the first two by-elections fought by the I.L.P. after 1900.

In the first of these by-elections, at North-East Lanark in

Scotland in August 1901, the decision of the local Liberal caucus to oppose Robert Smillie of the Lanarkshire Miners was widely deplored in Liberal circles, and Liberal Radicals in Parliament, other prominent Liberals outside and certain anti-war sections of the Liberal press all ignored the caucus choice to favour Smillie.[1] The Chief Whip's office privately washed its hands of the Liberal candidate, Cecil Harmsworth, who was regarded by many Bannermanites as a millionaire imperialist.[2] The Master of Elibank, holder of the great Gladstone's former seat at Midlothian, urged Smillie's election.[3] And according to Hardie, Irish members in the House backed Labour against a Liberal for the first time since the Liberal-Irish alliance of 1886.[4] Far from spurning, the I.L.P. actually sought this assistance, with Hardie, supposedly the most unbending of Independents, urging Liberals to give weight to Smillie's assurances that, if elected, he would 'vote straight on every Liberal measure' and would support 'every item of what [was] known as the Liberal programme.'[5] The result was a Tory victory by some 900 votes over Harmsworth, while the I.L.P. nominee secured the largest vote for Labour ever polled in Scotland. Then in a by-election at Wakefield in Yorkshire, in March 1902, in which Philip Snowden was defeated by a Tory, the Liberals again divided. When the local Liberal executive protested that Snowden's entry made it impossible to find a Liberal willing to stand and advised boycotting the polls,[6] many anti-war and radical Liberals in Wakefield spurned this advice. Twenty-six Liberal M.P.s and such Liberal journals as the *Manchester Guardian*, the *Yorkshire Observer* and the London *Daily News* backed Snowden, and the *Guardian* deprecated the attitude of those Liberals who would not vote.[7] Very soon after Wakefield at Bury in Lancashire in May 1902, where the Balfour Government suffered its first major by-election defeat, the local I.L.P., in an almost unprecedented action announced its support of the anti-war Liberal.[8]

All this co-operation in elections, however, was but temporary and local, and, as one might expect, attempts had been made to enlarge it into something both national and sustained. One such attempt, just after the General Election of 1900, led to the

formation of the National Democratic League or N.D.L. This
organization was largely the brain-child of W. M. Thompson,
editor of the Radical weekly, *Reynolds's Newspaper*. Among its
original supporters were trade unionists, left-wing Liberals
including David Lloyd George, and some socialists. Yet there
were few I.L.P. adherents, and the S.D.F. and Fabian response
was distinctly cold from the outset.[9] The N.D.L.'s general
purpose of amalgamating all democratic bodies for common
ends was vague, its programme was narrowly political, and its
organization, based on individual memberships at a shilling a
year, was loose and unstable. The S.D.F. considered it a mere
'half-way house' aimed at rehabilitating the Liberal party by
ridding it of its incorrigible Whigs and Imperialists. Hardie of
the I.L.P. shared this estimate.[10] Aside from this, in the early
days of the L.R.C. the League could be regarded as a threat to
the Committee as was, indeed, any group that might siphon off
L.R.C. trade unionists into the Radical camp. For a time the
League made gestures of friendship to the L.R.C., and as late
as 1903 there were proposals from 'Lib-Labs' within the
Committee to allow it to affiliate, but these were decisively
defeated.[11] Then as his own organization declined, Thompson
witnessed the L.R.C.'s growth with a mixture of bitterness and
trepidation. He attacked it as undemocratic, as the tool of a
socialist minority that worked in the Tory interest and as a
major obstacle to a broad progressive combination in England.[12]
Such attacks had little effect, however: Thompson's influence
was small. Anti-war sentiment had given the N.D.L. its initial
impetus, and, once the war was over it began to waste away,
its professed membership by November 1905 being down to a
mere 7,000.[13] After the General Election it disappeared.

An alternative project for uniting Liberal Radicals, socialists
and trade unionists, this time on a common basis of anti-
imperialism and political and social reform, was brought forward in August 1901, shortly after the North-East Lanark
by-election. Its champion was J. A. Hobson, the noted
economist. It is noteworthy that Hobson saw the nucleus of a
Labour party not in the L.R.C., which as yet did not possess
sufficient stature to draw his attention, but in the I.L.P., and it

M

was to this latter body that he addressed his appeal. It could not hope to succeed he cautioned if it chose to act alone.[14] The I.L.P. response to Hobson's proposal had been friendly if not enthusiastic. George Barnes, who was Secretary of the powerful Engineers, appears to have been the least sympathetic, arguing that the alliance would sidetrack and retard the growth of the L.R.C. MacDonald also hinted at this, though he was not averse to a conference. A lengthy defence of temporary alliances was made by J. Bruce Glasier, the Chairman of the I.L.P., but he could not, he said, discern any separate Radical party with whom, except on the war issue, the I.L.P. could make 'a covenant of common cause at the polls.' Hardie surprisingly had been the most enthusiastic. Claiming to have long advocated some such alliance, he pointed to the growing friendship among anti-war Liberals, Irish and Labour elements that had found expression at North-East Lanark. Toward a new alliance in Parliament, he said, there were already eighty-two Irish members, ten or a dozen Radicals and nine or ten Labour members.[15] Yet Hardie wondered if further combinations by the I.L.P. might not dull even more the temper of its socialist weapons,[16] and once the war had ended he appears to have become suspicious of all such schemes. In June 1902, when a meeting of Labour and Radical members was held in the House to make plans for united action on Labour and other questions, Hardie, in contrast to his earlier pronouncements, let it be known that he had opposed such a meeting and had played no part in convening it.[17] But if the coming of peace had weakened the appeal of such broad proposals as Hobson's, the demand for some understanding to prevent Liberal-Labour election clashes had in no way abated. On the contrary, with a general election impending, the feeling that only Government candidates would profit from triangular contests gained additional strength.

MacDonald, exercising an influence as L.R.C. Secretary that went far beyond what the creators of that office had anticipated, was peculiarly suited to seeking an electoral agreement with the Liberals. It might be argued that his solicitude for Independence was always equalled, if not excelled, by his resourcefulness in draining Independence of any political disadvantage. Yet anyone who had listened to or read MacDonald could hardly escape the conclusion that he was no intransigent and would regard Independence primarily as a political weapon. Impatient with doctrinaires who stood in the way of the broadest party structure, he had developed a philosophy of socialism so all-embracing that the programme or doctrine of no particular group was likely to confine him. Persuasive and skilful, he won many less eclectic socialists to his point of view. Socialism, he insisted, was not something alien and opposed to Liberalism; it was a natural outgrowth of Liberalism and incorporated the best of this older creed with the most promising features of the new doctrine. Also he appears to have discerned more clearly than did Blatchford, the Webbs, and even Hardie the new school of radical collectivism growing up within the Liberal party. Surely it was not quite the same party that Hardie had turned from in bitterness at Mid-Lanark or that MacDonald had himself abandoned in 1894. The Liberal split, the long period of introspection in opposition, had led to a searching examination of the older Liberal gospel of self-interest and found it wanting. There were many Whigs quite unaware of this change, but they were not the dominant element in the party, having grown steadily weaker since the defections of 1886. The theorists and spokesmen of this 'New Liberalism,' including J. A. Hobson, L. T. Hobhouse, H. W. Massingham and C. P. Scott were arguing, as did MacDonald, that the political democracy which Liberalism had won must now be translated into a social democracy, that Liberalism and socialism were not incompatible but complementary.[18] Perhaps the creed of the 'New Liberalism' was as deeply rooted in political expediency as in idealism, but, in any case, with Labour prodding, it was after 1905 to provide the basis for the great reforms of the Campbell-Bannerman and Asquith Governments leading in the direction of the social service state.

In completely failing to foresee this development, the Webbs, like Blatchford, revealed their political obtuseness. By 1904 the Webbs had lost all faith in Rosebery and his group while with the Campbell-Bannerman section, as Beatrice admitted in her diary, they were completely out of touch and held to be of no account. However, they believed that the 'C.B.' set would accomplish nothing if it did come into office; it would, they thought, mean the 'stalemate of progress.'[19] As for Blatchford, he showed greater sympathy with the Tory protectionist than with the Liberal free trader and in May 1903 was dismissing Campbell-Bannerman as 'an unhappy old drawler of platitudinous flapdoodle.'[20]

Hardie continued to predict that another Liberal Government would prove as disappointing as that of 1892-1894 and that Rosebery, not Campbell-Bannerman, would emerge supreme.[21] Nevertheless he supported MacDonald's policy of electoral arrangements, justifying this support on the grounds that only in power would the Liberals provide the rude awakening for those who still put their faith in the Liberal party.[22] Thus, it appeared, Hardie could obtain the fruits of compromise without compromising, could contribute to a Liberal-Labour victory without relinquishing his role as an arch critic of the Liberal party. Admittedly Hardie was not as adroit a politician as MacDonald and was incapable of many of the subtle adjustments, not to say the ambivalence, necessary to carry out the policy that had been embarked upon. Yet he must be regarded as politically obtuse if he failed to see, and guilty of subterfuge if he feigned not to see, that two parties dependent on each other for votes would almost certainly align on programme and policy. In Hardie the old habit of sweeping condemnation of the Liberal party persisted after it had ceased to reflect political reality.

Even though as L.R.C. Secretary MacDonald spoke for the trade unionists as well as for the socialists of the Committee, he had to proceed cautiously lest men in his own party criticize his approach to the Liberals as a betrayal. There was an S.D.F. fringe in the I.L.P. which consistently held that success was being bought too dearly and which regarded any I.L.P. leader who worked for a Liberal-Labour victory as neither believing in what the party professed nor practising what it enjoined Admittedly the Liberals were willing 'to allow a few carefully trained Labour cats to a share of the political cream in return for the Labour vote,'[23] but would not the Liberals then kick down the ladder by which they climbed to power? Ignoring the changes within the Liberal camp and the genuine reformist zeal building up in its ranks, these critics of any arrangement argued that the I.L.P. must not embroil itself with the older party merely for a temporary advantage. Sensitive to such criticisms, MacDonald and those who backed his efforts did much of their work behind the scenes, so that very often only a dim line separated their opportunism from deception.

From the Socialist point of view there had always been valid objections to the I.L.P. policy of concentrating its immediate energies and ambitions less on the socialist goal than on the instrument through which that goal might one day be reached— a united Labour party. Already this had obliged the I.L.P. to make considerable adjustment to the demands of its trade union ally. Electoral ties with the Liberals meant further adjustment though the ties in this case would be looser and less obvious. That Liberal and Labour partners in victory would remain in partnership thereafter to maintain that victory was fairly obvious, but it was a fact which MacDonald alone of the I.L.P. leaders seems to have fully grasped and accepted. But all the I.L.P. leaders, having risked absorption in a nebulous L.R.C. Labourism were ready to take further risks. Moreover, like the Liberals which whom they bargained, they thought less in terms of weakening their creed and the long-range effects of compromise than in terms of immediate votes and power. They were acting as politicians have usually acted and pursuing a policy of short-range opportunism designed to rout the Government and secure office for themselves.

There were, to be sure, Liberal opponents of any compact with Labour who demanded that Labour enter Parliament through the local Liberal associations or not at all. They were especially influential in the North where the challenge of Labour was greatest. Typifying their spirit were Alfred Illingworth of Bradford, who had raised his voice against Labour's claims since 1892,[24] and Samuel Storey, Chairman of the Executive of the Northern Liberal Federation, who warned that the surrendering of seats to the new party would mean 'the destruction of organized Liberalism in the North.'[25] In the headquarters of the Liberal Central Association in London, however, and among prominent Liberals inclined to a broader view of their party's interests, this parochial caucus spirit was frequently and publicly lamented. The Master of Elibank, for example, in criticizing Liberal opposition to Smillie at North-East Lanark argued that the Liberals must stand aside for such men in working-class constituencies: 'otherwise Radical electors [would] be driven more than ever into the extreme camp and what was once the life-blood of Liberalism . . . be dried up.'[26] Lord Tweedmouth early in 1903 dismissed as 'humbug' the notion that the Liberals in allying with Labour would be fostering class legislation; without an alliance, he insisted, the Liberals themselves could not hope to succeed.[27]

MacDonald, often under a pseudonym, 'Spectator,' which he used in writing a weekly column for the London *Echo*, began throwing out hints to such Liberal leaders as early as 1901. He observed that Harmsworth's running against Smillie 'postponed' that understanding between Liberalism and Labour which alone could insure a fighting opposition in Parliament and imposed upon the Labour party 'the painful duty of defeating a Liberal.'[28] When Wakefield Liberals refused to support Snowden, he described this as 'civil war' and suggested if only half a dozen Liberal associations could swallow their pride and be wise there need be no splitting of Liberal and Labour votes.[29] To the proposals for allying anti-war progressives, he countered with further pleas for free fights against the Tory, reminding his own following that the time had come to welcome some electoral arrangement and to 'steer [its] ship a little nearer to the land.'[30] For himself MacDonald was seeking from the Liberals a clear field for the second seat at Leicester, and when at first rebuffed, he warned that this augured ill for a general understanding and that unless the Liberals made some concessions Labour must pursue a policy of 'fighting for its own hand.'[31] But he never lost hope, being well aware that at the Liberal Chief Whip's office were men who, *mutatis mutandis*, shared his point of view.

Herbert Gladstone, the Liberal Chief Whip, was the youngest son of the great Prime Minister. He was educated at Eton and at University College, Oxford. In 1880, aged thirty-four, he entered Parliament for West Leeds. He was a Liberal whip, a junior lord of the Treasury and a financial secretary at the War Office before becoming an under-secretary in the Home Office in 1892. From 1892 to 1895 he served as First Commissioner of Public Works. When in 1899 he acceded to Campbell-Bannerman's request and became Chief Whip, it was regarded as a step down for an ex-Minister, but the sorry state of the party demanded a man of authority.[32] Measured by the results in 1906 Gladstone must be considered a success in this office, but in 1900 the poor condition of the Liberal party organization had made him an easy target for criticism. Hardie then regarded him as 'a person of barely average capacity'[33] and Henry Labouchere, a Liberal Radical, wrote Dilke in October 1900 that Gladstone was 'a hopeless head Whip . . . a mere fly on the Parliamentary coach.'[34] By the end of 1903, however, with party fortunes somewhat refurbished, Gladstone was no longer so vulnerable and in his handling of the party's relations with political Labour was revealing a breadth of outlook that proved him far removed from the narrow Liberalism of the Illingworth school. Beatrice Webb in her estimate of Gladstone in 1904 seems far too severe, and it should be remembered that where many of the political figures of this period are concerned, she was not a very shrewd judge. After entertaining Gladstone at dinner she commented in her diary, 'Herbert Gladstone is a heavy but pleasant "diner out"—with the sort of common sense which comes from years of experience of party wirepulling; but he is a mere party hack, absolutely unconcerned for any mortal thing (beyond his own comfort) but his party's success. He has some inkling of our ideas but dislikes them.'[35] This estimate should be contrasted with that of Gladstone's cousin, Lucy Masterman, who observes that in his opinions and outlook Gladstone was likely to agree with her husband, C. F. G. Masterman, who had a profound interest in social questions and in reform efforts in general.[36]

The Chief Whip derived his authority from the leader of the party, from the party as a whole, and from his control over certain party funds. His principal functions lay in House of

Commons duties, in holding conferences with party leaders, in overseeing and financially assisting organization and registration, in providing candidates when requested, and in raising money. He worked under the aegis of the Liberal Central Association, a rather shadowy body, supposedly containing all of the Liberal party in Parliament including the leaders and the whips. The National Liberal Federation (the N.L.F.), representing the party organizations in the constituencies, was designedly kept apart from the officialism of the Liberal Central, but the Federation could at any time bring pressure to bear on the central authorities through resolutions. The Secretary of the Federation, Robert Hudson, acted as a liaison officer between the Federation and the Chief Whip, that is, between the party in the country at large and the party headquarters and worked with Gladstone in friendship and in harmony.[37]

Reminded by his own associates that if the Liberals proved unaccommodating Labour could 'play havoc with the safer Liberal seats,'[38] Gladstone was prepared to urge upon the constituencies the claims of Labour. At Derby in 1900 where Bell had obtained the second seat he had been notably successful. He had to contend, however, with the stubborn opposition of the local caucuses unwilling to stand aside.[39] Were the question left to him alone, he boasted in 1901, he had no doubt but that he could come to terms with Labour in the course of half a morning.[40] Faced with the resistance of an Alfred Illingworth, Gladstone could do little, but he was by no means helpless. Though interference by the Chief Whip in the affairs of the associations was frowned upon, the democratic aspect of both the local and national machine being constantly boasted of in party propaganda, he could and did exert greater influence from the centre than was commonly acknowledged. With funds to dispose of he could mix strong admonitions with financial relief to hard-pressed locals. By consulting some Liberal magnate in the provinces and appealing to general as opposed to local party interest he might obtain important concessions, on occasion even a candidate's withdrawal. An eager candidate for Parliament who oppposed a Labour man regardless of behests from above was to find himself, in more than one instance, abandoned by party leaders aware of the displeasure of Liberal Headquarters and ignored by neighbouring Liberal candidates out of fear of Labour retaliation in their own constituencies.

Gladstone's attitude toward the rising Labour party was strikingly realistic in so far as immediate, if not long-range, Liberal interests were concerned. Putting little store in labels, he saw no reason to object to men who shared the Liberal view on leading questions simply because they ran as 'Labour' candidates. The argument that the emergence of a Labour party involved a great upheaval and the death of the older established parties he chose to belittle. 'The Labour party was, in fact, a new, vigorous political movement,' he said in 1903, 'directed to a certain side of politics but none the less it was political, and being political, it could not be separated from other parties whose sympathies ran concurrently with its own on most of the great political questions of the day.'[41]

Conspicuous among Liberals who shared Gladstone's view and who worked untiringly for an understanding with Labour was George Cadbury, the millionaire Birmingham chocolate manufacturer. It was a favourite remark of Cadbury that there should be a hundred Labour men in Parliament, but he was, above all, a good Bannermanite, and the type of Labour man he liked best was not the stubborn Independent but a Richard Bell or a Will Crooks through whom he saw hopes of uniting Labour and Liberalism in a single Party of Progress. His opinions were publicly voiced in the *Daily News* which he and others had purchased as a vehicle for the Liberal pro-Boers.[42] Prior to 1903 there had been references in the press to the friendly feeling that existed toward Labour at the Chief Whip's office. No really practical suggestion for a general electoral agreement had been made, however, until Harold Spender, engaged in writing a series of articles on Liberal election prospects for the *Daily News*, pointed out in an article in January 31, 1903, that if there were to be negotiations they would have to be complex with each constituency dealt with separately and with a start being made by Labour tabling the seats it wanted while the Liberal party tabled the seats it would hand over.

On receiving an intimation from MacDonald's office of a desire to explore such a possibility, an intimation relayed through Cadbury, Gladstone instructed Jesse Herbert, his chief lieutenant, to make further inquiries of MacDonald.[43] Then on the 8th of February he wrote to Campbell-Bannerman, 'I have some reason to think we may get them [the Labour people] to a working agreement about constituencies. But before we do I should like the principle to be discussed. Bryce used to be very stiff against any recognition of Labour candidates as distinct from Liberals. But it is a distinction we shall have to recognize and the sooner we can educate the constituencies to it the better—in my opinion.'[44]

The meeting between MacDonald and Herbert took place a few days later on 'neutral ground' so as to avoid the comments of those in the Labour party whom MacDonald said were 'ill-disposed' toward the Liberals. During the interview Herbert took the position of interested listener and made no commitments. MacDonald pointed out that working men of all shades of opinion, except for the miners and the S.D.F., were uniting behind the L.R.C. and that, with nearly a million members, it was assured of an annual income to its political fund of £5,000 to pay the salaries of its M.P.s and, in addition, provided the election were delayed another eighteen months, £120,000 for fighting elections. The majority of the members of the L.R.C. were men who had hitherto worked with the Liberal party and desired to continue to do so, MacDonald said, while the L.R.C. candidates were 'in almost every case earnest Liberals who [would] support a Liberal Government.' No alliance was asked for but only 'an exhibition of friendliness which [would] permit of good fellowship.' The Liberal party did not oppose Liberal League candidates, MacDonald noted; might it not act in the same manner toward the Labour party. If it refused, if it took an unfriendly attitude toward L.R.C. candidates, 'the L.R.C. [would] oppose the Liberal party not only in the places where the L.R.C. candidates [were] nominated, but also throughout the United Kingdom.'[45]

Thus did MacDonald combine friendly assurances with threat. His assurance that practically all L.R.C. candidates were 'earnest

Liberals' was for private hearing only. No I.L.P. official would have dared to state it publicly. It was shrewdly designed, however, to win favour as was also the reference to the Liberal League. At Gladstone's headquarters where Campbell-Bannerman's influence was paramount the League was still regarded with feelings ranging from distrust to hearty dislike with many Bannermanites preferring almost any Labour man to an out-and-out Roseberyite. Later on, after the tariff issue had drawn the Liberals more closely together, there would be less concern with the League, Gladstone noting in May 1903 that its power for mischief had become 'very small.'[46] The League could, perchance, even serve a purpose by providing a respectable bridge for Tories and Unionists who had supported the war but might now come over to the Liberals in opposition to the Education Act and Protection. But even allowing for all this, the League would still remain suspect, and what Herbert argued after his first interview with MacDonald served as argument for some of the more ardent followers of Bannerman for some time thereafter: if Liberal Headquarters could recognize the claims of the League which had money, why should it not recognize the claims of Labour which had numbers? Finally, MacDonald's stress on Labour's fighting fund must have greatly impressed the Chief Whip, for these were 'starvation years' of small and grudging contributions to the Liberal campaign coffers: twice in this period Gladstone had to borrow £5,000 for the party from his brother Henry.[47] One attractive result of any agreement, Herbert pointed out, was that if Labour were left alone in the number of seats it asked for, the Liberal treasury would be saved as much as £15,000.[48]

On the 12th of February, a few days after their meeting, MacDonald mailed to Herbert lists of twenty-five constituencies where the L.R.C. had placed candidates, seventeen where it would probably place candidates and ten under consideration. His accompanying letter was anything but obsequious in tone. London had not been fully considered, MacDonald wrote, and in Lancashire, due to the recent affiliation of the Lancashire textile workers, there would probably be additional nominations. The Liberal nomination of a miners' representative in East

187

Leeds (Yorkshire) without consulting any Labour organization beforehand was unsatisfactory. 'We do not accept that way of doing business,' he insisted, 'and before long we shall have something to say about it.'[49]

Until this time MacDonald alone had been in contact with the Chief Whip's office, but on the 25th of February Herbert was able to meet informally with Keir Hardie who assured him that he had been pretty fully informed by MacDonald of what had taken place and that nothing had occurred meanwhile at the Newcastle Conference that in any way changed the picture as MacDonald had presented it. As if to strengthen this assurance Hardie on the very next day, while speaking at York on behalf of an L.R.C. candidate, stated that Labour and Liberalism were as one in their desire to turn out the Government and that if the Liberals ran one candidate at York and left Labour the second seat this alone would be 'productive of good fellowship and would work to their mutual advantage.' Speaking in euphemisms, unable to be candid about the bargaining in progress, Hardie informed his York listeners that there could be no alliance or binding agreement or compromise.[50]

On the Liberal side Jesse Herbert revealed a readiness to ignore the larger issues involved in MacDonald's proposals and to measure them almost exclusively in terms of Liberal chances in the coming election. Though he thought the recognition of a separate group which would probably decline the Liberal whip was not to be taken lightly and asked if the Liberals should not prefer defeat rather than foster this growing power, he did not linger with these problems. It would mean the recognition of a vital change in the organization of parties, true, but would it, he noted, be other than 'the official recognition of a fact. . . .' 'I am concerned with the electoral prospects of the party and anxiously ask myself, "What would be the gain and the loss to the party at the General Election if a working agreement were arrived at with the L.R.C.?" There are some members of the party in and out of Parliament who would be estranged thereby, but they are few. Those employers of Labour who remained with the party when the Whig seceders went out on the Home Rule excuse, have (with few

188

exceptions) sincere sympathy with many objects of the L.R.C. The severe Individualists of the party who are wholly out of sympathy with the principles of the L.R.C. are very few. The gain to the party through a working agreement would be great, and can be measured best by a comparison of "no arrangement" with those of "an arrangement".'

'An arrangement' would mean that the future for both the Liberals and the L.R.C. would be 'very bright and encouraging.' It would mean votes for the Liberals from erstwhile Liberal working men and even from Tory working men. The main benefit, however, would be the effect on the public mind of seeing the opponents of the Government united. It would give hope and enthusiasm to the Liberals making them vote and work. It would make the Tories fearful and depressed and rob them of energy and force. If, on the other hand, there were 'no arrangement' and the members of the L.R.C. voted against Liberal candidates, 'the Liberal party would suffer defeat not only in those constituencies where L.R.C. candidates fought, but also in almost every borough, and in many of the Divisions, of Lancashire and Yorkshire. This would be the inevitable result of unfriendly action towards the L.R.C. *They* would be defeated, but so also should [the Liberals] be defeated.'[51]

In substance, Herbert was arguing in private as had Lord Tweedmouth and other Liberals in public, that without an agreement with Labour there could be no victory. Such strength and prominence had the L.R.C. gained in the eyes of key men in the Liberal machine, even at this early date, that they not only welcomed its friendly gestures; they believed in and feared its power to destroy them at the polls. This runs counter to the generally accepted view that practically no one fully appreciated the L.R.C.'s importance at this time, that even as late as 1906 its performance filled almost all political observers with astonishment. Quite the contrary was the case, however, among those Liberals who worked closely with Gladstone.

For a month after the first conversations, according to Mac-Donald, no one on the Committee except Hardie and himself knew what had taken place. Then on the 12th of March Mac-Donald and Herbert met once more in private. Asked by

Herbert who on the Committee should first talk with Gladstone, MacDonald suggested that he alone meet him since there were 'some very suspicious members who would have to be managed.' As to a place of meeting MacDonald was wary of going to the offices of the Liberal Central or of having Gladstone come to his office, 'for if it got breathed about,' he told Herbert, 'it would be all over the country in twenty-four hours,' nor would he go to Gladstone's home lest it appear that he had forced himself on the Chief Whip. Finally Herbert promised to arrange for a meeting at some hotel or other neutral place. 'We met, talked and parted on the most amicable terms,' reported Herbert to Gladstone. 'I told him nothing—save that the future arrangements (he used the word "arrangement") must be with you.'[52]

Gladstone proceeded immediately to draw up a secret memorandum on the nature of the proposed arrangement as he understood it. There was to be 'no compact, alliance, agreement or bargain,' but since there were no material differences between Labour and Liberalism on the main issues of Liberal policy, he was ready 'to ascertain from qualified and responsible Labour leaders how far Labour candidates [could] be given an open field against a common enemy.' Under no circumstances would he depart from the principle of working with and for recognized local Liberal associations. But he could use his influence with the associations 'to abstain from nominating a Liberal candidate and to unite in support of any recognized and competent Labour candidate who [supported] the general objects of the Liberal party.' He understood that the L.R.C. proposed to run about thirty candidates. This did not include Scotland nor the fifteen to eighteen candidates of the Miners' Federation nor were candidates of the S.D.F. to be considered. Going through MacDonald's lists, he concluded that it was possible to give the L.R.C. an open field in thirty seats. If in any constituency agreed upon the local association broke away, he would have to support the Liberal, but he would use 'every legitimate effort to secure [an] open field and to maintain it. . . .'[53]

Hardie, meanwhile, despite his approval of MacDonald's secret efforts, was continuing to brand current day Liberalism as a counsel of despair. What especially aroused his ire was a speech by John Morley in April in which the latter made a plea for more Labour representatives but asked that they come in 'at the strait gate,' that is to say, through the Liberal associations.[54] Wrote Hardie in an open letter to Morley: ' "Truly straight is the gate and narrow the way" by which Liberalism permits Labour to enter Parliament and few there be that enter therein. . . . You threaten Labour with the loss of the Liberal vote. . . . You, forget, however, that it is Liberalism which is dependent on Labour for support.'[55] In the Liberal press Hardie was marked down as an extremist and irreconcilable for such remarks, while Gladstone's headquarters, as the negotiations proceeded, at times doubted Hardie's good faith in carrying out the Labour side of the bargain.[56]

By May 1903, a drive to educate the local Liberal associations to accept the policy of Liberal headquarters was in full swing. At the annual meeting of the National Liberal Federation its executive professed to see an identity between Liberalism and Labour 'in all points of practical policy' and argued that it was the duty of Liberals everywhere to make 'reasonable accommodation.' A plea by Gladstone to the delegates of the associations for an understanding with Labour was seconded by Campbell-Bannerman who could see no reason for jealousy or friction between 'honest' Labour candidates and 'honest' Liberal candidates, 'both elements in the progressive force of the country.' All obstacles to Liberal-Labour unity would have appeared merely illusory had not Augustine Birrell, President of the Federation, warned that the constituencies could not be 'bullied' into concessions by Liberal headquarters.[57]

The launching of Chamberlain's tariff campaign in May, while nearly disrupting the Government party, provided another 'point of practical policy' on which L.R.C. and Liberal forces were in essential agreement. It was MacDonald's opinion that this would make it easier for Liberals to stand aside for Labour,[58] but since the defence of free trade helped to lessen the feuds among the Liberals and to raise their confidence considerably, it might well have had just the opposite effect. The electoral pact was not sealed but still in its initial stages, and many

Liberals were inquiring why concessions should be made to a party dominated by what appeared to them an unfriendly I.L.P. Efforts were of course being made to assuage these Liberal doubts, especially by L.R.C. trade unionists, one of whom pointed out in an article in the Liberal *Westminster Gazette* that the L.R.C. candidates were trained officials, practical men, 'averse to the shadow hunting of intransigeant parties like the I.L.P.,' men who 'would never be its catspaw.'[59]

If, with their own prospects so much improved, some Liberals now assumed that the L.R.C. could be safely ignored, a by-election in Barnard Castle (Durham) in July 1903 served to dispel this assumption. Not only did the L.R.C. win its first victory over both Liberal and Tory at Barnard Castle; its candidate, Arthur Henderson of the Ironfounders, won wide Liberal endorsement, and the Chief Whip's office tried in vain to secure the Liberal candidate's withdrawal.[60] The fact that the L.R.C. might prove less tractable in the wake of this victory and that the dissolution of Parliament appeared imminent no doubt made Gladstone anxious for an early final settlement with MacDonald. Negotiations between the two party headquarters and in the constituencies progressed rapidly, and by the 7th of August Gladstone was able to forward to Campbell-Bannerman a list indicating that, now, in at least thirty-five seats where L.R.C. candidates were *fixed* or *likely to be chosen* the Liberals could, with 'no difficulty anticipated,' allow these candidates a free field.[61] 'You will see,' he wrote in an accompanying letter, 'that in the great majority of cases there is no friction or danger. In fact, up to the present there are not more than six constituencies where the difficulty is at all serious or active. People are talking great nonsense about the need for an understanding and arrangement, but, if they would only hold their tongues and allow us to work the thing quietly, we should be all right.'[62]

In the months following, in the press and on the platform, pleas continued to be made for a Liberal-Labour understanding that already existed, while MacDonald guardedly stated for public consumption that the voters who were being influenced by the L.R.C. 'could not help being influenced by friendly acts done to the Committee.'[63] By the end of the year Gladstone's office had achieved an excellent rapport with Labour in almost every constituency where it had investigated or intervened, and Bryce was writing to Campbell-Bannerman that the Liberals could turn to other issues 'now that the claims of Labour had been settled.'[64]

## NOTES

1. For a partial list of the Liberal supporters see the *Labour Leader*, Sept. 21, 1901.

2. H.G. to C.B., Sept. 24, 1901. C.B., vol. xi.

3. *Manchester Guardian*, Sept. 21, 1901.

4. Hardie in the *Glasgow Herald*, Sept. 11, 1901.

5. In a letter to the *Manchester Guardian*, Sept. 23, 1901.

6. *Daily News*, Mar. 7, 1902. The *Clarion* of Mar. 21, 1902, lists the *Leeds Mercury*, the *Wakefield Herald* and the *Yorkshire Mercury* as Liberal papers urging abstention.

7. Regarding the 26 Liberal M.P.s see the *Daily News*, Mar. 24, 1902; *Manchester Guardian*, Mar. 26, 1902.

8. N.A.C. Minutes, May 26 and 27, 1902.

9. The Fabian Executive with only two dissentients decided to send no one to the N.D.L. founding conference. Fabian Executive Minutes, Oct. 12, 1900.

10. See the S.D.F. weekly *Justice* for Feb. 9, 1901, and Aug. 2, 1902. For Hardie's attitude toward the N.D.L. see his letter to Victor Fisher in *Reynolds's Newspaper*, July 21, 1901.

11. The vote was 118 to 48. *L.R.C. Annual*, 1903, 25-26.

12. In *Reynolds's, passim*, 1902 to 1906.

13. *ibid.*, Nov. 12, 1905.

14. Hobson's articles in the *Echo*, London, Oct. 15 and Nov. 7, 1901, and in the *L.L.*, Oct. 19, 1901.

15. Barnes and MacDonald in the *Echo*, Oct. 17, 1901; Glasier in the *L.L.*, Oct. 26, 1901; Hardie in the *Echo*, Oct. 16, 1901.

16. In the *Labour Leader*, Oct. 19, 1901.

17. *Daily News*, June 12 and *L.L.*, June 14, 1902.

18. See especially J. R. MacDonald, *Socialism and Society*, London, 1905.

19. Beatrice Webb's Diaries: Entry of Mar. 1, 1904.

20. In the *Clarion*, May 22, 1903.

21. Hardie's letter to Lord Tweedmouth, *L.L.*, Feb. 21, 1903. Only in retrospect would Hardie admit the full importance of the 'strong leaven' of Socialist Radicalism in the Liberal party with which Campbell-Bannerman threw his influence. Had C.B. been twenty years younger, Hardie was to write, he might have come over to the Socialists. *The Socialist Review*, vol. i, August, 1908, 238.

22. *L.L.*, April 24, 1903.

23. H. Russell Smart in the *L.L.*, May 23, 1903.

24. Fenner Brockway, *Socialism over Sixty Years: The Life of Jowett of Bradford*, London, 1946, 37-38.

25. In a letter to the *Daily News*, July 6, 1903. Equally unsympathetic with Labour's claims was the President of the Northern Liberal Federation, Sir Charles Furness. See his speech to the Council of the Federation as reported in the *Newcastle Chronicle*, April 20, 1903.

26. In a letter to the press quoted in *Justice*, Oct. 2, 1901.

27. Speech to the annual meeting of the General Council of the Scottish Liberal Associations, Edinburgh, Feb. 13, 1903. *Westminster Gazette*, Feb. 14, 1903.

28. As 'Spectator' in the *Echo*, Aug. 22 and 29, Sept. 5 and 26, 1901.

29. *ibid.*, Mar. 6, 1902.

30. Writing as Secretary of the L.R.C. in the *L.L.*, Oct. 26, 1901.

31. Signed letter to the *Daily News*, Mar. 25, 1902.

32. In the Liberal Cabinet formed in December, 1905, he was Home Secretary. Then in 1910 he became a viscount and was appointed the first Governor-General and High Commissioner of the Union of South Africa. He retired in 1914 and died in 1933. (D.N.B.) There is a memoir by Sir Charles Mallet, *Herbert Gladstone*, London, 1932, which, unfortunately, contains only a brief treatment of his work as Chief Whip and only a few references to matters directly relating to this study.

33. *Labour Leader*, Jan. 27, 1900.

34. Labouchere to Dilke, Oct. 30, 1900. Dilke papers, vol. xxix, 208.

35. She continued: 'The deciding fact is, as he frankly asserted, "people with advanced opinions do not pay" and he looked at me as much as to say, "How much have you ever subscribed to party funds I should like to know?" His look was so unmistakable that I found myself explaining that most of us were poor—"Moreover," I added, "as far as I am concerned I have never been a Liberal, and my husband is not in politics but only in local administration." ' Beatrice Webb's Diaries: Entry of June 8, 1904.

36. Lucy Masterman, *C. F. G. Masterman*, London, 1939, 104.

37. This material is based in part on a memo note of Herbert Gladstone listing his principal duties (H.G. papers, vol. cxiv, 8) and on some typewritten remarks regarding his work with Hudson (H.G., vol xxiv, 155). See too J. A. Spender, *Sir Robert Hudson, A Memoir*, London, 1930, 63.

38. Philip Stanhope to H.G., Aug. 7, 1902. H.G., vol. lxvii, 8.

39. Letter to a correspondent printed in the *Newcastle Daily Chronicle*, May 2, 1903.

40. Speech at Leeds, Oct. 8, as reported in *The Times*, Oct. 9, 1901.

41. Address to Liberal agents at Scarborough, May 16, 1903. *National Liberal Federation Annual*, 1903, 99.

42. On Cadbury see A. G. Gardiner, *Life of George Cadbury*, London, 1922.

43. Jesse Herbert Memorandum, Mar. 6, 1903. H.G., vol. xxviii, 132.

44. H.G. to C.B., Feb. 8, 1903. C.B., vol. xi, 247-248. Regarding James (afterward Lord) Bryce, he had in the past protested vigorously against a party based on class and had argued that rather than see the two party system superseded he would prefer to see working men join the Tories. See Bryce to H.G., Mar. 24, and 28, 1892. H.G., vol. xv, 28-31. See also H. A. L. Fisher, *James Bryce*, 2 vols., New York, 1927, vol. i, 299; and Conrad Noel, *The Labour Party*, London, 1906, 39.

45. Herbert Memorandum, 132-141.

46. H.G. to C.B., May 18, 1903. C.B., vol. xi.

47. Sir Charles Mallet, *Herbert Gladstone; A Memoir*, London, 1932, 194.

48. Herbert Memorandum.

49. MacDonald to Herbert, Feb. 12, 1903. H.G., vol. xxviii, 142-143. For the lists see H.G., vol. cxvi, 31-33.

50. Herbert Memorandum. For Hardie's speech see also the *Yorkshire Observer*, Feb. 28, 1903. In the I.L.P. there were protests against the speech. Hardie was definitely proposing a compromise and a binding agreement, argued one member of the party, and if it came to pass the Labour party would become 'merely a wing, and that a broken wing, of the Liberal party.' E. R. Hartley in a letter to the *L.L.*, Mar. 14, 1903.

51. Herbert Memorandum.

52. Herbert to Gladstone, Mar. 12. 1903. H.G., vol. xxviii, 144-147.

53. Gladstone Memorandum, Mar. 13, 1903. H.G., vol. cxvi.

54. Speech at Newcastle, April 18, as reported in the *Daily News*, April 20, 1903.

55. In the *Labour Leader*, April 25, 1903.

56. Herbert to Gladstone, Sept. 1, 1903. H.G., vol. xxviii, 155. See H. W. Massingham on Hardie in the Liberal *Speaker*, April 18, 1903.

57. *National Liberal Federation Annual*, 1903, 39, 52, 101.

58. As 'Spectator.' *Echo*, June 3, 1901.

59. *Westminster Gazette*, July 28, 1903.

60. Henderson's most prominent Liberal supporter was Robert Spence Watson, a former President of the National Liberal Federation. Among Liberal newspapers backing him were the *Daily News* and the *Northern Echo*. On the Chief Whip's intervention see particularly Gladstone's letter to Hubert Beaumont, the Liberal candidate, July 1, 1903. H.G., vol. lxviii, 77.

61. The list is in the Campbell-Bannerman papers, vol. xii, 2.

62. H.G. to C.B., Aug. 7, 1903. C.B., vol. xii, 1.

63. In an article entitled 'Liberalism and Labour' in the *Speaker*, Aug. 8, 1903.

64. Bryce to C.B., Dec. 28, 1903. C.B., vol. vi, 254.

# CHAPTER XI

# Barnard Castle

THE Barnard Castle Division of South Durham covered an area of nearly 600 square miles and might well be said to have tested the physical endurance of a parliamentary candidate as much as his political capacity. Lying mostly in the slopes and foothills of the Pennine Range it embraced moorland and dales, farmlands and coal fields. The agricultural population was large and there were many cattle raisers. but the majority of workers were coal miners and quarrymen. Methodism was strong in the hamlets and mining villages, Liberalism, the only political creed the miners knew. What hold the Conservative party enjoyed had been considerably weakened by the passage of the Education Act and Chamberlain's protectionist proposals. In the political life of South Durham and also of North Yorkshire a family of Quaker industrialists, the Peases, had long exercised a predominant influence. But since Arthur Pease had separated from his brother Joseph on Home Rule, that influence had waned. Arthur and his son after him sat as Unionists for Darlington.[1] Sir Joseph, the Liberal, sat for Barnard Castle. There for some seven years, Arthur Henderson served him as election agent.

Born to poverty in Glasgow in 1863, Henderson had migrated to Newcastle and there at twelve served as an apprentice in an iron foundry. In the Ironfounders' Society he had risen to a position of leadership serving as a district delegate to branches in Northumberland, Durham and Lancashire and gaining a considerable reputation for his skill as a conciliator in industrial disputes. He was also known, like many others in the Labour movement, for his activity as a lay preacher, having been inspired by the noted evangelist, Gypsy Smith, and converted to Wesleyanism. An ardent Liberal, he had turned increasingly from trade union work toward politics, though still maintaining an official connection with his union, and had been elected to the Newcastle Town Council and appointed a J.P. In the General Election of 1895 he was sufficiently well known politically to be considered as a possible running mate to John Morley for the two Newcastle seats, but the Liberals chose a wealthier aspirant instead. Removing to South Durham in 1896 he had entered the service of Sir Joseph Pease as secretary-agent at a salary of £250 a year. The Barnard Castle constituency was operated from Darlington, and there Henderson took up residence, and ran successfully for the Darlington Town Council and for the Durham County Council. In 1903, aged thirty-nine, he became Mayor of Darlington. Methodical and painstaking in his work as election agent, he came to know every corner of the Barnard Castle Division and to be thoroughly familiar with local Liberal party machinery.[2]

Late in 1902 the Ironfounders, who had affiliated with the L.R.C. at the outset, decided to run a candidate for Parliament and for this purpose agreed to levy every member threepence a quarter. As in other large unions—the Ironfounders had a membership of over 18,000—the branches nominated candidates who campaigned within the union for election. Henderson in this particular instance received the majority of the branch nominations and in the election polled first in a field of six. There was some criticism of his candidature on the ground that he was no longer actively associated with the Ironfounders, and a few branches even demanded another ballot, but Henderson in November 1902 became the union's official nominee and turned to seeking a suitable constituency.[3] While he was so engaged, in February 1903, Sir Joseph Pease, now old and infirm, intimated that he would not stand for re-election for Barnard Castle.

Henderson might well have been invited by the Liberals to run as Sir Joseph's successor had not the L.R.C. constitution as revised at Newcastle explicitly forbade such a step. Even before Newcastle, Sir Joseph's son Jack, M.P. for Saffron Walden, had regretted that Henderson, a good Liberal, might be lost to the party and compelled to adopt the same attitude as Shackleton at Clitheroe.[4] It was not the Liberals, therefore, but a Labour League, recently formed in the division, that on April 1, 1903, adopted Henderson. Some four thousand trade unionists— miners, quarrymen, cokemen, mechanics and others—were represented at the meeting. Only the Durham Miners' Executive remained aloof, John Wilson, M.P., and his colleagues being averse to L.R.C. policy. The President of the Durham Miners' Association, Alderman House, however, eventually came out wholeheartedly for Henderson.[5]

The S.D.F. could not stomach the new candidate, *Justice* describing him as 'a camp follower of the Liberal party' with 'no ideas at all apart from those of capitalist Liberalism.'[6] Nor could the I.L.P. leaders view his selection without some misgivings. He had always opposed the socialist and extreme Labour section, and when Curran had run for Barnsley against a Liberal in 1897, Henderson had branded the I.L.P. 'a national curse.'[7] As late as January 1903, Glasier regarded him as unreliable, 'a sleek, backboneless customer,'[8] and his attitude while serving as Hodge's agent at Preston had not been reassuring. By the time of the by-election in July, however, most I.L.P. members, though allowing that Henderson was not a candidate after their own heart, had to admit that for such a recent convert from Liberalism, he was 'remarkably straight on independence.'[9]

When Henderson was chosen, there was as yet no Liberal candidate, and there was hope that he might receive the same treatment as Shackleton. The majority of the local official Liberals were in no mood to practise self-abnegation, however, and only a short time had passed before their Selection Committee decided by a vote of eight to six, indicating a strong minority opinion, that one Hubert Beaumont be invited to address the Liberal Association with a view to adoption. At London Liberal headquarters, news of a probable Liberal candidate was greeted with alarm, one of Gladstone's colleagues, who had spoken with Henderson, arguing that the introduction of Beaumont would be an act of sheer folly. 'It would have the worst possible effect on the working-class electorate and lay the Liberal Association and Party open to the charge of active hostility to Labour interests in the case of a Labour candidate already in the field,' he wrote, ' . . . the only thing that I can see to do is to bring the strongest pressure on Beaumont himself to induce him to retire from a rather undignified position and to avert a worse than useless struggle which would have far-reaching and unfortunate results. Don't let us play Keir Hardie's game for him.'[10]

In the light of his record it was difficult for anyone to classify Henderson as an enemy of the Liberal party, and it soon became obvious that even within the Liberal Association itself he had many champions. When the Association met on April 25 to hear Beaumont's address, thirty-four members were in favour of supporting Henderson. Yet sixty-five opposed, and a resolution to adopt Beaumont was then put and carried by fifty-eight to thirty-six.[11] A three-cornered fight now seemed inevitable. The Tory, making his third try for the seat, was Colonel William Vane, the brother of Lord Barnard of Castle Barnard, one of the greatest landowners in the division. Then on June 23rd the venerable Sir Joseph passed away, thus necessitating an immediate contest.

Even at this late date the younger Pease was hopeful that the Liberal-Labour split might be repaired. He pointed out to Beaumont the danger of going forward at the very moment the Liberals were endeavouring to reach an agreement with Labour throughout the country and inquired of Gladstone if the difficulty might be solved by men like Sir David Dale for the Liberals and John Burns for Labour acting as arbiters?[12] But all such efforts proved hopeless, and finally Pease's son, despite his affection for Henderson, felt obliged to endorse the official Liberal nominee. As pressure continued to be exerted upon Beaumont to withdraw, he became increasingly uneasy. He knew that most Liberal M.P.s would refuse to speak on his platform out of fear of the Labour people in their own constituencies and that he risked the permanent displeasure of Liberal headquarters. He insisted, however, that he was bound to fulfil his promise to the local association and that the onus for the fight lay with the L.R.C.[13] which he described as 'an entirely outside Socialist body.'[14] Yet as the Liberal chances of holding the seat

grew dimmer, Beaumont's father, who had been in Parliament
for thirty years, confided to Charles Trevelyan that his son
would have been only too glad to escape running were he not
kept to his pledge by the association. Trevelyan, with this
intelligence, asked Gladstone to use his influence to open the eyes
of the association to the true situation.[15] But as a matter of
long practice, open intervention on the part of the Chief Whip
was to be avoided, and Gladstone pointed out that it was for the
local Liberals themselves to decide 'whether this disastrous
division between those who ought to act together against the
common enemy [was] to continue.'[16] 'If Beaumont withdraws
in the interest of the party,' he wrote to an M.P. who was in
touch with Beaumont, 'and in such a way as to secure the defeat
of the Tory candidate and the election of Henderson who is
sound on Free Trade, Educn., and Temperance and the leading
questions which interest progressive politicians, he will deserve
the utmost support which it is in the power of the party
organization to give him to secure his entry into Parliament . . .
the Labour party would certainly be under distinct obligation to
a man who retired in favour of a Labour candidate.'[17] Still
Beaumont delayed, torn between pressure to surrender and
pleas to fight on, and as the contest became more heated, withdrawal became all but impossible.

The divisions in Liberal ranks were reflected in the party's
press. Cadbury's *Daily News* backed Henderson, and the
*Northern Echo* of Arnold Rowntree, according to the *Ironfounders'
Monthly*, rendered the Labour candidate 'magnificent service
. . . right through the campaign.'[18] The *Manchester Guardian*
expressed no opinion regarding the respective rights of the two
candidates though on the morrow of the election it described
Henderson as 'the more thorough though the less official Liberal
of the two.'[19] Prominent in supporting Beaumont were the
*Daily Chronicle*, the *Newcastle Leader* and, among the Harmsworth papers, the *Leeds and Yorkshire Mercury*.

Having refused himself to run for Barnard Castle, Samuel
Storey, Chairman of the Executive of the Northern Liberal
Federation and former M.P. for Sunderland, was the most
prominent northern Liberal in the planning of Beaumont's

campaign. Apparently as an election manoeuvre only, Storey offered Henderson, on Beaumont's behalf, a clear run against the Tory if only Henderson would pledge himself to support the Liberal party apart from purely Labour questions. Henderson replied that he could not pledge himself to the Liberal party since the Ironfounders who financed his campaign were made up of all shades of political opinion but that if the Liberal party attempted to give effect to the programme he outlined it would receive his unqualified support.[20] Henderson's programme which stressed trade union legislation, a universal system of old age pensions, thorough reform of the Poor Law administration and amendment or repeal of the Education Act, differed in no important respect from Beaumont's. Their main difference was that Henderson was an out-and-out opponent of Chamberlain's tariff proposals while Beaumont, though insisting he was a free trader, welcomed Chamberlain's demand for an inquiry into fiscal policy.[21] To Henderson, on the other hand, 'every vote given for an inquiry was a vote given for a tax on food.'[22] The Beaumont camp made still another offer of withdrawal—if Henderson would agree to support John Wilson and other 'Lib-Lab' candidates of the Durham miners. 'I say emphatically and deliberately,' Henderson replied, 'that if the Durham Miners by their vote return me as a Labour candidate I unhesitatingly promise to go and support the Durham miners' Labour candidates in return.'[23] The President of the Durham Miners' Association, Alderman House, publicly accused Storey of having earlier made an agreement with him that if Henderson pledged support of the Durham miners' candidates no Liberal would be put forward.[24]

When Beaumont and Storey dismissed both of Henderson's replies as unsatisfactory and evasive, an honoured veteran of their party called them to account. Robert Spence Watson, ex-President of the National Liberal Federation, could find nothing evasive in Henderson's replies; they were, he said, a full and satisfactory acceptance of the offers made, and he warned that the course which the Beaumont group was pursuing was likely to prove a serious blow to the Liberal party in the coming General Election.[25] Later Henderson, to great advantage no doubt, distributed Watson's chastisement as part of his election literature.[26]

As sections of the Liberal press continued to vie with the party managers in urging Barnard Castle Liberals to sink their differences and unite behind Henderson, the opponents of such compromise were aroused to stronger protest. The Liberal agent at Clitheroe urged Beaumont never to step aside as had Philip Stanhope at Clitheroe the year previous. 'What has been the result in our Division in the past twelve months, since our constituency was given away?' he wrote to the chairman of Beaumont's Election Committee. 'In the first place, our organization is falling to pieces like a rope of sand, our subscriptions have fallen down twenty-five per cent, we cannot get a meeting together except, perhaps, with the view of winding up the business of the Association, and most of our active supporters and workers are openly declaring that they will vote Tory if there is a Tory candidate in the field. Now, after all this sacrifice, which was brought about mainly by the Heads of the Party in London, what effect has it had upon the Labour party. It has had one effect only, and that is that they have been more aggressive. . . . If the Liberal party can only be made strong by giving away its strongest positions, all I can say is that its day of usefulness is gone, and the party which was described by Mr. Gladstone as the great instrument of progress, is no more.'[27]

When Beaumont sent this letter to the Chief Whip, Gladstone was already in receipt of a similar warning from Alfred Illingworth, who had already accused Liberal headquarters of strangling West Bradford in 1900 in the interests of the I.L.P. candidate, Jowett. 'I see what is being done from Parliament Street in Beaumont's case,' he wrote. '. . . Excuse my saying that for you to give advice it is necessary that you should be posted up and know local conditions or fatal consequences may follow mistakes.' He then informed Gladstone that the party in West Bradford had decided to reassert itself and would fight Jowett in the General Election, that if it did not fight this time, it would, in his opinion, be extinguished.[28]

There were still other criticisms of Parliament Street but

probably none as extreme as that of Storey. In a letter to the pro-Henderson *Daily News*, he insisted that some of the Liberal leaders and Whips were 'nursing into life a serpent which [would] sting their party to death. . . . I venture to warn you and the Party Whips and those M.P.s who would apparently cast Barnard Castle to the wolves in the hope, perhaps, of keeping them from their own doors, that the effect of surrendering to this new party will be the destruction of organized Liberalism in the North.'[29] Echoing this sentiment and noting that Beaumont 'had been deserted by the Liberal members all over the country and apparently also by the Liberal Executive,' the *Leeds and Yorkshire Mercury* felt obliged to censure Gladstone. Let the 'Socialist wreckers' win in Barnard Castle, it said, and 'there is not a Liberal constituency in the country safe from their attack.'[30]

The readiness of many Liberal newspapers to characterize the Henderson candidature as the work of 'Socialist wreckers' and to place upon Hardie the obloquy of the fight was, in a sense, rather ironic. Rather than master-minding the contest, the I.L.P. socialists found themselves ignored by Henderson just as they had been ignored by other recent L.R.C. candidates. What the I.L.P. leaders found especially irritating was the tendency of their own men in the Barnard Castle Division to urge that no prominent members of the party appear lest it 'spoil the game.'[31] Hardie, having anticipated this boycott, thought it legitimate to try to force the situation,[32] and, finally, after MacDonald and others had talked with Henderson, he did consent to have Snowden and other I.L.P. speakers if they could be obtained.[33] Nevertheless, he still depended chiefly on trade unionists like Shackleton, Crooks, and Hodge for his platform support.

At Clitheroe, at Woolwich, at Preston, and now at Barnard Castle, the I.L.P. leaders had been kept in the background. Glasier expressed to Hardie his regret at these signs of exclusion. 'I quite share your feeling of disappointment at the tendency to boycott the I.L.P. shown at recent L.R.C. elections,' he wrote. 'It is not a wholesome sign and the apprehension on the part of some of our friends that our presence "will spoil the game" is a forewarning of feebleness and perhaps of faithlessness. It was not by such a spirit that our pioneer work has been accomplished. . . .' But Glasier's faith in the validity of the larger I.L.P. objective, which he as much as anyone had helped to define, remained unshaken. 'I feel sure . . . that this timid spirit will not prevail; the rank and file even of the Trade Unionists will not suffer it. There is also the better thought; that it is preferable that our members should have the simple trust and grace to rely upon the influence of their work rather than that they should show the opposite spirit of seeking to see themselves on the front of everything.'[34]

As the campaign advanced in intensity, Beaumont expended much of his ammunition against the Labour candidate almost to the point of ignoring the Tory, an especially bitter note being sounded when Henderson was accused in a Liberal flysheet of having kept from the Liberal Association important papers he had in his possession as Liberal election agent. Henderson denied the charge, threatening suit if it were repeated.[35] Meanwhile, the Tories flooded the division with literature of the Imperial Tariff League, and though Beaumont continued to favour Chamberlain's inquiry, a conspicuously displayed Liberal poster urged the voters to 'Vote for Beaumont and the Big Loaf.'[36]

In a division so large the Liberal and Tory candidates had a great advantage in using motor cars, still something of a novelty in this section of the country, and by day and night they drove to remote towns where, as often as not, the whole local population would appear to hear them. Henderson had to depend largely on railway service and on a pair-horse landau, though when election day came, as one correspondent suggested, perhaps Beaumont's motor cars unwittingly carried many of Henderson's supporters to the polls.[37] The result of the polling was for Henderson 3,370, for Vane 3,323, and for Beaumont 2,809, thus giving Henderson forty-seven votes to the good against the Tory and 561 as against Beaumont. Despite the small majority it was the most striking vindication of the policy of independence that the L.R.C. had yet experienced. Clitheroe could partly be explained on the grounds of Tory and Liberal self-denial; Woolwich as proof of the virtues of the unity of all progressives. Barnard Castle, in which Labour fought both parties, was unique.

In the division itself resentments ran high, the reaction to Labour's victory among Beaumont's following being expressed by the *Leeds Mercury* when it stated in an editorial that Henderson entered the House 'with such credit as attaches to a trusted officer who on the eve of an engagement goes over bag and baggage to the enemy.'[38] In London Robert Hudson observed to the Chief Whip that though Henderson would be as right as could be in the House he was afraid that the result would make for trouble with the Labour people generally and in the North in particular.[39] Henderson himself was inclined to agree, feeling that the attacks on him personally would anger trade unionists elsewhere and make for reprisals rather than for conciliation with the Liberals.[40] At L.R.C. headquarters MacDonald knew that the victory would have a salutary effect in discouraging Liberals from opposing Labour in earmarked constituencies, but, working assiduously to implement the general agreement with Gladstone, he hoped that Barnard Castle would not jeopardize his efforts by encouraging a great increase in the number of L.R.C. candidates. Some forty Labour fights were anticipated, and for the moment at any rate that was enough.[41]

A remarkable insight into the weaknesses of the L.R.C. position and of the true nature of Henderson's victory was shown by the *Newcastle Leader*, a newspaper that had endorsed Beaumont. It pointed out that if in a General Election Henderson faced only one opponent, as was likely, he would need at least 1,500 more votes than he had obtained in the by-election and that he would have to seek them either from the Tories or from the Liberals. In view of the official attitude of the L.R.C. as a foe of both parties he could expect the support of neither. Thus, whatever his theoretical attitude might be, he would have to seek by his practical conduct an open or secret alliance with the Liberal or Tory Party. As illustrating the L.R.C. position generally, it said, Henderson's case showed that co-operation, even when repudiated in appearance, had to be sought in reality unless the Labour party were to be merely a destructive force.[42]

What the victory meant to the I.L.P. socialists was somewhat in doubt. 'Henderson's victory is a most portentous one,' wrote Glasier to Hardie, 'though it is not easy for us to say how far its portent is a good one for us. Let us however accept its gift with sturdy faith that providence has placed it in our hands. It will enormously improve the position of all the L.R.C. candidates and out of the mass of these we have enough reliable Socialists to insure the Socialist policy of the new party in the House.'[43]

Just after the election, a handbook for L.R.C. election agents was published in which Henderson wrote the sections on registration while MacDonald wrote those on organization.[44] Clear and to the point it was widely used, but it made no pretence at replacing the standard manuals on these subjects. In 1904 Henderson was chosen treasurer of the L.R.C. In 1905 he succeeded Shackleton as chairman. The skill and experience he had gained as a Liberal agent, now placed at the disposal of the Committee, helped it to avoid legal pitfalls and to build a more effective party machine. Henderson was a strong advocate of local Labour associations affiliating with the central body, pointing out that it was impossible for a trades council to cover the whole of great county divisions like Barnard Castle and Clitheroe. In 1904 it was decided that local associations could affiliate where there was no trades council, but as a matter of fact very few did, and the Committee for some time to come depended on the trades councils, often in collaboration with I.L.P. branches, as its chief agents in the constituencies.[45]

## NOTES

1. John Penny, 'The Pease Dynasty,' *L.L.*, Dec. 4, 1903, and 'Barnard Castle' in the *Clarion*, Jan. 1, 1904.
2. Edwin A. Jenkins, *From Iron Foundry to War Cabinet*, London, 1933, 7-10; M. A. Hamilton, *Arthur Henderson*, London, 1938, 32.
3. *Annual Report of the Friendly Society of Ironfounders*, 1902; *Ironfounders' Monthly*, Nov. and Dec., 1902, Jan. and April, 1903.
4. J. A. Pease to H.G., Dec. 19, 1902, H.G., vol. lxvii, 140.

5. *Daily News*, July 20, 1903; J. M. Paulton to H.G., April 14, 1903. H.G., vol. lxviii, 6; *Newcastle Daily Chronicle*, July 7, 1903.
6. *Justice*, July 11, 1903.
7. Quoted from the *Barnsley Independent* of Oct. 2, 1897, by *Reynolds's*, July 19, 1903.
8. Glasier to Hardie, Jan. 26, 1903.
9. Quoted from the *I.L.P. News* by the *Leeds and Yorkshire Mercury*, July 27, 1903.
10. J. M. Paulton to H.G., April 14, 1903. H.G., vol. lxviii, 6.
11. *Newcastle Daily Chronicle*, April 22, 1903.
12. Sir J. W. Pease to H.G., June 29, 1903. H.G., vol. lxviii, 69.
13. Beaumont to H.G., June 28, 1903. H.G., vol. lxviii, 65.
14. *Leeds and Yorkshire Mercury*, July 8, 1903.
15. Charles Trevelyan to H.G., July 7, 1903. H.G., vol. lxviii, 95.
16. H.G. to Beaumont, July 1, 1903. H.G., vol. lxviii, 77.
17. J.G. to Richard Rigg, M.P., July 7, 1903. H.G., vol. lxviii, 91.
18. *Ironfounders' Monthly*, Aug. 1903.
19. *M.G.*, July 27, 1903.
20. *Daily News*, July 4, 1903; *Leeds and Yorkshire Mercury*, July 3, 1 903.
21. *Westminster Gazette*, July 18, 1903.
22. *Leeds and Yorkshire Mercury*, July 23, 1903.
23. *Newcastle Daily Chronicle*, July 8, 1903.
24. *Daily News*, July 10 and 21, 1903.
25. R. S. Watson to Beaumont, July 20, as printed in the *Daily News* of July 24, 1903.
26. *Speaker*, Aug. 1, 1903.
27. T. Catterall, to the Chairman of Beaumont's Election Committee, July 2, 1903. H.G., vol. lxviii, 89.
28. A. Illingworth to H.G., July 17, 1903. H.G., vol. lxviii, 105.
29. *Daily News*, July 6, 1903.
30. *Leeds and Yorkshire Mercury*, July 9, 1903.
31. John Gowland of the I.L.P. branch in Crooks (Durham) to Glasier, July 6, 1903.
32. Hardie to Glasier, July 9, 1903.
33. Glasier and MacDonald to Hardie, July 15, 1903.
34. Glasier to Hardie, July 13, 1903.
35. *Leeds and Yorkshire Mercury*, July 16, 1903.
36. *Shields Daily News*, July 24, 1903.
37. *Daily News*, July 25, 1903.
38. *Leeds and Yorkshire Mercury*, July 27, 1903.
39. R. Hudson to H.G., July 28, 1903. H.G., vol. xxxiii, 12.
40. Interview in the *Daily Chronicle*, July 27, 1903.
41. As 'Spectator' in the *Echo*, July 29, 1903.
42. *Newcastle Leader*, July 27, 1903.
43. Glasier to Hardie, July 26, 1903.
44. *Notes on Organization and the Laws of Registration and Elections*.
45. L.R.C. Minutes, Sept. 28, 1904; *L.R.C. Ann.*, 1905, 43.

# CHAPTER XII

# A Time of Test and Doubting

THE year 1903 was the climactic year in the history of the Committee. The movement had been consolidated, its membership disciplined through a stricter definition of Independence, the sinews of war insured through the inauguration of the Parliamentary Fund, and a fair showing in the coming General Election made all but certain as a result of the agreement with the Liberals. All this can be seen in retrospect. Yet for those at L.R.C. headquarters who waited impatiently for the downfall of a Government that refused to fall, the two years before the General Election were filled with tension and nerve-wracking uncertainty. Candidates complained of the hardship and cost of an intolerably prolonged campaign; the statements and actions of certain L.R.C. members made Independence seem little more than an elaborate bluff; and as new candidates pressed for position, the Liberal-Labour understanding threatened at times to disintegrate into a local scramble beyond the control of the party chiefs.

So long as Balfour was absorbed in an attempt to mend his own party's fences on the fiscal question, there was little likelihood of any major legislative endeavour lest it further divide the Unionists. When the Government did act, it displayed its usual propensity for broadening the target for its opponents. Such was the case with the Licensing Act of 1904, which fulfilled Balfour's pledge to the licensed victuallers. It provided that when a liquor license was taken away for reasons other than misconduct, the license owner should be compensated out of a fund levied on the trade. The Temperance Forces joined with the Liberals in denouncing the Act as a 'brewers' Bill' and as 'endowing the trade.' Labour argued that another monopoly had been strengthened, and the L.R.C. called for public control through the municipalization of the drink traffic.[1] Not only on Free Food League platforms, but on those of the United Kingdom Alliance, Labour and Liberal candidates could now attack the Government in concert.

Resentment to the Licensing Bill was as nothing, however, compared to the fury and indignation aroused when the Government approved the importation of Chinese Labour in the Transvaal. Had Chamberlain remained at the Colonial Office, it is hard to imagine that such a blunder would have been committed, nor would Balfour have condoned it had he been at all familiar with the mind of Labour. The first indentured Chinese arrived in South Africa in June 1904, and by the time of the General Election some 50,000 were at work in the Rand mines. The mine owners argued necessity due to a shortage of Kaffir labour, while the Archbishop of Canterbury spoke of a 'regrettable necessity,'[2] but the British trade unionist could only see the Rand magnate treating labour as a mere commodity, 'blackleg' labour destructive of wage standards and of trade unionism itself. That this was free trade at work with a vengeance was conveniently ignored, and a cartoon of a Chinaman borne on the bent back of a South African white expressed in crude form the fear and resentment of the British worker at this economic threat and this insult to his dignity. Reports soon reached England that the compounds in which the Chinese were kept were sinks of indescribable immorality and cruelty, and the exaggerated picture of the manacled coolie and the flogging overseer became familiar not only on election posters but in some constituencies was even acted out in costume. 'Chinese slavery,' as catching and as damning a phrase as 'the dear loaf,' reduced the Government's stock to its nadir. With leaflets like 'Slavery in the Transvaal,'[3] the L.R.C. exploited its advantage to the full.

The year 1904 opened inauspiciously for the Committee when it suffered a discouraging setback in a triangular by-election contest at Norwich in Norfolk. Since Tory-held Norwich was one of the two-member constituencies where the Liberals were allowing Labour one clear run in the General Election, the local I.L.P. was uncertain whether to fight or hold its hand. Hardie was strongly for fighting no matter what the Liberals did and mistakenly thought that they would stand aside if this were made clear.[4] An I.L.P. candidate, George Roberts, was therefore put forward. Aged thirty-two, Roberts had served on the Norwich School Board and was a member of the Typographical Society and chairman of the Norwich Trades Council. The Liberal Party headquarters did its best to secure his withdrawal, Jesse Herbert pointing out to MacDonald that if the seat were lost due to division the free trade cause would be grievously injured and Roberts' success at the General Election jeopardized while if Roberts waited, the Liberals would support him later and both Norwich seats might be won. When MacDonald, ill at Lossiemouth, replied that he could do nothing, Herbert privately expressed the wish that Roberts would get 'such a beating as [would] teach the L.R.C. a deserved lesson.'[5]

In the more conservative L.R.C. circles there were misgivings about opposing the Liberal, and Will Crooks found excuses for not appearing on Roberts' platform.[6] Shackleton, however, agreed to speak, much to the concern of Kay Shuttleworth, the late Liberal member for Clitheroe, who feared that Liberals would turn against Shackleton in his own constituency.[7] Henderson also appeared and to Glasier's relief 'spoke perfectly straight and without the least strain of apology.'[8] It was the I.L.P. speakers who added zest to the campaign. Roberts made no concessions to Liberal feelings and denounced the division between the older parties as fictitious. The time was approaching, he said, when the main divisions of parties would find Labour on one side, anti-Labour, including Liberal and Tory, on the other.[9] Snowden belittled the notion that Liberals anywhere were sacrificing seats to Labour[10] and took to task those who accused the Labour party of isolating itself, of playing Ishmael. 'They were glad to be a party of Ishmaelites . . .' he asserted, 'Who was Ishmael? They were told that he was landless, he was homeless, but they were also told that the Lord had compassion upon him and the Lord said, "I will protect thee; I will strengthen thee; I will multiply thee and out of thee I will raise a great nation and a great people".'[11]

When the Liberal won Norwich by 1,820 votes over the Tory and by 6,136 over Roberts, even optimists in the Liberal party were surprised.[12] Roberts blamed most for his defeat the 'subtle misrepresentations' of those Liberals who confused the basic issue 'by expressing their association with and love for the Labour movement.'[13] Gladstone described the victory as 'triumphant' and told C.B. that it would help with the Labour men 'who under the promptings of Hyndman's Socialists [had been] threatening mischief.'[14] 'Labour has been saved in spite of itself from damaging its own interests,' commented a Liberal daily, '. . . the Norwich figures raise a clear warning to Labourists wishing to force their candidatures on unwilling constituencies.'[15] In the *Speaker*, H. W. Massingham wrote that if the Liberals had not won, there might have been Liberal-Labour fights everywhere thus irreparably damaging Labour's chances at the General Election.[16] Commenting further on Norwich in a letter to the *Labour Leader*, he argued that it proved that the Labour party must co-operate with the Liberals and that since nothing in the way of reform could be expected from a Liberal party in which Rosebery would be dominant, Radicals everywhere were anxious that Labour should win. 'At least the world in which you live is alive.' Massingham wrote. 'Sometimes I think the world in which I move is dead.'[17]

In the same month as Norwich a miners' candidate named John Johnson was returned as a Liberal in a by-election in Gateshead in Durham. It was not only the decision of the Durham Miners to find seats for at least two of their own men that made the official Liberals concede the seat; there was a distinct possibility of an I.L.P. candidature if a miner had not run.[18] The suggestion of a prominent Liberal that an understanding might be arrived at with MacDonald to leave Gateshead for Labour on provision that the Liberals be left alone in Norwich had come to nothing.[19]

To add to MacDonald's worries there appeared in the press while the Norwich campaign was still in progress a letter from one of Gladstone's assistants referring to the electoral pact. Addressed to an unnamed member of the Labour party in Accrington it stated that Gladstone's efforts had already resulted in 'an arrangement for some forty or fifty Labour candidates in constituencies where the Labour candidate [would] have a fair field and be supported by the Liberal party,'[20] and that in the comparatively few places where friction had arisen Gladstone would 'continue to do his best in the interests of unity.'

Possibly this communication, which would obviously considerably embarrass MacDonald, was meant to remain private. On the other hand, it may have been a deliberate plant aimed at reminding the Committee of the dangers of the unco-operative attitude shown at Norwich. MacDonald thought it best to issue a strong denial. He made no reference to the 1903 negotiations, to the assurance of L.R.C. support for Liberal candidates nor to the efforts of his office to keep seats not clearly earmarked for Labour from locally being challenged. 'There is no such thing as an arrangement between the Liberal party and ourselves,' he wrote in a letter to the *Manchester Guardian*. 'The Liberal party knows that in certain constituencies we are going to run men, and in some of these constituencies pressure has been brought from Parliament Street upon the local Liberal associations, so that no Liberal candidate will be run in opposition. That is exactly all that has happened, and nothing more.'[21]

Hardie had been unable to participate in the Norwich campaign. He had collapsed with appendicitis in October 1903, and was convalescing at his home in Cumnock, Scotland. As spring came on and his old strength did not return, he decided on a trip to the Continent, the necessary funds having been raised by friends in and outside the party.[22] MacDonald, also recuperating from illness, accompanied him for part of the journey. Though Hardie admired and defended MacDonald, he regarded him as something of a *poseur* and was not averse to criticizing him among intimates. In a letter to Glasier from the Riviera in April 1904, Hardie wrote: 'Mac by the way is not an ideal travelling companion. In all the arrangements he discussed his own plans apparently without regard for my inclinations, and altho he always at once and with the utmost readiness fell in with any suggestions of mine, this was not

the same as thinking first of the weaker brother. He wanted
to see everything not so much I think from any real interest,
as to be able afterwards to talk at dinner tables about what he
had seen.'[23]

One result of Hardie's illness was his final surrender of the
*Labour Leader* to the I.L.P.; the work of financing and editing
it was now too great a drain on his strength. There had long
been criticisms of the quality of the paper, MacDonald early in
1903 regarding it as tottering, dull and inaccurate,[24] and
Hardie's reluctance to part with it had been met with increasing
impatience by other leaders in the party. As early as June 1902,
Glasier had written him, 'I feel strongly that with your commanding position as public leader of the party, it is a matter of
great political principle that if we have an official organ of the
party it should not be—or seem to be—a duplicate of your
voice and opinions. . . . The movement is being starved of news
and matters of interest concerning itself. The *Leader* for some
reason appears to have no deep interest in the branches, the
Council or the general political activity of the party. From the
references or rather lack of references in its pages one would
hardly imagine that there was an I.L.P. at all.'[25]

The paper was purchased and taken over by the National
Council early in 1904.[26] MacDonald for a time had the leading
hand in editing it with 'absolute powers to accept or decline
any copy' sent to him.[27] The offices of the paper were moved
from Glasgow to London. At the end of 1904 Glasier became
the chief editor. The *Leader*'s circulation greatly increased in
the next four years due less perhaps to the improvements in
its contents than to the growing interest in and importance of
the Labour party generally. Glasier was able to devote most
of his time to the editorship; in 1903 his three-year term as
chairman of the I.L.P. had expired. He was succeeded as
chairman by Snowden who in 1906 was to give way to Mac-
Donald.

The work at the L.R.C. Office grew heavier and MacDonald,
never robust, easily depressed, and wondering if perhaps the
movement was not advancing too rapidly,[28] soon showed the
effects of strain and overwork. He was ill or in poor health

in late 1903 and the early part of 1904. In May he was operated on for appendicitis and in the next few months was obliged to let Henderson and Shackleton supervise much of the work.[29] Meanwhile, to defray increased operating costs at headquarters, affiliation fees had been raised from 10s. to 15s. per thousand for trade unions and socialist societies, and from £1 to £1 10s. for trades councils. MacDonald had been voted a salary of £150 a year and £125 for his able young assistant, James Middleton. The cramped quarters at 3 Lincoln's Inn Fields were now obviously inadequate, and at the end of March more spacious offices were acquired at Victoria Mansions, 28 Victoria Street, under the shadow of the House of Commons.

Contributions to the Committee's parliamentary fund were below expectations with some unions arguing that there were obstacles to such contributions in their rules and others still insisting that they should be responsible only for their own candidates. When the L.R.C. Conference of 1904 voted to make contributions compulsory and retroactive,[30] some of the smaller unions withdrew,[31] and in April 1904, according to MacDonald's estimate, over a third of the membership had still not begun the required payments.[32] This situation was made worse by the fact that critics of the Committee, and especially W. M. Thompson of *Reynolds's* and the National Democratic League, were eager to exploit opposition to the compulsory levy and to question the legality of any trade union contributions to the L.R.C. This question was not to be fully dealt with in the courts until 1909 when the Law Lords in the famous Osborne decision decided that compulsory levies by a trade union for political purposes were illegal, thus at a stroke cutting off most of the Labour party's financial resources, but the question nearly reached the courts in 1905. First of all a newly appointed Registrar of Friendly Societies threw a scare into the movement by deciding that, under the Trade Union Act of 1876, running members for Parliament was not a legitimate 'object' to be included in a trade union's rules. Soon afterward, however, it became clear that it was the form rather than the action itself that the Chief Registrar found unacceptable and that a trade union might list such activity under 'methods.'[33] The Railway

Servants sought the counsel of Sir Edward Clarke and Sir Robert Reid on the question and were advised that parliamentary levies were legally enforceable so long as rules to provide for them were properly passed by the union members.

When the Canning Town (London) branch of the Plumbers' Union, acting on Thompson's advice, sought an injunction to restrain its executive from making payments to the L.R.C., MacDonald was anxious that the action be fought as a test case. He prevailed on the L.R.C. Executive to guarantee £50 to the Plumbers Union[34] for expenses and went himself to the Manchester County Court where the case was heard on November 17, 1905. If the Plumbers' Executive won, MacDonald argued, a statement could be sent out to give the L.R.C. affiliates a feeling of security. If it lost, the L.R.C. could point to the decision as a new campaign against the trade unions reminiscent of Taff Vale.[35] As it turned out, however, the case settled nothing. A few days before the hearing the Canning Town branch dropped its claim to restrain the executive. Though a majority of the Plumbers Union had voted in favour of a levy, the society had no rules on the subject, and in the court hearing it was simply decided that the Executive would not levy the Canning Town branch until the rules were changed. The Committee, thereupon, assured its members that a parliamentary levy could be legally compulsory if rules so provided and urged immediate action on the part of all trade unions to see that this was done. It further assured member societies with no parliamentary levy that they could continue to subscribe to the L.R.C. from their general funds if they had in their 'objects' general powers to advance the interests of their members.[36] By this time, the General Election was little more than a month away, and here the question rested.

When Hardie returned to his duties in the House in July 1904, he was dispirited by the lack of aggressiveness displayed by the L.R.C. members. 'The group doesn't appear to be making much of a show,' he wrote to Glasier, 'and J. R. M. [MacDonald] writes me a somewhat disquieting note concerning their tendency to merge in the Liberals. Would that the election were over. We would then see more clearly where we are and what we do.'[37] The sorry fact was that the L.R.C. group was too small and too cautious to make much of a show, for Henderson, Shackleton and Crooks were by nature incapable of those dramatic bids for attention, through exaggeration and violence of speech, of which Hardie was master—the only means, wanting outstanding ability, by which small groups can grasp the limelight. As for Bell, he had now for all practical purposes gone over to the Liberals. At Norwich not only had he refused to speak for Roberts, stating in a letter that it was 'wicked to split the Progressive vote at such a time';[38] he had also sent a telegram of congratulation to the Liberal victor. Called to account both by the L.R.C. and his own union, he would not recant, and continuing in his refusal to sign the revised L.R.C. Constitution, he was removed from the L.R.C. lists.

As for the tendency to merge in the Liberals, the Labour members were almost bound to work closely with Liberals in the House if only to secure a place on the ballot for Labour measures. In 1904 and 1905 even the bills to amend trade union law had to be introduced by Liberals. Furthermore, assuming that they had tried to work alone and to ignore Liberals and 'Lib-Labs', the members of the L.R.C. group would have found it difficult to agree amongst themselves on many important questions. Shackleton, in response to the desire of the Lancashire cotton operatives, was opposed to amendments to the Factory Act raising the age limit of child labour. Henderson had pledged the Durham miners not to vote for any Miners' Eight Hours Bill.[39] On woman's suffrage there were also differences. On the instructions of the I.L.P. Conference of 1904 the National Council of the party drafted a Woman's Franchise Bill which Crooks agreed to sponsor in Parliament,[40] but the L.R.C. Conference in 1905 opposed the measure and favoured an Adult Suffrage Bill instead. It was argued that Crooks's Franchise Bill would increase the power of the propertied classes by enfranchising upper- and middle-class women leaving the great majority of women voteless and that a woman's suffrage platform would mitigate against the L.R.C.'s election prospects.[41] Both Hardie and MacDonald decried this attitude, pointing out that though adult suffrage might be more desirable the case for it was somewhat vitiated by its being virtually impossible of attainment.[42] Many trade unionists, however, were inclined to be critical of suffragette methods and to regard Mrs. Pankhurst's call for female revolt as no concern of theirs.

It was irksome to Hardie that Burns continued to be regarded as the leader of Labour in the House, especially since Burns still regarded the L.R.C. group with suspicion, rarely took the group into his confidence, and ignored Hardie's appeals to him to throw his weight behind the newcomers.[43] On one occasion, according to Hardie, Burns advised Crooks against signing one of Hardie's measures because, he said, it was poorly drafted.[44] Then in March 1904, without consulting any member of the L.R.C. group beforehand, Burns moved an amendment to Shackleton's motion for the payment of 'standard' wage rates in government shipyards and factories. The amendment, though desirable, was proposed so late in the evening that when Shackleton requested closure just before the House rose, his request was opposed on the grounds that the amendment had not received adequate discussion.[45] Explaining what had occurred, Shackleton let slip the remark that Burns was not of the Labour group nor recognized by it and at the Trades Union Congress in September placed on Burns the blame for the failure of the motion. Burns thereupon lowered his guns for a verbal barrage on the L.R.C. 'These social movements for the benefit of the nation, the elevation of the race,' he wrote, 'cannot, and must not, be confined to, and captured by, a small clique of professorial prigs, middle-class men on the make, masquerading as Labour leaders, securing Liberal votes, manipulating Radical enthusiasm, exploiting Socialist sentiment, and eking out a precarious political existence out of trade union funds to which they have not subscribed. It does not help them in their travesty of political independence and impotent isolation from others that they have subscribed to conditions which bemean a man, and make the Parliamentary representative a mechanized automaton, and, whilst professing independence, make him really but a dependent beggar with two hundred bits of gold.'[46] No one in the movement could match such an outburst. Burns in delivering it had revealed either an abysmal misunderstanding of the L.R.C. or a readiness to deliberately misinterpret and discredit it. He had never been prone to let accuracy destroy the polish of a well-turned phrase. 'Burns is becoming quite a pathetic figure,' Glasier had said in private, 'his vanity has quite eaten his moral energy up. He will wake up some of these days and discover he is a man of the past.'[47]

Efforts to secure changes in the laws affecting trade unions proved disheartening. A bill, previously discussed by the L.R.C. and the trade unionists in joint committee, was introduced by Shackleton in 1903. Limited in object, it dealt solely with legalizing picketing and persuasion, and Asquith, in making a concise statement of the Bill's aims, emphasized that the trade unions did not seek complete immunity for their funds. A second reading was defeated by twenty votes when the Government agreed to the appointment of a Royal Commission.[48] In any case, many trade unionists regarded as worthless any measure not assuring the protection of their funds, and the Trades Union Congress in 1903 registered its disapproval of Shackleton's bill by demanding legislation fully embodying the pre-Taff Vale position.[49] Such a measure, drafted by the Parliamentary Committee of the T.U.C., was introduced in 1904[50] and with the invaluable support of Sir Robert Reid passed a second reading by thirty-nine votes,[51] the Parliamentary Committee having effectively lobbied both the major parties. Balfour, however, would allow it no further facilities. In 1905, with members becoming ever more sensitive to Labour's threat in their own constituencies, a similar Bill passed the second reading by a majority of 122, many of its opponents absenting themselves from the House, and although many Liberals, including Asquith, expressed grave concern with the clauses allowing complete immunity of funds, the 'No' votes were all Unionist.[52] In Committee, however, the Bill was crippled by amendments, and the Labour members asked for its withdrawal. This request was refused, the efforts of the Employers' Parliamentary Council were completely successful, and the Committee, from which Liberals and Labour members had withdrawn, proceeded to hack the Bill beyond recognition.[53] In so doing they accomplished nothing beyond making anti-

Taff Vale sentiment outside all the stronger. The death of the bill meant the triumph of the agitation for it. As for the Royal Commission, it was condemned by Labour as packed and partial, even though Sidney Webb was one of its members, and a joint committee of the L.R.C. and the Parliamentary Committee advised that the commission be boycotted. The advice was followed, and the commission conducted its inquiries in the absence of any important trade union witnesses. According to Webb, the Commission was believed to have been privately told not to report until after a General Election lest its report embarrass the Government.[54] The report was not finally made public until February 1906.

Bell's defection was only one of the reasons for a gnawing fear in 1904 that the L.R.C.'s independence might go crumbling. In the summer of that year Henderson, Crooks and Shackleton all appeared on free trade platforms where Liberal candidates were running in by-elections and were widely criticized for what some regarded as a breach of the Newcastle resolution. Their action, said the *Labour Leader*, had 'tied a millstone around the neck of the L.R.C.'[55] while the S.D.F. organ, *Justice*, with Bell also in mind, commented that these incidents 'have disrupted the Labour party; four out of the five members who composed it . . . have gone over to the Liberal party to which they have always really belonged.'[56] When Henderson and Shackleton explained that they had appeared as free traders, not as supporters of the Liberal candidates, the L.R.C. Executive accepted this explanation but decided that in the future the executive alone should decide what action was to be taken in such cases.[57]

There were still other offenders besides the L.R.C. members of Parliament. John Hodge, the Committee's candidate for Gorton, was informed by the Executive that the Constitution would not permit him to support Winston Churchill, Liberal candidate in the neighbouring North-West Manchester division. Yet he was reported to have appeared on Churchill's platform.[58] James Sexton of the Dockers, candidate for Central Hull, was severely censured by the *Labour Leader* for close collaboration with the local Liberals and for inviting J. Havelock Wilson of the Seamen's Union and W. E. Harvey of the Derbyshire Miners, both critics of L.R.C., to speak in his behalf. Although the L.R.C. Executive refused to share the I.L.P. view and saw nothing in Sexton's actions of which it could disapprove,[59] it is worth noting that Sexton withdrew from Central Hull and did not find a seat elsewhere. Yet another problem was the reluctance of certain L.R.C. candidates to sign the constitution, and while Bell, John Ward and W. C. Steadman had to be removed from the L.R.C. lists on this account, Crooks, and Isaac Mitchell of the Engineers did not sign until more than a year after Newcastle and even for some months after the 'resign' clause had been removed.

Had the L.R.C. trade union section produced a more dynamic leadership ready to exploit these difficulties and had its members in the House been as insistent as Bell on their own particular points of view, the I.L.P. might have lost much of its influence on the Committee, an influence that had always partly depended on trade union inertia, not to say cloddishness. Indeed the ineffectiveness of the L.R.C. trade unionists in Parliament was, from one point of view, of distinct advantage to the I.L.P. As Glasier reminded Hardie in June 1904, there had been 'a danger that the non-socialist wing of the Labour party would break the start and rush the field' and that the I.L.P. would encounter difficulties in claiming recognition as 'the active and forward force of the movement.' 'The present complacent attitude of the Trade Union M.P.s, however, makes the position riper than ever for the I.L.P.,' said Glasier, 'and I feel sure that things everywhere point the way to our taking a more active and confident lead than we have been doing for some time. The rank and file of the L.R.C. candidates are with us, and I entirely agree with the remark you made at Cumnock that we can take their support for granted. . . . I have absolutely no fear of a Labour-Liberal régime taking place. There is positively neither the conditions nor the mind in present day history to sustain such a policy. Everywhere our strength lies in the hope of a *new* party.'[60]

Glasier's confidence was based partly on the realization that even those trade unionists opposed to the Newcastle resolution were usually unwilling to embarrass the Committee or hamper its work. The Trades Union Congress had lost prestige. The powerful Engineers Union, with five candidates running under L.R.C. auspices, and also the Ironfounders, were not even attending the Congress in 1903 and 1904; the old party in the Congress now seemed limited to London and the coal mining districts; and even the miners were divided, the Lancashire and Cheshire group having joined the L.R.C. while other miners' groups inclined in that direction. Aside from this, the Congress had no clear plan of political action so that trade unionists everywhere were accepting the Committee as the true heart of the political Labour movement. Nor did many of them belittle the socialist contribution to its success. This is why attempts to exclude the socialists continued to be overwhelmingly defeated at L.R.C. Conferences, such a proposal in 1904 failing even to find a seconder,[61] and why in the Trades Union Congress it soon became recognized that any resolution critical of L.R.C. policy had little chance of passage. When in 1904 the T.U.C. was presented with another resolution to make L.R.C. membership the same as that of the Congress, it was generally conceded that this was a useless gesture, and Richard Bell, as Chairman of the Congress, acquiesced in a ruling of its General Purposes Committee that the resolution could not be considered since the Congress had no jurisdiction or control over an 'outside body.' This clear recognition of the L.R.C. as an entirely separate and independent organization did not mean, however, that the Congress was relinquishing all control over the political side of the movement, for its Parliamentary Committee still claimed the right to endorse and support trade unionist candidates regardless of whether they were affiliated to the L.R.C.[62]

To the I.L.P. section of the Committee these Congress decisions were not altogether reassuring.[63] It was obvious that L.R.C. trade unionists, in their drive to retrieve their former legal status, would not be willing to confine their support to L.R.C. candidates alone, and that if the Parliamentary Committee and the L.R.C. Executive were to act separately on such crucial matters as the Trade Union Bill, the whole movement might be confused and compromised at the General Election.

Suggestions for combining the L.R.C. and the Congress provided no answer, for until the miners willingly joined the L.R.C., welding the two organizations together would present insuperable difficulties. It was therefore necessary to seek agreement for united action at the polls.

With this objective, representatives of the L.R.C., the T.U.C. and the General Federation met at Caxton Hall, London, on February 16, 1905. Already at a by-election at West Monmouth in the preceding November, the L.R.C. Executive had decided that the Newcastle resolution did not forbid L.R.C. support of a Labour candidate outside L.R.C. auspices. At first the Executive had been pretty equally divided on the question, Hardie, Shackleton, Henderson and Hodge approving support; Pease, Clynes, Gee of the Weavers and Stephenson of the Engineers opposing. But when the candidate, Tom Richards of the South Wales miners, assured MacDonald that he was a 'Labour' candidate, supported but not sponsored by a local Liberal Association and that if returned he would support the formation of a Labour group in the House,[64] the opposition dwindled, and many L.R.C. men participated in the West Monmouth campaign.

The agreement reached at Caxton Hall had four main clauses. The first provided that all L.R.C. candidates should be supported by all sections of the Labour movement; the second, that candidates approved by the Parliamentary Committee of the Congress should receive the support of the Labour Representation Committee insofar as its constitution would permit and on the lines followed at West Monmouth; the third, that in no case would candidates run by either the Congress or the L.R.C. oppose one another; and the fourth, that in constituencies where no Labour candidates were running, the policy of abstention would in no sense be recommended to the local organizations.[65]

The L.R.C. had definitely the better part of the bargain, for while the trade unionists promised L.R.C. candidates unconditional support, the L.R.C. promised reciprocal support only under a specific set of circumstances. MacDonald interpreted the second clause as meaning that if a candidate was paid by a Labour organization, ran purely as a Labour candidate and pledged himself to work with the L.R.C. party in Parliament, then the Committee could advise its officials and candidates to give such a candidate their backing if they so chose. The decisions of the L.R.C. Conference at Liverpool, said Mac-Donald, bound the L.R.C. Executive to go no further.[66] George Bernard Shaw, whose comments on the L.R.C. at this time reveal that he only faintly grasped the nature of the independent position and underestimated the strength which the Committee had attained, wrote that the socialists had won a point at Caxton Hall but had abused their advantage and were forcing the trade unionists to revolt.[67] It would seem that even given the restrictions of Clause 2, the I.L.P. leaders were at first determined to interpret the agreement as rigidly as possible, for in early December 1905, they decided to recommend that members of the party support L.R.C. and socialist candidates only, which, it was stated, implied abstention from supporting all others.[68] At the end of December, however, at a General Election conference of the party, it was finally set down that each I.L.P. branch should be left to decide for itself about supporting other candidates,[69] and it seems highly doubtful that where L.R.C. or socialist candidates were not in the field, any large number of I.L.P. members refrained from voting for Liberals, trade unionist or otherwise. In more than one instance the I.L.P. leaders themselves gave the Liberals at least an indirect support, as was to be expected once they became involved in the agreement between the Liberal Chief Whip and L.R.C. headquarters. MacDonald had given assurance that his people would support the 'Lib-Lab' Broadhurst at Leicester; Hardie had advocated the policy of casting the second vote for the Liberal at York; and in some two-member constituencies the I.L.P. candidates were to give extremely broad hints that votes should be swapped with the Liberals.

## NOTES

1. Speech of Shackleton, *L.R.C. Ann.*, 1905, 39; L.R.C. resolution, *L.R.C. Ann.*, 1905, 55.
2. The 'Lib-Lab' Broadhurst exchanged letters with the Archbishop criticizing his use of these words. Broadhurst Correspondence, vol. vi, 4-6.
3. L.R.C. Leaflet No. 11.

4. Hardie to Glasier, April 1, 1903.
5. Jesse Herbert to H.G., Dec. 31, 1903. H.G., vol. xxix, 53.
6. 'Crooks has funked,' wrote Glasier to Hardie on Jan. 6, 1904. 'Snowden . . . wrote him a strong letter but there is no reply.'
7. Kay Shuttleworth to H.G., Jan. 16, 1904. H.G., vol. lxix, 140.
8. Glasier to Hardie, Jan. 15, 1904.
9. *Eastern Morning Gazette*, Norwich, Jan. 2, 1904.
10. On this point see also Snowden in *L.L.*, Feb. 6, 1904.
11. *Eastern Morning Gazette*, Jan. 16, 1904.
12. The Liberals had been resigned to losing if Roberts persisted. H.G. to C.B., Jan. 13, 1904, C.B., vol. xii, 73. Roberts' vote of 2,400 was not a mean achievement, according to the L.R.C. Executive, since there had not been more than 1,500 trade union voters on the register before the election. *L.R.C. Ann.*, 1904, 20.
13. *Eastern Morning Gazette*, Jan. 16, 1904.
14. H.G. to C.B., Jan. 18, 1904. C.B., vol. xii.
15. *Shields Daily News*, Jan. 16, 1904.
16. *Speaker*, Jan. 23, 1904.
17. *L.L.*, Jan. 30, 1904.
18. *Clarion*, Jan. 29, 1904; *L.L.*, Jan. 30, 1904. Prior to Gateshead, John Wilson was the only representative of the Durham miners in Parliament.
19. Cyrus Hardy to H. W. Massingham, Dec. 29, 1903. H.G., vol. lxix, 80. The Liberal Leif Jones had asked to be considered for Gateshead, claiming that the Labour people owed him something for having made way for a Labour man at South Glamorgan, Wales. Leif Jones to H.G., Dec. 29, 1903. H.G., vol. lxix, 81.
20. *Daily News*, Jan. 13, 1904.
21. *Man. Guardian*, Jan. 15, 1904.
22. Stewart, *Hardie*, 215-216.
23. Hardie to Glasier, April 10, 1904.
24. MacDonald to Glasier, Jan. 24, 1903.
25. Glasier to Hardie, June 25, 1902.
26. N.A.C. Minutes, Jan. 25 and 26; Mar. 21 and 22, 1904.
27. N.A.C. Minutes, April 3, 1904.
28. 'Spectator,' *Echo*, June 10, 1903.
29. *L.R.C. Quarterly Circular*, June, 1904.
30. *L.R.C. Ann.*, 1904, 40.
31. So that membership stood at 900,000 at the beginning of 1905 as compared with 969,000 at the beginning of 1904. *L.R.C. Ann.*, 1903, 22.
32. MacDonald letter to members of the Executive, April 22, 1904. At the beginning of 1904 there was a balance of £2,260 on hand in the Parl. Fund. During the following year subscriptions to the fund amounted to £4,491, *L.R.C. Ann.*, 1905, 30.
33. On the question of registration and parliamentary funds see *Reynolds's* Oct. 29, 1905; MacDonald in the *L.L.*, Nov. 3, 1905; *The Labour Record and Review*, Nov. 1905, 273; and *The Leicester Pioneer*, Dec. 23, 1905.
34. MacDonald to members of the L.R.C. Executive, Oct. 25, 1905.
35. MacDonald to member of the L.R.C. Executive, Oct. 27, 1905.
36. MacDonald circular letter, Nov. 27, 1905.
37. Hardie to Glasier, July 1904.

38. Letter of Jan. 11 as reported in *Reynolds's*, Jan. 17, 1904.
39. Shackleton speech to the Bradford L.R.C. Conference, *L.R.C. Ann.*, 1904, 50.
40. *I.L.P. Ann.*, 1904, 30; 1905, 17.
41. *L.R.C. Ann.*, 1905, 55-57.
42. Hardie in *L.L.*, Feb. 3, 1905; MacDonald as 'Spectator' in *Echo*, Feb. 1, 1905.
43. See Hardie's 'Open Letter to John Burns,' *L.L.*, Mar. 28, 1903.
44. Hardie to Glasier, July 16, 1903.
45. Parl. Debates, Commons, 4th series, vol. 132, Mar. 23, 1904, cols. 553-580; *Daily News*, Sept. 9 and 10, 1904.
46. *T.U.C. Ann.*, 1904, 83; Burns' statement in the *Daily News*, Sept. 9, 1904.
47. Glasier to Hardie, Mar. 2, 1903.
48. Parl. Debates, Commons, 4th series, vol. 122, May 8, 1903, cols. 204-268; no Liberal voted against the second reading. See MacDonald's comments on the weakness of the Bill, 'Spectator,' *Echo*, Mar. 25 and April 1, 1903.
49. *T.U.C. Ann.*, 1903, 67-71.
50. Since none of the Labour members were successful in the ballot, Richard Bell induced a Liberal, Mr. Paulton, M.P. for Bishop Auckland, to introduce the Bill. *General Secretary's Annual Report, Amalgamated Society of Railway Servants*, 1904, 21.
51. Parl. Debates, Commons, 4th series, vol. 133, April 22, 1904, cols. 958-1008; Winston Churchill gave a strong support to the second reading, cols. 998-1001.
52. Parl. Debates, Commons, 4th series, vol. 142, Mar. 10, 1905, cols. 1054-1107.
53. *L.L.*, May 12, 1905.
54. Webbs, *Trade Unionism*, 1920 edition, 605.
55. Quoted in *Daily News*, June 25, 1904.
56. Quoted in *Reynolds's*, July 10, 1904.
57. L.R.C. Minutes, June 30, 1904.
58. L.R.C. Minutes, May 12, 1904; *M.G.*, June 17, 1904, *Clarion*, July 1 and 13, 1904.
59. *L.L.*, July 22 and 29, Aug. 5, 1904; L.R.C. Minutes, Sept. 28, 1904.
60. Glasier to Hardie, June 17, 1904.
61. *L.R.C. Ann.*, 1904, 37.
62. *T.U.C. Ann. Report*, 1904, 117.
63. See *L.L.* editorial, Sept. 16, 1904.
64. MacDonald letter to member of the L.R.C. Executive, Oct. 21, 1904.
65. Report of the Joint Conference at Caxton Hall, Feb. 16, 1905, in L.R.C. papers. A sub-committee of representatives of the national bodies represented at Caxton Hall was appointed to meet regularly to discuss common action on election, legislative and other problems, with Shackleton, Henderson and MacDonald representing the L.R.C. *L.R.C. Quarterly Circular*, April 1905.
66. 'Spectator' in *Echo*, Feb. 22, 1905.
67. In *Reynolds's*. Feb. 25, 1905.
68. N.A.C. Minutes, Dec. 6, 1905.
69. Conference of Dec. 30, 1905, *I.L.P. Ann.*, 1906, 17-18.

# CHAPTER XIII

# The Question of Socialist Tactics— The Unemployment Bill

EXCEPT for the Marxists, British socialists had seldom looked to the Continent for inspiration or guidance, regarding their socialism as uniquely English both in origin and in method. In theory at least the I.L.P. tended more to the Fabian view of the solidarity of classes than to the Marxian concept of the class struggle, and in its propaganda was a strong admixture of religion, of simple chapel Christianity, with which the free-thinking socialist of Western Europe could rarely sympathize. In 1904 a German Marxist and a close student of the British movement, Max Beer, in a polemical exchange with George Bernard Shaw, derided I.L.P. doctrine as mere 'Nonconformism sicklied o'er with the pale cast of socialist thought.'[1] While in England trade unionism had preceded the formation of the existing socialist societies, on the Continent organized socialism had come first and to a considerable degree had shaped the trade union movement in its own image. This helps to explain the relative sterility of the S.D.F. Marxists, unable to command trade union support and therefore more prone to a doctrinaire attitude than their continental brothers. It also partly accounts for the nebulous quality of the socialism of the I.L.P. allied with the trade unions and cautiously attempting to steer them toward political independence.

Though the I.L.P. had no exact counterpart on the continent, it was by no means alone among contemporary socialist parties in emphasizing the parliamentary method. Since the failure of the Paris Commune in 1871, the notion of the violent overthrow of the state had lost much of its appeal for a large section of the socialists in all parliamentary countries and had yielded to a growing acceptance of peaceful persuasion, of long range efforts to capture the machinery of government through the vote. The gains had been substantial, especially in Germany and France, but the greater the gains the more apparent had become the wide chasm separating socialist platform agitation, still based in part on a revolutionary concept, from socialist absorption in laborious parliamentary efforts to secure ameliorative legislative reform. In Germany, Bernstein tried to bridge this chasm by preaching a Fabian gradualism and a revision of Marx. In France and Belgium middle-class socialists like Jaures and Vandervelde sought to synthesize revolutionary doctrine and evolutionary practice and meanwhile defended alliances with non-socialist parties for temporary ends. Opposition to this revisionism had mounted steadily, however, with Marxists of a stricter school, including Bebel and Kautsky in Germany and Guesde in France, deprecating involvement with non-socialist ministries as alien to the prosecution of the class war. By 1904, when the quarrel over parliamentary tactics was carried to the International Socialist and Labour Congress at Amsterdam, a deep rift was obvious in the European movement.

The British section at Amsterdam of 103 delegates was the largest of its kind ever sent from England and included trade unionists, Fabians, members of the S.D.F. led by Hyndman, I.L.P. delegates included Hardie and Glasier, and MacDonald and Shackleton representing the L.R.C. Never before had the British so closely identified themselves with an international socialist controversy as they did on this occasion, reading into the debates justification or criticism of their own particular policies at home. At Dresden the previous year the Germans had passed a resolution condemning Bernstein's revisionism. Now at Amsterdam, in combination with the Guesdists, they sought to extend that resolution internationally and implicitly to condemn Jaures and the policy of co-operation with other parties. To most of the British trade union and I.L.P. delegates the Guesdists were the French equivalent of the S.D.F. attempting to stereotype tactics and enforce a dogma on socialist parties everywhere. They therefore threw their support behind

Jaures, the defender of such co-operative efforts as they themselves were pursuing within the L.R.C. Though the Guesdist resolution was accepted by the Congress it was by the smallest majority, with a heavy vote from non-parliamentary countries, and according to MacDonald, it could not be justly considered a condemnation of Jaures.[2] Amsterdam demonstrated, claimed the *Labour Leader,* that in co-operating with non-socialists in the L.R.C., the Independent Labour Party had the approval of every continental socialist leader of note.[3]

In reporting on the Congress Hardie and Glasier both penned strong indictments of the class war theory. To Glasier the fact that a class war existed was 'no more a prediction of Socialism than . . . the fact that nations go to war and that Orangemen fight Catholics is a prediction of the brotherhood of man.' Socialism was not the prosecution of class war but 'a process of universal social growth,' of the increase of 'mutual help and solicitude.'[4] 'I am more than ever convinced,' he confided to Hardie, 'that the continental movement has fallen into a species of mere radicalism, and that it is marching by watchwords rather than by either faith or right. The half of these bourgeois leaders abroad strike me as utterly unregenerate from our Morris, Ruskin, Burns point of view. . . . The cause of Socialism not only in our country but in the world will receive a new character of freedom if only we set out I.L.P. or British (should I not say Scottish?) conception above all German formulas.'[5]

The call at Amsterdam for the unity of all Socialists led Jaures and Guesde in 1905 to ostensibly sink their differences in a united socialist party. In England it gave renewed impetus to the proposals for S.D.F.-I.L.P. fusion, its foremost advocate in the I.L.P. being S. G. Hobson. Hardie argued that the demand for unity, while it applied to countries like France and Germany where there were warring socialist factions within Parliament itself, could not apply to England where the S.D.F. was a small dissentient body outside the general movement.[6] Glasier, dismissing Hobson as 'a born intermeddler,' doubted that the L.R.C. was anxious to welcome the S.D.F. or that any alterations should be made in the L.R.C. constitution to meet its objections. 'We all know that in good time the word Socialist will be acknowledged by the L.R.C.,' he told Hardie, 'but for us to urge the change in the interest of a little fractious body like the S.D.F. would be curious opportunism. We should do nothing to precipitate any form of union with the S.D.F. Hyndman, Quelch and many more are too inveterately S.D.F. to be greatly changed at heart; and any revival of S.D.F.ism, however mild in form, would be a fatal mistake.'[7]

MacDonald, in analysing the Amsterdam debates, drew lessons for the L.R.C. from the fact that Jaures had given parliamentary support to the Combes ministry, and in an article in the Liberal *Speaker*, went so far as to suggest that if the next Liberal Cabinet 'were anti-Imperialist and were sound on Trade Union legislation, the Labour party would be perfectly justified in giving it general support and in protecting it from defeat.'[8] In a reply that sharply questioned MacDonald's version of the Congress, Hobson insisted that such support would constitute a betrayal of the L.R.C.'s independence.[9] Almost equally vexed by the article, less probably for the sentiment expressed than for the fact that MacDonald had expressed it publicly, Glasier wrote Hardie, '. . . how varied is the pitch on which he [Mac-Donald] winds his tune. He is so able and competent and hard-working that one grudges to find fault with him. . . . I agree with you that the reference to the likelihood of the Labour party giving a general support to the Liberal party is quite unfortunate, and I marvel that Mac or anyone with statesman-ship in our ranks should write these kind of things.'[10] No doubt as a corrective to the *Speaker* article, Hardie expressed an exactly opposite view in the *Labour Leader*. 'I cannot conceive of any set of circumstances as likely to arise within my lifetime which would lead me to agree to any alliance with any party now existing,' he wrote. 'Temporary tactical understandings with, say, the Irish party, or any other independent section of politicians, I can understand; but a working agreement with Liberals or Conservatives would spell ruin.'[11] But what Hardie professed was certainly no true reflection of what the I.L.P. actually practised. In view of the electoral deal with the Liberals and the Liberal leanings of many L.R.C. trade unionists, there was an obvious divergence between such pronouncements and the actual machinery by which the I.L.P. was seeking to prosper at the polls.

In the same month as the Amsterdam Congress there was another Liberal-Labour by-election clash when a representative of the Scottish Miners named John Robertson entered a three-cornered fight in North-East Lanark, the same seat contested by Smillie in 1901. As at Norwich, the Liberal won and Labour received the lowest poll. The L.R.C., though not responsible for Scottish constituencies, provided a number of speakers, and the L.R.C. M.P.s issued a manifesto in Robertson's behalf. One notable result was that Robertson received a thousand more votes than had Smillie even though Smillie had enjoyed the benefit of official Irish support which now was thrown to the Liberal. Scottish labour as yet returned no man to Parliament, the L.R.C. agreement with the Liberals did not apply outside England and Wales, and Labour in Scotland was to have no success whatever in bargaining with the Liberals for clear runs in the impending General Election. This was due in part to local Liberal stubbornness and the inability of the Liberal Chief Whip to bring any strong influence to bear in Scottish constituencies and also to the fact that the Scottish miners were more inclined to socialism and more extreme in their criticism of the Liberal party than the miners south of the Tweed. While Mac-Donald remarked that opposition to Robertson was 'suicidal to Liberalism' Hardie warned that it would have been prudent for the Liberals to declare a truce at least until the General Election. Was it to be supposed, he asked, that Labour would not retaliate?[13]

North-East Lanark was the tenth seat wrested from the Unionists since Chamberlain had begun his protectionist campaign. Aware that its time was rapidly running out and that it would soon have to go to the country, the Balfour Government now showed an increased readiness to conciliate Labour. Yet public, press and all sections of Parliament were showing greater sympathy with working-class demands and greater sensitivity to working-class distress since the Boer War had ended, and, even granted organized Labour's political awakening, the government's change in attitude cannot be explained on purely political grounds. It testified rather, to something more important—to an increased awareness of social problems and to deeper feelings of social responsibility among all sections of Society. Investigations like those of Booth in London and the Rowntrees in York were sinking into the public conscience. Unemployment was certainly not as acute in 1904 and 1905 as it was ten years earlier, yet now, in sharp contrast with that earlier period, agitation for the unemployed found a readily responsive public. Poverty was ceasing to be regarded as akin to crime, the result merely of indigence and to be treated as such. New light was being thrown on the harshness and chaotic condition of the Poor Law and on the injustice of reducing to second-class citizens through disenfranchisement those obliged to seek relief. By August 1905, Balfour was prepared to appoint a Royal Commission to inquire into the operations of the Poor Law, there having been no inquiry of this kind since the 'thirties.

From the winter of 1904 onward the I.L.P. centred much of its energy in unemployment agitation. Some form of state assistance outside the Poor Law was now widely held to be inescapable, but exactly what form this assistance should take was a matter of much debate. John Burns, as early as October 1903, in a report of the London County Council, favoured the advanced preparation of schemes of public works.[14] Hardie in January 1905 estimating the number of unemployed in the United Kingdom as 760,000, urged afforestation projects, public works, especially the cultivation of neglected lands, and a law to prohibit aliens from working at anything but trade union rates.[15] Everywhere in Labour circles there were demands for the creation of a Ministry of Labour.

The first notable effort to alleviate unemployment centred in London and was largely the work of Walter Long, President of the Local Government Board. A scheme, which he introduced in November 1904, provided for joint committees of guardians, councillors and members of charity organizations in each metropolitan borough and a central committee to act as their adviser and guide. The local committees received applications for work and divided these into two classes, the temporarily distressed, unable to find employment, and the ordinary applicants for regular poor law relief. In dealing with the former group, the central committee collected funds, distributed information regarding employment, and also provided for special works—gardening, street-making, road sweeping, farm work and the like. By voluntary subscription over £50,000 had been subscribed for these projects by April 1905.[16] Meanwhile, Long had set in motion a plan to extend such distress committees beyond the metropolitan area.

The sudden interest of the Liberal party in the unemployment problem, beginning in December 1904, no doubt stemmed partly from a fear lest the Balfour Government gain credit for some timely alleviative measure. Campbell-Bannerman, with an unemployed deputation on hand when he spoke at Manchester at the beginning of the month, was at a loss for anything to say,[17] but Gladstone shortly thereafter came to grips with the question in a speech to his constituents at West Leeds. Professing to see no objection to the Government's taking a hand in organizing works when thousands were unemployed and existing machinery was unable to cope with the situation, he suggested a survey of the whole country to determine what improvements from a national point of view, such as harbour and reclamation works, could be undertaken through state initiative.[18] When the speech was well received, C. B. repeated the same formula in an address in East London at the end of the year. Other Liberal leaders, however, were soon raising warning signals against any far-reaching commitments. Bryce cautioned that it must not appear that the Liberals admitted that it was the duty of the state to provide work.[19] John Morley could offer no remedy at all. Like some outmoded philosopher of the Charity Organization Society he decried the deteriorative effects of public employment on the worker's character and raised the bogey of the Paris National Workshops of 1848 which, he warned, had dislocated industry and ended in 'a most bloody and terrible catastrophe.'[20] All of the Liberal leaders appeared timid in the face of any really practical proposals for national works. When a scheme for the building of a network of canals was being bandied about, C. B. wrote to the Chief Whip, '. . . it would (I presume) only be done by the state, which wd. be a *very* new departure and wd. mean ultimately the taking over of the Railways and therefore a couple of million in government employment and . . . the first effect wd. be to scare every railway shareholder in the country.'[21]

In February 1905 in the King's speech the Balfour government promised a bill to deal with the unemployed. In April two measures, an Aliens Bill and an Unemployed Workmen's Bill, both aimed at wooing the working-class vote, were introduced in Parliament. Another bill, to amend and extend the Workmen's Compensation Act, was also introduced and was to pass through all stages in the House of Lords in the following Session and to be discussed in the Commons, but in July 1904 it was withdrawn. The Aliens Bill, meeting with only half-hearted resistance from the Liberals, finally became law on August 11, 1905. It was opposed by the Labour M.P.s and by some sixty Liberals led by Sir Charles Dilke. Chamberlain in defending the bill as a working-class measure found a splendid opportunity to chide those Liberals who ignored their own free trade precepts by supporting it. It was, he insisted, a partial vindication of his own position. The Bill 'is an effort to protect the working classes of this country against the labour, the underpaid labour, of a class of immigrants sent here,' he told the House. 'After all, then, we see that the other side have made some progress in regard to fiscal reform . . . the step is very little indeed to another Bill which I hope will be introduced before long to prevent the goods these people make from coming into the same competition.'[22]

The argument of an L.R.C. memorandum that England had the smallest alien population of any industrial country in the world,[23] would not have impressed the average trade unionist if the Aliens Bill had placed really effective curbs on underpaid immigrant competition. In areas of heavy alien concentration like East London resentment toward such competition was intense; Hardie had condemned the use of low paid Polish labour in the Scottish mines;[24] the Trades Union Congress had long demanded limitations on the entry of destitute aliens; and even the British labourer's opposition to indentured Chinese in the

Transvaal was based less on humanitarian considerations than on the indirect threat that such a practice represented to his own wage standards. But the Bill did not provide effective curbs, Labour spokesmen asserted, and was therefore a sham measure. In such ports as the Home Secretary might designate immigration officers and boards were to deal with aliens arriving in batches of more than twenty and could exclude steerage passengers who were unable to prove that they had means of decent subsistence or who were lunatics or criminals or might from infirmity become charges on the public rates. Those who could prove that they sought political asylum, however, were not to be excluded merely for want of means. An amendment to the Bill moved by Hardie to include among undesirables those aliens brought in to replace British workers during trade disputes was defeated.[25] As for the treatment of criminal and diseased aliens, this had nothing to do with the labour aspect of the alien problem. If it professedly aimed at alleviating unemployment, it was argued, the measure was fraudulent, and a joint committee of trade union representatives and the L.R.C. resolved in January 1905, that '. . . proposals like the Aliens Bill [were] misleading and calculated to divert attention from the real cause of the evil, namely the existence of monopoly and the burdens which the non-producing sections place on the industrial classes, together with the lack of such an organization of industry as will prevent alternate periods of overwork and unemployment.'[26]

Debate on the Aliens Bill was irritating to the Labour members. It delayed consideration of the Unemployed Bill which, it was widely feared, might be pigeon-holed and left to a later session. Hardie with other L.R.C. members harried Balfour with constant demands that the Bill be brought before the House. In May protest demonstrations were organized in London and the larger towns by a joint committee of the T.U.C., the General Federation and the L.R.C., and the Government faced the prospect of having unemployed armies marching on London. Balfour, who had weathered much stronger agitation when Chief Secretary for Ireland and had not quailed before passive resistance to the Education Act, was the least likely of men in the Government to be hustled by outside demonstrations. In the House on May 18th Hardie asked the Prime Minister if he was aware that 700 unemployed were about to begin a march on London from Leicester while similar demonstrations were in progress from Glasgow, Newcastle, Leeds and Manchester and whether he would undertake the second reading of the Unemployed Bill and insure its passage in the present session.

MR. BALFOUR: I have read the reports referred to, but I venture to say that the arrangements of this House with regard to its own business ought not to be modified in one way or another by any external considerations. (Ministerial cheers).

MR. KEIR HARDIE: It is only force which carries any measure of this kind through this House. (Ministerial cries of 'Oh!').

MR. BALFOUR: I take exactly the opposite view. It is not force which carries any measure through this House. It is, I hope, a reasonable and cautious public opinion. Any such demonstrations of force as the Hon. Member described are inimical and not favourable to the prospects of the Bill. (Ministerial cheers).

MR. WILL CROOKS: Will the Prime Minister exclude from his mind any demonstration and fix a day for the second reading? There is no more force about this than there was about the Brewers' Bill. (Opposition cheers).

MR. BALFOUR: I do not think the brewers came marching to London. (Loud laughter).

MR. DAVID SHACKLETON: Their demonstration is behind you. (Opposition cheers).

Mr. Balfour said he could not say more than that he earnestly hoped the Bill would become law this session.

MR. KEIR HARDIE: I am not advocating force; I am only pointing out that these men, having grown desperate, and seeing the indifference with which this measure is treated, have no resource left but force if they are not reassured.[27]

The original bill as introduced by Gerald Balfour, who had succeeded Long at the Local Government Board, provided for distress committees to be set up in London, in seventy-one county boroughs except where the board granted exemptions, and in other places where local councils or boards of guardians might apply. The local distress committees were to look after labour registries and sort out applicants for work into employable and non-employable and pass the former on to the central authority and the latter to the poor law authority. Land could be acquired by the central authority, and standard trade union rates were to be paid to those put to work, but weekly earnings were to be less than those earned in the open market. Funds for these undertakings were to be raised by voluntary contributions and by a rate which was not to exceed one penny in the pound.[28]

Hardie defended the measure. It affirmed three great principles, he argued—that it was the responsibility of the community to provide work for those unemployed due to causes for which they were not primarily responsible, that the cost for this was to be a public charge and not a private charity, and that help was not to involve disenfranchisement or loss of any rights of citizenship.[29] Yet Labour was not united on the Bill and even as Hardie in the House pressed Balfour for a second reading a conference of all the trade union sections and the L.R.C. only narrowly avoided advising rejection of the Bill,[30] deciding instead to press for amendments. While stating that the recognition of public responsibility and the removal of disenfranchisement were sound principles on which to base the Bill, the conference held that the Bill should not be accepted by organized labour unless it applied to the whole country, unless the Exchequer found most of the cost, and unless all limitations on rates of wages were removed, these limitations constituting a serious menace to trade union standards.[31] According to MacDonald, the bill's insistence on partial employment was 'an invitation to the committees to cut down hourly wages to philanthropic levels' regardless of the payment of standard trade union rates. Even attempts to amend the bill were hopeless, he thought, and would probably kill it.[32]

When on the 20th of June the Bill passed its second reading by 228 to 11, a speech by Hardie gave the Government a powerful assistance. The Liberal Front Bench could not have missed his jibe when he expressed satisfaction that 'a government had at length arisen which was prepared to make the unemployed question a matter of serious discussion in the House.' Urging country-wide establishment of the new authorities and changes in the wage scale clauses, Hardie warned his listeners, 'If no provision were made for the coming winter, the cursings and the groanings of the hungry and the dying, the despairing and the suicides, might well embitter the lives of those who were responsible should they succeed in wrecking the Bill.'[33]

In July, while the Bill was in the perilous Committee stage and seemed about to be abandoned to make way for the Aliens Bill, outside agitation continued. On July 9th a mass unemployment demonstration organised by the L.R.C. was held in Hyde Park.[34] On the 17th over a thousand wives of unemployed workers marched to the House of Commons where Balfour received their deputation. At the end of the month a demonstration in Manchester was dispersed by the police.[35] In redrafting the measure, the Government removed the obnoxious wages clauses and made the Bill practically compulsory for the whole country, but in addition it took away what many regarded as the Bill's most vital principle—providing work at the public expense. Land was to be acquired for farm colonies but work was to be paid for only from charitable contributions. Leaving the rates untouched was apparently the one sure way of assuring a wide if grudging Tory support.

In the ranks of Labour some like Crooks favoured the Bill, even in its emaciated form, as a partial gain, while others, including S. G. Hobson, argued that the more defective the act, the more sweeping would be its subsequent amendment.[36] MacDonald shared neither view. 'To grasp something immediately may postpone a satisfactory settlement for a generation,' he wrote; 'to accept a Bill which is to break down in the expectation that that will lead to something better is a characteristic blunder of every amateur politician. The Labour party should not allow the threats of Mr. Balfour to induce it to accept this Bill without amendment.'[37] When the Bill came to a vote on August 4th, Hardie criticized it as trifling with a great social problem, yet admitted that it made a beginning, and, in deference to Crooks, said he would not divide the House against it.[38] Many trade unionists were alarmed by its passage, however, James Sexton in an address to the T.U.C. the following month pointing out that it would give the employer the chance to point to an over-supply of labour as an excuse for cutting wages and to use the registering of the unemployed as a means of recruiting blackleg labour.[39]

The consideration of the Bill in the House of Lords exasperated Hardie and led him to pen a violently bitter attack on the Lords in general and on the Archbishop of Canterbury in particular. Lansdowne had assured the Lords that there was no danger that it would create a fresh class of 'privileged paupers.' '. . . what is the House of Lords,' asked Hardie, 'but an assembly of "privileged paupers?" The loafers and wastrels who cheered his [Lansdowne's] statement, what are they but vermin, many of them unclean vermin, who fatten on the nation because of their privileges? . . . And thereafter uprose the graceless Archbishop of Canterbury, a sprawling, ungainly figure, with a fleshy, expressionless face, and a noisy, empty voice. He wore his full canonicals. From his neck hung a gold chain on which was hung a gold cross. A cross of gold! As he from time to time raised his fleshy right hand, a great gold signet ring showed itself on his third finger. When he moved his left hand a gold ring gleamed upon the little finger of that hand. Upon him descended the coloured light from the painted windows overhead, whereon kings and queens and courtesans are displayed in gaudy colours. And for twenty minutes he mouthed stale nothings. He the representative of the Carpenter of Nazareth! He, with the fifteen thousand a year upon which he ekes out his miserable existence! Not one word of hope or pity for the poor, with whom his Master claimed kinship. Not a word to disturb the serenity of the atmosphere of their lordships' house, or give them one twinge of conscience over their bursting coffers replenished at the cost of the heart's blood of the poor. What wonder that the people of England have turned in disgust from a church of which this is the head.'[40] There was much of the worst of Hardie here—his demagoguery, his almost unhealthy puritanical streak, but also much of the best—his burning indignation at indifference to suffering, his deep faith in a simple Christianity.

The hope that in the hands of capable administrators the Unemployed Act might yet be made to yield surprising results was soon crushed when in October the Local Government Board finally issued its regulations. Destitution, rather than unemployment, appeared to be the test for coming under the Act, and the rates of pay were to be below standard rates.[41] Meanwhile, there was increasing talk, from General Booth of the Salvation Army and others, favouring emigration of the unemployed, and the National Council of the I.L.P. felt obliged to call on the distress committees 'to resist the proposals now being made for transporting the unemployed to other lands, as though they were criminals or undesirable aliens.'[42] A national fund campaign had been inaugurated for the work projects under the Act with the Queen contributing £2,000. By the end of 1905 it had reached £125,000. When the *Daily News* praised the Queen for contributing on an heroic scale, Hardie described this as 'so much fudge.' 'The Queen received £30,000 a year from the nation as pin money,' he said, 'and to give £2,000 of that to stave off something like a social revolution [could not] be described as being heroic.'[43]

### NOTES

1. Max Beer in the *Clarion*, Dec. 16, 1904.
2. MacDonald in the *Speaker*, Aug. 27, 1904.
3. *L.L.*, Aug. 26, 1904.
4. Hardie in the *L.L.*, Sept. 9, 1904; Glasier in the *L.L.*, Nov. 11 and 18, 1904.
5. Glasier to Hardie, Sept. 2, 1904.
6. *L.L.*, Aug. 26, 1904.
7. Glasier to Hardie, Sept. 2, 1904.
8. *Speaker*, Aug. 27, 1904.
9. Hobson in the *Speaker*, Sept. 3, 1904.
10. Glasier to Hardie, Sept. 2 and 8, 1904.
11. *L.L.*, Sept. 9, 1904.
12. As 'Spectator' in the *Echo*, July 20, 1904.
13. Speech of Aug. 2 as reported in the *Glasgow Herald* of Aug. 3, 1904.
14. W. S. Adams, *Edwardian Heritage*, London, 1949, 217.
15. Speech at York, Jan. 31, 1905 as reported in the *Yorkshire News*, Feb. 4, 1905.

16. *Reformers Year Book*, 1906, 142.
17. C.B. to H.G., Dec. 19, 1904. C.B., vol. xii, 142.
18. Speech at Leeds, Dec. 5, as reported in the *Daily News*, Dec. 6, 1904.
19. Bryce to H.G., Dec. 14, 1904. H.G., vol. xv, 80-81.
20. Speech at Walthamstow, Nov. 20, as quoted in *Reynolds's*, Nov. 26, 1905.
21. C.B. to H.G., Jan. 2, 1905. H.G., vol. xii, 42.
22. Parl. Debates, Commons, 4th series, vol. 145, May 2, 1905, col. 764.
23. *L.R.C. Ann.*, 1905, 62.
24. Speech at North East Lanark, Aug. 2, as reported in the *Glasgow Herald* of Aug. 3, 1904.
25. Parl. Debates, Commons, 4th series, vol. 149, July 10, 1905, cols. 131-134.
26. Report of the Special Conference on the Unemployed, Jan. 25, 1905, *L.R.C. Ann.*, 1905, 64.
27. As reported in the *Labour Record and Review*, June 1905, 117.
28. *L.L.*, June 2, 1905.
29. *L.L.*, May 26, 1905
30. According to MacDonald as 'Spectator' in the *Echo*, May 24, 1905.
31. *L.L.*, May 26, 1905.
32. As 'Spectator' in the *Echo*, May 31, 1905; in the *Leicester Pioneer*, June 9, 1905.
33. Parl. Debates, Commons, 4th series, vol. 147, June 20, 1905, col. 1180.
34. *L.R.C. Quarterly Circular*, July, 1905.
35. *Daily News*, July 18 and Aug. 2, 1905.
36. Hobson's letter of July 7 printed in *L.L.*, of July 21, 1905.
37. As 'Spectator' in the *Echo*, July 26, 1905.
38. Parl. Debates, Commons, 4th series, vol. 151, Aug. 4, 1905, cols. 428-429.
39. *L.L.*, Sept. 8, 1905.
40. *L.L.*, Aug. 11, 1905.
41. *L.L.*, Oct. 20, 1905.
42. *L.L.*, Oct. 6, 1905.
43. *Daily News*, Nov. 15, 1905.

# CHAPTER XIV

# The General Election of 1906

THE decision of the Balfour Government to resign in December 1905 was in part prompted by the expectation that the Liberals would be deeply divided over the question of self-government for Ireland. In Liberal enthusiasm for Home Rule one could trace a descending scale from John Morley to Lord Rosebery, but even the Morleyites were unwilling to commit their party to the Irish cause as fully and unreservedly as had the great Gladstone. His commitment had all but destroyed the party and had left it for nearly twenty years in barren and discordant opposition. No longer were the Irish representatives in Parliament regarded as virtually a Liberal appendage, and the mere thought of again returning to office dependent on the Irish M.P.s for survival had nightmarish qualities even for many Liberals in genuine sympathy with Irish demands. If another Home Rule Bill were introduced it would certainly be thrown out in the Lords, and this, thought Asquith, 'would wreck the party for another twenty years.'[1] Yet no matter how frightening the Irish nettle, the Liberals could not simply ignore it. There were more than one hundred seats outside Ireland where the Irish vote might decide an election[2] and where the promise of some concession in the direction of Home Rule was well-nigh irresistible.

Labour was in a less delicate position in seeking Irish support; it had no anti-Home Rule section to conciliate. An outright alliance between Labour and the Irish, such as Hardie and Glasier envisioned, might spark little response in the movement, for pressing social reforms and the revision of trade union law were not to be side-tracked to make way for Home Rule.[3] But the fact remained that Labour candidates were staunch Home

Rulers almost to a man, and Irish leaders like John Redmond, Gavan Duffy and Michael Davitt had made it clear that Labour therefore deserved preferential treatment. In the General Election, the United Irish League urged the Irish in Great Britain to vote for Labour candidates except where Labour opposed an old and tried friend of Ireland or where such a vote assured the return of a Unionist.[4] Since in some fifteen seats coveted by the L.R.C. the Irish vote could easily prove crucial,[5] this official Irish blessing was highly valued.

In seeking some formula for Ireland that would appeal to the widest segment of his party, Campbell-Bannerman took comfort in the knowledge that even ardent Roseberyites were inclined to regard their leader's pronouncements on Ireland as a little too blunt and unbending. As one member of the Liberal League put it, now that the Liberal coach was again on the road, Rosebery, by his outspoken opposition to Home Rule, threatened to plunge it 'into an Irish bog.'[6] 'C.B.' was at a loss to fathom why Liberals should shout, as did Haldane, that they must have a clear majority without the Irish: even if it were true, why offend the Irish unnecessarily? Haldane, the 'wonderful intriguer and diplomat' was displaying 'no more tact than an hippopotamus.'[7] It was 'C.B.'s' view that the party could best face the country with a 'step-by-step' policy for Ireland. There would be no all-embracing Home Rule measure, but Home Rule would not be lost sight of, and progress toward it would be gradual. On November 23, 1905, he embodied this formula in a speech at Stirling, having consulted with Grey, Haldane and Asquith and secured their agreement beforehand.[8] Of this agreement with his supposed colleagues Rosebery, when he spoke at Bodmin two days later, was apparently unaware. He objected to 'C.B.'s' 'raising the banner of Home Rule,' thus impairing the unity of the free trade party and indefinitely postponing discussion of social and educational reforms. 'Emphatically and explicitly and once and for all,' he announced, 'he could not serve under that banner.'[9]

Even as Rosebery spoke, Haldane at Frodsham was stating that the wise and Liberal course was 'to leave the people of Ireland to educate themselves in the administration of their own affairs.'[10]

Lord Rosebery, it soon became obvious, stood practically alone, and since he had hastily slammed the door in his own face with apparent disregard to party unity, his predicament aroused little sympathy. Campbell-Bannerman had no intention of reopening the door by more clearly defining what he had meant at Stirling. The speech had been vague in many respects, but, as the Chief Whip noted, so long as 'C.B.' and the Irish leader Redmond clearly understood each other and Redmond could not argue that he had been misled into giving Liberals the Irish vote, was it worth while endangering some thirty or forty Liberal seats by too closely defining the real situation?[11] What Rosebery's self-inflicted isolation meant to the Bannermanites was well expressed by Jesse Herbert. 'The party will rejoice that it is saved by Lord R[osebery]'s own flaming indiscretion from any entanglement with him & thus will be preserved from the evil it has dreaded, the possibility of having to sacrifice to Cabinet exigencies the legislative objects for which alone it is worth while to put our leaders into office.'[12]

That Rosebery's speech would actually strengthen rather than weaken the Liberals, Balfour could not be expected to foresee. Rather it appeared to him that the Liberals were again sinking into internecine squabbles and that Ireland might be a most effective issue for a Unionist appeal to the country. Balfour's long and skilful efforts to unite his own party by bringing Chamberlainites and the Unionist free traders together on some common ground of compromise were meanwhile crumbling under the persistent hammering of Chamberlain in favour of his full programme. Indeed the Chamberlainites had captured the National Union of Conservative Associations which on November 14 had passed an undiluted protectionist resolution.[13] As bad as was the situation, to Balfour there seemed no prospect that there would be a more favourable time to step down. On December 4, therefore, he tendered his resignation to the King.

Among the Liberals there were doubts as to the advisability of accepting office before a dissolution of Parliament, especially since it was believed that Balfour would soon be forced to take this step, but the Chief Whip, though anxious to escape the burdens that fell on him if the General Election were delayed, saw grave dangers if 'C.B.' declined. The King might send for Rosebery who would try to form a Liberal or a Coalition Government. 'In either case that wd. be disastrous for *our* candidates,' he wrote to Bannerman. 'If Rosebery also declined, A. B[alfour] wd. have a splendid chance of recovering ground & at any rate might work through the next session.'[14]

'C.B.', in no mood for shirking responsibility, accepted office on December 5. From his personal point of view there was an advantage in this acceptance before an election, an advantage which he himself may not at first have discerned. Rather than risk the results of facing the electors with a divided Liberal front, the Liberal Leaguers, Asquith, Grey and Haldane, were all finally won over to abandoning their demand that 'C.B.' go to the Lords (which he would not do) and leave Asquith to lead in the Commons. Asquith was the first to give way when he agreed to go to the Exchequer, and then Haldane and Grey assented by taking the War Office and Foreign Office respectively.[15]

The Cabinet appointments were impressive—few Cabinets in British history had so many men of intellect and ability—and though Labour spokesmen regretted the absence of Dilke and found the Cabinet too heavily weighted with Liberal Leaguers, they were somewhat reassured by the presence of Sir Robert Reid as Lord Chancellor, Lloyd George at the Board of Trade, Morley at the India Office, Gladstone at the Home Office, Sidney Buxton as Postmaster-General and Augustine Birrell at the Board of Education. John Burns at last received his reward in the Presidency of the Local Government Board, and appointment that met with a mixed response in Labour and Socialist circles, though it was generally conceded that it marked his complete severance from the Labour section in the House. Hardie used the strongest terms in criticizing some of the new ministers. 'The most prominent radical in the Cabinet,' he wrote, 'is John Morley whose distrust of the people is only equalled by that of John Burns.' As for Asquith and Haldane, they were, he extravagantly asserted, 'cold-blooded reactionaries of the most dangerous type.'[16] On December 21, Campbell-Bannerman in a major address at Albert Hall promised Labour an amendment of trade union law and a 'carefully conducted experiment to find out how best to mitigate unemployment.' It was certainly not much, but Glasier commented in a letter that 'C.B.' had 'made a good start.'[17]

The General Election began on January 12 and spread over nearly three weeks. The long-laid plans, the electoral pact, the registering, the canvassing, the speechmaking, at last were put to the test. Pamphlets and posters on Licensing, the Education Act, Free Trade, on Chinese Labour and Taff Vale, poured from Liberal and Labour committee rooms. Prominent in the campaigns of L.R.C. candidates were giant coloured posters, one of which entitled 'Guarding His Own' shows a pugnacious bulldog, the Labour party, guarding a bone marked 'Industrial Constituencies.' The most striking L.R.C. poster, 'Taff Vale Justice' depicts an ermine-coated judge handing to 'Capital' a knotted cat o'nine tails while a figure of 'Labour' stands by handcuffed with fetters marked 'Judge-made law.'

The L.R.C.'s Election Manifesto declared that the election was to decide whether or not Labour was to be fairly represented in Parliament. 'Landlords, employers, lawyers, brewers, and financiers are there in force. Why not Labour?'

## IS THERE NO NEED?

The Trade Unions ask the same liberty as capital enjoys. They are refused.

The aged poor are neglected.

The slums remain; overcrowding continues, while the land goes to waste.

Shopkeepers and traders are overburdened with rates and taxation, whilst the increasing land values, which should relieve the ratepayers, go to people who have not earned them.

Wars are fought to make the rich richer and the underfed school-children are still neglected.

Chinese labour is defended, because it enriches the mine owners.

The unemployed asked for work; the Government gave them a worthless Act; and now, when you are beginning to understand the causes of your poverty, the red herring of Protection is drawn across your path.

Protection, as experience shows, is no remedy for poverty and unemployment. It serves to keep you from dealing with the land, housing, old age, and other social problems!

There was no reference to socialism here. It was a broad and generalized appeal to the trade union vote raising only those issues on which the widest agreement seemed possible. It was less specific, in fact, than the manifesto of the Trades Union Congress which began, 'For the past ten years monopoly has been unchecked, and a Government which came into office to give old age pensions to the aged poor has impoverished the people to benefit the idle rich,' and went on to urge votes for Labour and all other candidates who supported a programme that would restore unions to their pre-Taff Vale status, extend and amend the Workmen's Compensation Act, abolish Chinese labour, and establish a state pension fund for those who were sixty or over. It further demanded extension of the Housing of the Working Classes Act, making returning officers' fees a public charge, adult suffrage, and the establishment of an eight-hour day.

The I.L.P. in its manifesto, while declaring itself socialist, and denouncing the Education Act, the capitalist press and the private liquor traffic, laid down a programme that was essentially reformist. Included were woman's suffrage and the abolishing of the House of Lords and of property qualifications for voting. Even the S.D.F., while repeating the usual formula of public ownership of the means of production laid emphasis on 'a series of palliatives of the existing capitalist anarchy.' The most important were state maintenance of children, state organization of the labour of the unemployed, and pensions, 'instead of Workhouse Pauperization,' for the aged and incapacitated.

While the election was still in progress and trade unionists everywhere were making Taff Vale the primary test in judging non-Labour candidates, the Royal Commission on Trades Disputes completed its report. 'There might be an advantage in withholding publication until the elections are over,' wrote Herbert Samuel to Gladstone. 'The report will not advocate the acceptance of all the demands of the Trade Unions and its publication would probably be the signal for questions on points of detail being put to Liberal candidates who have yet to be elected, with the result that they may pledge themselves in ways that may prove inconvenient later.'[18] Not until the second week in February was the report finally published. But whether or not it was deliberately held back, so many Liberal candidates had in fact pledged themselves to the full trade union demands that the Liberal Government when it came into office was obliged to scrap its own Trades Disputes Bill and, despite the protestations of legalists like Asquith and Haldane, accept the Labour Party's substitute granting complete legal immunity to trade unions from all civil actions arising from strikes.[19] Nothing was to testify so forcefully to Labour's new power as this early success. Even the Unionist-controlled House of Lords thought it prudent not to tamper with the measure.

As the returns poured in after January 12 it soon became clear that a great Liberal tide was sweeping all before it. No Conservative or Unionist was returned for a Welsh borough, and the situation was almost the same in Scotland. In Lancashire the Unionists lost no less than thirty-two seats while two of the fifteen who were elected were Free Fooders. Yorkshire boroughs went almost solid for free trade. Even the Home Counties gave the Liberals a majority. In practically all the largest and most populous industrial centres but not in Chamberlain's Birmingham, the Unionists went down. Balfour himself was defeated in Manchester, whilst elsewhere political nobodies were astonished to find themselves replacing well-known Unionists. Only in the Midlands was the Liberal tide checked. It was not simply a political defeat; it was a rout. Without the Irish or Labour, the Liberals numbered 377, 84 to the good over all other parties combined. The opposition was reduced to 157 including 109 Chamberlainites, 32 Balfourites, 11 Unionist Free Fooders and a few who were uncertain where they stood on protection. The Irish were the usual united 83. The real surprise of the election was the triumph of Labour. Of 50 nominees of the Labour Representation Committee, 29 were elected. Of miners and 'Lib-Labs' there were 24. No 'Lib-Lab' and no miner running outside L.R.C. auspices had been defeated. The total number of 'Labour' men in the House was thus 53.

## NOTES

1. Asquith to C.B., Oct. 22, 1905. H.G., vol. x, 117.
2. Re Irish seats in Great Britain see H.G., vol. cvxi, 151-155.
3. See the article by 'A Labour M.P.' in the *Leicester Pioneer*, Dec. 30, 1905.
4. *Barrow-in-Furness Dalton News*, Jan. 13, 1906.
5. The Irish vote was especially important in such places as Halifax, Gorton, Ince, East Leeds, Northeast and Southwest Manchester, Newcastle, Stockport, Sunderland and St. Helens.
6. J. Lawson Walton to H.G., Mar. 18, 1905. H.B., vol. lxxi, 127.
8. *The Times*, Nov. 24, 1905; J. A. Spender, *Great Britain*, 246.
9. *Daily News*, Nov. 27, 1905.
10. *Daily News*, Nov. 28, 1905.
11. H.G. to C.B., Nov. 30, 1905. H.B., vol. xii, 199-201.
12. Jesse Herbert to H.G., Nov. 27, 1905. H.G., vol. xxix, 177.
13. J. A. Spender, *Great Britain*, 245.
14. H.G. to C.B., Nov. 30, 1905. H.G., vol. xii, 201-202.
15. Spender, *Great Britain*, 248-250.
16. *L.L.*, Dec. 22, 1905.
17. *The Times*, Dec. 22, 1905; Glasier to Lizzie, Dec. 22, 1905.
18. Herbert Samuel to H.G., Jan. 18, 1906. H.G., vol. xliii, 89.
19. J. Lawson Walton, the Attorney-General in the new Government, had been opposed by a Labour candidate, Albert Fox of the Locomotive Engineers, in South Leeds. During the campaign, Fox's election agent, Alfred Mattison, had taken photographs of election posters one of which urged 'VOTE FOR WALTON AND A TRADES DISPUTES BILL.' When Walton on March 30, 1906, defended the more restrictive Government measure in the House, Hardie was able to remind him of a speech in which he had earlier favoured the trade unionists' measure and to hold up Mattison's photographs to the House to press home his point. Alfred Mattison's Diaries: Note Book 3.

# CHAPTER XV

# The L.R.C.–Liberal Electoral Pact
# in the General Election

••••••••••••••••••••••••••••••••••••••••••••••••••••••••••••••••••••••••••••••••••••••••••••••••

THE Liberal-Labour electoral pact negotiated and sealed in 1903 had been only slightly modified thereafter. Applying everywhere but in Scotland, which was outside the L.R.C.'s jurisdiction, it paid both sides handsomely in 1906 and accounted not only for Labour's impressive showing, its emergence as a major political force, but also, according to the private admissions of key Liberal leaders, for the overwhelming nature of the Liberal victory.[1] Given the nature of the pact and the by-election clashes of Liberal and Labour candidates at Norwich and North-East Lanark in 1904, a number of Liberal-Labour fights had been taken for granted. Yet of forty-two L.R.C. men fixed in England and Wales at the beginning of 1904 only eleven faced Liberals; of forty-three at the beginning of 1905, only twelve; of forty-five who entered the lists in 1906, only fifteen.[2]

This is a remarkable lack of variation in view of the long campaign, the mounting Liberal confidence and the eagerness of Liberal and Labour aspirants to rush the field. It can only be explained by the constant and, on the whole, successful efforts of L.R.C. and Liberal headquarters to keep local ambition in check and to avoid recrimination for the sake of the larger goal. A complete picture of how the pact was implemented and enforced locally in the different constituencies will never be obtained, for the pact's success, of necessity, depended largely on secrecy, but there is sufficient evidence, especially in private correspondence, to provide a fairly informative account.

### LANCASHIRE

Nowhere was the attempt to avoid Liberal-Labour rivalry more fully realized than in Lancashire where the L.R.C. made its maximum and most fruitful effort fighting for sixteen seats and losing only three. In only one of these sixteen seats did Labour encounter Liberal opposition and that seat, Eccles, was one of those lost. The other two losses were in Liverpool where so firmly established was the Tory machine that defeat appeared all but certain. Since 1886 the Tories had been predominant in both the boroughs and the county divisions of Lancashire, so that the Liberal readiness to stand aside for Labour was not unexpected. Liberal organization in some places was notoriously weak, and in 1900 out of a total of fifty-eight seats for all of Lancashire, the Liberals had won but twelve. From this glaring failure it was inevitably concluded that perhaps Labour could better woo the Lancashire working man from his loyalty to the Tories, and Shackleton's victory at Clitheroe gave support to this view. Still, once the Protection issue was raised, the Liberal position appeared anything but discouraging, for the great majority of employers and operatives in Lancashire were pronounced free traders, and by the time of the election, a thriving textile industry was offering striking rebuttal to Chamberlain's prophecy that free trade meant ruin for cotton. The more Liberal prospects improved the more difficult it became for Liberal headquarters to keep Labour's claims unchallenged. The L.R.C., on the other hand, did its best to prevent expansion beyond its initial claims. Gladstone had given assurances of thirteen of the clear runs in August 1903. Two others, in Barrow and South-West Manchester, were arranged shortly thereafter.

Some of the worst hitches in implementing the pact were encountered in the Manchester area. Aside from the seats in Manchester itself, those in the neighbouring Salford division and one in Gorton were involved. In late 1903 Gladstone could see no obstacle to the L.R.C.'s claiming Gorton, South Salford and one of the Manchester divisions, preferably the North-East. To MacDonald everything in the Manchester district appeared to be 'settling down splendidly'[3] when in December 1903, the

Liberals in Gorton prepared to bring out a candidate. At first reluctant to back such an enterprise, Gladstone finally felt obliged to promise his official support,[4] but Liberal candidates in the neighbouring constituencies, had grave misgivings: they felt that the Gorton entry by opposing Labour was risking their necks as well as his own. They therefore refused to assist him, Winston Churchill being among them, and apparently it was the prospect of being practically isolated during the campaign that in December 1905, decided the Gorton Liberal to withdraw.[5]

Overshadowed by Manchester were the three Salford seats. When, instead of adopting a man for South Salford, which had been left open in the electoral pact, the Manchester and Salford L.R.C. chose to contest Tory-held West Salford, where a Liberal was already adopted, MacDonald assured Herbert that he was mortified by the 'mistake' and would bring pressure to correct it.[6] At this juncture a prominent Liberal leader in the South protested any transfer of the Labour man to his division. All efforts at settlement appeared deadlocked[7] when the L.R.C. man in West Salford withdrew to go to North-East Manchester, the L.R.C. candidate there having retired due to illness.[8] This left no Labour candidate in any of the Salfords. Even so, the I.L.P. Executive in December 1905, strongly disapproved the suggestion of an I.L.P. branch that another man be put forward in the West,[9] and in the General Election the Liberals contested and won all three of the Salfords without Labour opposition.

The L.R.C.'s readiness not to press its claims in Salford stemmed partly from the fact that the Liberals were willing to leave two divisions open in Manchester, the North-East and the South-West, rather than only one as Gladstone had originally indicated. Acceptable to L.R.C. headquarters, this arrangement was temporarily threatened when a local I.L.P. and *Clarion* group in East Manchester decided to put someone forward, but the candidature aroused little enthusiasm,[10] was deprecated by the I.L.P. leadership[11] and soon collapsed.[12]

Further to the north, at Accrington, the L.R.C. leaders made a persistent effort to avoid opposing the Liberal. Here Thomas Greenall of the Lancashire and Cheshire Miners had been introduced. MacDonald in September 1903 suggested that he change to South Salford, but Greenall proved obstinate.[13] Some of the Accrington Liberals felt that he could do little harm anyway, since most of his miner supporters were confirmed Tories, but the Liberal candidate was not so sanguine and urged Gladstone to work through Shackleton and other Labour leaders to secure Greenall's removal.[14] Greenall found that a refusal to co-operate had certain disadvantages. It appears that Shackleton was unwilling to assist him in his campaign,[15] and until another L.R.C. man was chosen at Newton, the L.R.C. Executive did its best to get Greenall to go there. By early December 1904, the Executive felt obliged to deny reports that undue pressure had been exerted on Greenall,[16] but by the end of the same month he had, nevertheless, withdrawn,[17] and he did not run elsewhere.

There were occasions when the I.L.P. tried to dissuade Socialist candidates other than those under L.R.C. auspices from challenging Liberals. At Rochdale (Lancashire), for example, the Liberal was opposed by a Unionist and S. G. Hobson, supported by the local S.D.F. and I.L.P. Rochdale was a good prospect for the Liberals, who had lost it by only nineteen votes in 1900, and Gladstone had been unwilling to concede MacDonald's request that it be given to the L.R.C. Distrusting MacDonald and ridiculing Hardie's defence of the L.R.C. Secretary as 'the brains in the movement,' Hobson was not surprised when the I.L.P. leaders held aloof from Rochdale. 'Hardie asked me to withdraw,' he writes. 'I asked why. He thought I ought to stand for a more hopeful constituency. I smiled pleasant incredulity. He was annoyed. Bruce Glasier came at the special request of the I.L.P. National Administrative Council to ask me to withdraw. I asked why. He said the Labour Party was going to be a big thing, and they meant to be in it. I was a source of embarrassment, and of course I should not be forgotten. John Penny, the Secretary of the Party, came to ask me to withdraw. I asked why. "Because," said he, "we want Rochdale to bargain with for somewhere else".'[18]

In Barrow-in-Furness MacDonald at first worked to prevent a Labour candidature, that of Charles Duncan, but in the end it

was the Liberals who gave way. Neither Hardie[19] nor Mac-
Donald was impressed by Duncan, and MacDonald asserted
in private, according to Herbert, that Duncan was being run in
the Conservative interest and with Conservative money. The
Liberal grooming himself for Barrow, assured by MacDonald
that he would do his best to get Duncan removed, rather
stupidly told of this assurance on a public platform, and though
MacDonald disavowed it, the story so incensed the Labour
people in Barrow that MacDonald could exert little influence
there.[20] When Duncan was sponsored by the Engineers, the
L.R.C. had no alternative put to place him on its roster. Labour
had made striking gains in municipal elections in Barrow,[21]
the local Liberals found Duncan not at all inconsiderate of their
feelings, and by election time he had secured official Liberal
support.[22]

### YORKSHIRE

Many Liberals were inclined to regard Yorkshire as their
special preserve and the introduction of Labour candidates as
something akin to poaching. In 1900 twenty-five Liberals and
the miner Ben Pickard had been returned as against twenty-six
Tories, marking the first time since 1885 that the Liberals had
failed to attain a majority. Losing control in the boroughs they
still kept a respectable lead in the colliery villages and smaller
mill towns of the counties. This was especially true in the West
Riding where most of the L.R.C. men fought and where the
county divisions returned only one Conservative in 1906. Since
the Yorkshire worsted trades had been hard hit by American
and Continental tariffs, free trade was not as sacrosanct as in
Lancashire, making Labour and Liberalism far less scrupulous
about treading on each other's toes. Five of the eight L.R.C.
candidates placed in Yorkshire had to face Liberal as well as
Tory opponents, and the L.R.C. won only three seats. Two of
these, East Leeds and Halifax, a double-member constituency,
were won with Liberal support. In the other, West Bradford,
Fred Jowett, who had lost this seat by only forty-one votes in
1900, had to face both the major parties. The main threats to

the electoral pact in Yorkshire were in Bradford, Leeds and Wakefield.

In spite of the presence of Alfred Illingworth's candidate in West Bradford the I.L.P. did not retaliate by contesting other Bradford seats, for the L.R.C. plan here, as in many other places, called for focusing all available trade union and socialist strength on a single effort. Moreover, in the general agreement of 1903 Gladstone had held out no hope of a clear run in West Bradford. When in the spring of 1905 the S.D.F. brought out a candidate for the Eastern division the *Labour Leader* deplored this 'eleventh hour attempt' as subversive of L.R.C. policy and as sowing 'distrust in the good faith and motives of the [Labour] party.'[23] Particularly irritating to the I.L.P. leadership was the fact that the S.D.F. standard bearer was none other than a maverick member of their own party and its most outspoken critic of electoral arrangements with the Liberals, E. R. Hartley. The Liberal in the Eastern division won in spite of Hartley, and apparently his presence did not detract from Jowett's support. Jowett's election, perhaps the most impressive of all the L.R.C. gains, was not begrudged him even in prominent Liberal circles. 'I am not sorry for Jowett's notable Labour victory. . . .' Gladstone wrote the Prime Minister. 'He is a good man and his victory justifies our official attitude though it deals a formidable blow at Alfred Illingworthian Liberalism.'[24]

In Leeds the Liberals controlled three out of the five divisions. Herbert Gladstone represented the West, Sir Joseph Walton, the South, and the North had been captured by the Liberals as one of the first fruits of the Education Act in a by-election in 1902. Labour, if less organized than in Bradford, was making steady and impressive gains in contests for municipal office, and could hardly be denied the right to a clear run in the Eastern division.[25] A miners' representative named Parrott brought out with Liberal backing in the East in February 1903, was not satisfactory to the L.R.C. and was replaced by an L.R.C. candidate, James O'Grady of the Furniture Makers. The change was resented by the Liberals in the East, however, and by the spring of 1904 they were ready to adopt their own candidate, Sir William Butler. Liberal-Labour fights in other Leeds divisions appeared certain. Walton in the Southern division felt that the East Leeds people were not only risking leaving the Tory in possession of their own division but were imperilling him and Gladstone. As both party whip and local member, Gladstone was in a particularly touchy position, and Walton thought that if some Labour man could not be found whom the Liberals would support, Gladstone might well wash his hands of the Liberal entry in East Leeds.[26] Yet Gladstone reportedly backed Butler, once he was adopted, and the *Labour Leader* accused him of having surrendered to the pressure of the Harmsworth element which, through the *Leeds and Yorkshire Mercury*, consistently attacked Labour candidates, even Parrott.[27]

In March 1905, when a Labour Conference was called in Leeds to consider running in the South and West in retaliation for Butler's intervention, Arthur Henderson, then Chairman of the L.R.C., brought to the conference a recommendation of the National Executive that West and South Leeds should be left alone and all efforts concentrated on returning O'Grady. As in the case of Bradford this recommendation was undoubtedly based not only on a policy of concentrating effort but on the un-publicized desire not to endanger the general Liberal-Labour understanding. The local Labour people were not impressed with Henderson's arguments, 'respectfully disagreed' with the London Executive, and refused to have their hands tied.[28] In November 1905, only six weeks prior to the day of election a trade unionist, Tom Fox, was brought out in South Leeds.

Walton, who after the Labour Conference in March had regarded the danger to Gladstone and himself removed, now talked of a rising Labour tide in Leeds that would in time submerge them. 'It can scarcely be that Trades Unionists are to fight the seats held by Liberals who have all their lives advocated their cause,' he wrote Gladstone. 'Otherwise some change of policy should be adopted throughout the country in dealing with the constituencies where the Liberals have given their men a run.' Could some influential Liberal work against the candidature through Fox's union? he wondered; otherwise, would it not be well to threaten the I.L.P. with reprisals in seats such as Barrow?[29] The I.L.P. leaders were also disturbed by

Fox's candidature. 'Leeds men seem to have got the bit between their teeth and to be off helter-skelter,' Hardie told Glasier. 'But for James O'Grady in East Leeds whose chances are imperilled I would wish them luck.'[30] Eventually O'Grady did gain his clear run, for Butler withdrew, and despite a widespread feeling among Liberals that O'Grady must be opposed, if only to keep Labour preoccupied and so weaken their menace in the South and West,[31] no one was adopted in Butler's place. The L.R.C. in London wanted no further trouble. When on December 14 the L.R.C. Executive endorsed Fox for the Southern division, it passed a resolution declining to sanction any further candidates for Leeds.[32]

One of the Yorkshire seats that MacDonald was positive the L.R.C. would contest when he gave his first lists to Herbert, was Wakefield which Snowden had fought in the by-election of 1902. Impatient with the procrastination of the local Labour organizations in finding a candidate, MacDonald warned them that if the Liberals acted the Labour people would have themselves to blame, and at the beginning of September 1903, he told Herbert that the Liberals would be justified in going ahead.[33] But hardly had he done so when Wakefield trade unionists and socialists finally acted and chose Dr. Stanton Coit, a member of the I.L.P.[34] Coit was left unchallenged until August 1905, when the local Liberals decided to run Alderman Snape, whose candidature Will Crooks deplored as a 'crime.'[35] Though Snape ignored the pleas of the Liberal Chief Whip's office to step down, he did offer to go to East Leeds to oppose O'Grady. The offer was greeted with derision, 'He [Snape] wants East Leeds,' Herbert wrote Gladstone, 'and sets up his own impudent interference at Wakefield as a reason for being given East Leeds. He talks of "the difficulty at Wakefield." *He* is the only difficulty. The Labour people fought Wakefield at the Bye in 1902 since when it has been understood they should have a fair and undisputed field at the next General. Their candidate Dr. Stanton Coit is a very able and reputable man. Snape has thrust himself into the field there. As the Tory polls more than half the available Register the chances for Snape are ridiculous. He has no claim to ask for consideration because of any difficulty at Wakefield—unless it be granted that a man may use his own wrong-doing as a reason for a favour.'[36]

A local Liberal newspaper, the *Wakefield Express*, was virulent in its attacks on Coit and the I.L.P. Then when Snape was given the boycott treatment by neighbouring Liberal candidates and party officials, a treatment that had forced the Liberal in Gorton, Lancashire, to withdraw, the *Express* turned its ire on Gladstone whom it claimed had some compact with the Labour party of which the Wakefield Liberal Association was ignorant.[37] For Snape's poor showing in the election, behind Coit and the Tory victor, the *Express* held the Chief Whip responsible. He had prevented the local Liberals from opposing Snowden in 1902, it said, had shortly thereafter 'filched' away to another contituency a prospective Liberal candidate and had then secured the isolation of the man finally chosen and so destroyed the party's chances.[38]

### THE NORTH-EAST

In Northumberland and Durham the election of miners' M.P.s like Burt, Fenwick and John Wilson had resulted less from Liberal abnegation than from the ability of the miners to swamp certain constituencies. A narrow Liberal caucus spirit was prevalent in the region and was typified by Sam Storey, the prime mover in opposing Henderson in the Barnard Castle by-election. For a time Storey was Chairman of the Northumberland and Durham Liberal Federation, but in late 1903 he resigned this post and declared himself a protectionist.[39] His attitude towards Labour candidates was shared by the President of the Northern Liberal Federation, Sir Charles Furness, a manufacturer and shipowner whom Hardie dubbed 'the Pierpont Morgan of England,'[40] and in the spring of 1903 Furness was publicly expressing impatience with Liberal failure to place candidates in constituencies where Labour was making its bid.[41] Durham Liberals were particularly unyielding, feeling secure in their majority, especially in the counties, but Henderson's victory at Barnard Castle was a warning against the policy of no concession, and the Durham Miners, by

R

returning Johnson for Gateshead in 1904, were demonstrating a growing determination to be represented by their own kind. The L.R.C. fought six seats in Northumberland and Durham and lost three. The three successes, all with Liberal support, were at Barnard Castle, where Henderson was again returned, and at Newcastle and Sunderland, both two-member constituencies. Perhaps also to be classified as an L.R.C. victory was the election of the miners' candidate, J. W. Taylor, at Chester-le-Street, for Taylor joined the L.R.C. immediately after his election. The Durham Miners, out of deference to the Liberal member, Sir James Joicey, one of the biggest mine owners in the North, had refrained from nominating anyone in this constituency, but when Joicey was elevated to the peerage the miners decided to place Taylor in the vacancy.[42] When Taylor had to face a rapidly chosen Liberal replacement as well as a Unionist, the miners were quite naturally resentful, but the Liberals were not united in opposing Taylor, one Liberal paper, the *Northern Echo* supported him all the way, and he secured a comfortable majority.

The three L.R.C. defeats in the North-East were at Darlington, Stockton and Jarrow. After Isaac Mitchell, one of the five candidates of the Engineers, had been chosen as L.R.C. candidate for Darlington in April 1903, Liberal headquarters saw virtually no hope of securing him a clear run, but in December 1903, the local Liberal Executive in Darlington, claiming to have failed in its efforts to find a candidate, urged local Liberals to throw their support to Mitchell.[43] That the town was favourably disposed toward Labour seemed to be indicated by the election of Henderson as Mayor of Darlington in 1903, but the Unionist, nevertheless, retained his seat, though only by 488 votes. Gladstone also saw serious obstacles in 1903 to any L.R.C. claimant in Stockton which MacDonald in February of that year listed as 'under consideration' by the Committee. In April, however, Frank Rose of the Engineers was placed in Stockton, and McKinnon Wood, the Liberal being groomed for the seat, was reluctant to go forward in these circumstances. In May he sought MacDonald's aid in securing some settlement, but MacDonald said he could do little and that what was needed was pressure on Rose from the Engineers.[44] Wood then sought John Burns' assistance, to influence the Engineers' Executive, but Burns could do nothing,[45] and in June McKinnon Wood withdrew to stand for a Glasgow constituency.[46] The Liberals then chose a Mr. Ferdinand Mendl who, according to MacDonald's report to Liberal headquarters, could never command the support of the local Labour people.[47] In the resulting three-cornered contest Rose came in at the foot of the poll but took enough votes from the Liberal to insure a Conservative victory.

At Jarrow, where Gladstone in 1903 saw no hope of an arrangement, Pete Curran of the Gasworkers and the I.L.P. engaged in the only straight fight between a Liberal and an L.R.C. nominee. Curran's prospects were not encouraging. The Liberal member, Sir Charles Palmer, had represented Jarrow since 1885 without opposition and as head of the Palmer Shipbuilding Co., he was regarded as a good employer and, now in his eighties, was widely venerated.[48] It was virtually impossible for Curran to put any sting into his campaign by attacking his opponent who privately confided to the Prime Minister that he was only sacrificing retirement in order that there would not be a three-cornered fight that would give the Socialist Curran a chance of success.[49] Sir Charles retained his seat by over 2,900 votes.

## THE MIDLANDS AND THE SOUTH OF ENGLAND

In the Midlands there were two L.R.C. successes and two defeats. All were clear runs as set down in the 1903 agreement. At two-member Leicester MacDonald and the 'Lib-Lab' Broadhurst split their votes and trounced the Tories.[50] At Grimsby, Lincolnshire, which the Liberals had failed to contest in 1900, the L.R.C. introduced Tom Proctor of the Engineers, after MacDonald had informed Herbert that the local working people could not support the Liberal candidate Haldinstein, 'a Jew and a Liberal Leaguer.' Haldinstein thought seriously of withdrawing and said he considered it a waste of money to go on, but Jesse Herbert urged him not to panic.[51] In the resulting three-cornered fight the Unionist won with a larger vote than that of the two other contestants combined, with Proctor coming in last.

In the Home Counties, Norfolk and Greater London put together there were only eight L.R.C. candidates, five of whom were returned. Only one of the winners, but all three of the losers, had to face both the major parties. Labour had made small progress in propaganda and organization in this area except in parts of London, while the Liberals had won only five of seventy-three Home Counties seats in 1900 and in London had fared hardly better. In Deptford, London, the L.R.C. candidate Clery, who in 1902 had accepted adoption by the local Liberal Association, was shunted by the L.R.C. leadership in favour of C. W. Bowerman of the London Society of Compositors.[52] When the local Liberals nominated one Herbert Vivian to oppose Bowerman, neither the Chief Whip's office nor the London Liberal Federation gave Vivian its blessing, 'Lib-Labs' including Burns condemned his intrusion,[53] and he received the embarrassingly low poll of 726 while Bowerman achieved a substantial lead over the Tory.

The L.R.C. defeats in the South of England were in Gravesend (Kent), Croydon (Surrey), and Portsmouth (Hampshire). Though none of these seats was covered by the 1903 agreement, the Liberal opposition in all three was almost exclusively local in origin. The officials of the Home Counties Liberal Federation deplored triangular contests as virtually hopeless, not dreaming that this land of Toryism could go Liberal. Earl Carrington, Chairman of the Federation, was friendly toward Labour's claims,[54] and W. M. Crook, its Secretary, was inclined to favour Liberal forbearance wherever such claims were strong and persistent. Crook regarded many of the Liberal associations in Kent as money grabbers pursuing politics as a profitable source of income.[55] Gravesend he considered hopelessly corrupt, and when early in 1905 unfavourable publicity forced the Liberal candidate's withdrawal, Crook suggested that a good Labour man backed by Burns and Will Crooks would have a much better chance of beating the Unionist than would any Liberal.[56] Just before the General Election, however, local Liberals hurried a candidate into the contest against the L.R.C.'s choice, James Macpherson of the Shop Assistants. Little spade-work had been done by Labour in Gravesend: there was no I.L.P. branch, and although there were many riverside and cement workers, trade union organization was relatively weak.[57] The Unionist won by a large majority while Macpherson received only 873 votes, the lowest of any L.R.C. nominee. A Conservative also kept Croydon where in 1900 no Liberal had run, and although Lulu Harcourt early in 1904 thought that the Liberals had best leave Croydon alone,[58] this was a seat that the Liberals would undoubtedly have won had there been no L.R.C. candidate.[59] The Liberal finished only 638 votes behind the Conservative while the L.R.C. man polled 4,007. At Portsmouth, a double-member constituency in Unionist hands, Crook was desirous of giving one seat to Labour, and in late 1903 there was a Liberal plan afoot to place W. C. Steadman of the Barge-builders in Portsmouth.[60] Since Steadman would not run as an Independent, however, the local L.R.C. group opposed him, and William Sanders of the I.L.P. and the London County Council was selected. When it appeared that the local people would put two Liberals forward, Crook in November 1904 wondered if Sanders might not be allowed a clear field at Walthamstow where another Liberal-Labour split was impending and feared that otherwise both the Portsmouth seats would be lost.[61] In Walthamstow the Labour aspirant withdrew giving the Liberals a clear run, but in Portsmouth while Sanders polled better than either of the Unionists both Liberals kept the field and both were victorious.

## WALES

Wales was a Liberal stronghold, and late in 1903 when the L.R.C. was considering placing at least two men in Glamorganshire and one in Swansea, Gladstone had seen obstacles to all of these proposed candidatures. Though a local I.L.P. branch helped secure adoption of J. Littlejohns at Swansea, he would have had to face a Liberal Radical, and he was dropped after Hardie expressed concern lest the effort end in fiasco[62] and

Glasier warned the Swansea group that a small vote for an I.L.P. man in South Wales would be disastrous.[63] As a result of Liberal unwilligness to surrender hopeful Welsh seats only two L.R.C. men ran in Wales, Hardie to keep his seat in the double-member constituency of Merthyr, James Winstone of the South Wales Miners in a bid for Monmouth Boroughs. Both were three-way fights. Winstone polled below the Unionist and the Liberal victor. At Merthyr a clear run for Hardie seemed assured until a second Liberal, a Cardiff shipowner, entered the field on the very eve of the election.[64] His action was not to the liking of D. A. Thomas, Hardie's partner in victory in 1900 nor, according to Thomas, was the late entry approved by the Liberal Chief Whip.[65] With the Liberals divided, the South Wales miners voting for Hardie, and no Unionist in the running, Hardie won the second seat, 3,700 votes behind Thomas but over 2,400 votes ahead of the Liberal intruder.

In all of England and Wales all but three of the L.R.C. victors had had clear fields against the Unionist, and only in a single instance was a seat fought by the L.R.C. and set down as clear in 1903 challenged by a Liberal. This was at Deptford, London, where the Liberal, as has been noted, was denied official blessing, polled miserably and did not prevent the L.R.C. man from winning. There were thirty clear runs in all, twenty-five of which had been listed by Gladstone in the initial agreement. In two the difficulty anticipated by Gladstone in 1903 had been removed.[66] In three, L.R.C. men were fixed and had clear runs obtained after the initial agreement.[67] As regards seats where the Liberals in 1903 were willing to stand aside but which the L.R.C. failed to contest, in two, Whitehaven and East Worcestershire, the L.R.C. appears to have abandoned interest. In three, the candidates were 'Lib-Labs' removed from the L.R.C. lists for their failure to sign the Newcastle constitution— Richard Bell at Derby, John Ward at Stoke-on-Trent, and W. C. Steadman at Central Finsbury. In one, Oldham, the L.R.C. candidate at the last minute proved unwilling to go forward.[68] In one, South Salford, the L.R.C. was compensated for its withdrawal with an additional clear run in nearby Manchester.

Nine of the L.R.C. clear runs were in double-member constituencies where Liberal and Labour forces, in all but three cases, pretty evenly split their votes. In Preston and Blackburn, both in Lancashire, there were many 'plumpers' for the L.R.C. candidate, indicating converts from Toryism willing to vote Labour but not Liberal.[69] York, on the other hand, was the only two-member seat covered by the electoral pact where a large number of Liberals failed to give their second vote to Labour but instead plumped for the Liberal. The L.R.C. candidate, G. H. Stuart of the Postmen's Union, maintained a more independent attitude and was not as solicitous of Liberal support as L.R.C. candidates elsewhere. This partly accounts for his defeat. He himself placed part of the blame on Will Crooks who openly urged Labour in York to give its second vote to the Liberal, thus making Stuart's independent stand seem like mere intransigence.[70]

In view of the landslide nature of the Liberal victory it might be suggested that the Liberals had been mistaken in yielding so many seats to the L.R.C., that they had overestimated the damage an unfriendly L.R.C. could do them. But the agreement with Labour, as Gladstone himself noted, was one of the major explanations of the landslide, producing a 'solidarity of voting especially in the big towns' that the Liberals had 'scarcely dared hope for.'[71] Jesse Herbert was elated by the pact's effectiveness. The results, he said, were 'astoundingly good' and to be found 'in the figures of every Liberal candidate because of the friendliness of the Labour leaders.' Summing up the results of the agreement, he wrote to Gladstone:

'All the L.R.C. men and all the other Labour men we supported won except in Birmingham, Darlington, Liverpool and York and the only one to be regretted is Darlington, for Mitchell is a good man.

The only seats won by the L.R.C. men where a Liberal also stood were seats to which Labour was entitled, viz., W. Bradford, Deptford and Merthyr.

The only seats which ought to have been won by a Lib.

but were lost because of the presence of an L.R.C. man were Croydon and Stockton.

An L.R.C. man would have won Wakefield had not a Liberal stood.

The only Liberal seat won by Labour not L.R.C. was won by a miners' candidate at Chester-le-Street, and properly so won. . . .

The sum of the matter is that in England and Wales, Liberals and Labour hold 367 seats, i.e. a majority of 239, and there are only two cases in which we have any just ground of complaint against the Labour people, and one case in which they have just ground of complaint against us.

Was there ever such a justification of a policy by results?'[72]

## NOTES

1. See footnote 71.
2. *L.R.C. Ann.*, 1904, 19; *L.R.C. Ann.*, 1905, 26
3. As 'Spectator' in the *Echo*, Dec. 2, 1903.
4. Charles Hatch, the candidate, to H.G., Nov. 19 and 23, 1905. H.G. vol. lxxii, 112 and 118.
5. Hatch to H.G., Nov. 27, 1905; Hatch to Alderman W. H. Wainwright, Dec. 1, 1905. H.G., lxxii, 122 and 139.
6. Herbert Memorandum of interview with MacDonald on Sept. 6, 1903. H.G., vol. cxvi. Glasier had refused to let his name be put forward in the Western Division in view of Liberal readiness to leave the Southern division vacant. Glasier to Hardie, Aug. 8, 1903.
7. Jesse Herbert to H.G., Sept. 18 and Oct. 5, 1903. H.G., vol. xxviii, 12; vol. xxix, 175.
8. *Clarion*, Oct. 23, 1903.
9. N.A.C. Minutes, Dec. 18, 1905.
10. See John Penny's article on Manchester Labour prospects, *Clarion*, Sept. 11, 1903.
11. Wrote Hardie to Glasier on Nov. 29, 1905: 'I think if we take a firm stand . . . and not only issue a sort of mandamus to the branches but also communicate with the *Clarion* people, we can stop the threatened folly in East Manchester.' The Local L.R.C. did not support the East Manchester entry, and on December 2 the I.L.P. Executive voted to notify the I.L.P. branches concerned that they were 'honour bound to work in harmony with the local Labour Representation Committee.' N.A.C. Minutes, Dec. 2, 1905.
12. According to the *Daily News* of Mar. 14, 1904, there was at one time a compromise plan to remove the Labour candidate from East Manchester in return for the withdrawal of the Liberal at Gorton.
13. Herbert Memorandum of interview with MacDonald on Sept. 6, 1903. H.G., vol. cxvi.

14. J. F. Leese to H.G., Sept. 21, 1904. H.G., vol. lxx, 115.
15. *M.G.*, Jan. 14, 1904.
16. L.R.C. Minutes, Dec. 2, 1904.
17. *Reynolds's*, Jan. 1, 1905.
18. S. G. Hobson, *Pilgrim to the Left*, 111. Hobson claims to have planned for other joint efforts of I.L.P. and S.D.F. branches but to have been thwarted by the I.L.P. leaders. There would have been at least six such candidates, he asserts, out of which the nucleus of a truly Socialist party might have been formed. *ibid.*, 112.
19. 'Charles Duncan was here for over an hour. He was very disappointing.' Hardie to Glasier, Aug. 1, 1903.
20. Herbert Memorandum of interview with MacDonald on Sept. 6, 1903. H.G., vol. cxvi.
21. In 1904 it returned all of the six Labour nominees for the Board of Guardians. *North Western Daily Mail*. Barrow, Mar. 30, 1904.
22. *North Western Daily Mail*, Dec. 30, 1905. When asked by a heckler if he was a socialist, Duncan answered that Haldane and John Burns were socialists and that he was a socialist just the same as John Burns and in no different sense of the word. *Barrow-in-Furness Dalton News*, Jan. 10, 1906. Asked if he would vote on the Liberal, or Conservative side of the House, he answered, 'On the Liberal, of course.' *North Western Daily Mail*, Jan. 3, 1906.
23. *L.L.*, Mar. 10, 1905.
24. H.G. to C.B., Jan. 14, 1906. C.B., vol. xii, 291-292.
25. The Liberal M.P. in neighbouring Colne Valley whose own seat offered a tempting Labour prospect thought that Labour was perhaps entitled to two seats in Leeds. James Kitson to H.G., Feb. 28, 1904. H.G., vol. ii, 16.
26. J. Lawson Walton to H.G., Dec. 12, 1904. H.G., vol. lxx, 178.
27. *L.L.*, April 14, 1905.
28. L.R.C. Minutes, Feb. 15, 1905; Walton to H.G., Mar. 18, 1905. H.G., vol. lxxi, 127.
29. Walton to H.G., Nov. 5 and 28, 1905. H.G., vol. lxvii, 92 and 127.
30. Hardie to Glasier, Nov. 29, 1905.
31. James Kitson to H.G., Dec. 7, 1905. H.G., vol. ii, 122.
32. L.R.C. Minutes, Dec. 14, 1905.
33. Herbert Memorandum of interview with MacDonald on Sept. 6, 1903. H.G., vol. cxvi.
34. Jesse Herbert to H.G., Sept. 8, 1903. H.G., vol. xxviii, 163.
35. *Daily News*, Aug. 28, 1905.
36. Jesse Herbert to H.G., Sept. 5, 1905. H.G., vol. xxix, 112.
37. *Wakefield Express*, Jan. 6, 1906.
38. *ibid.*, Jan. 20, 1906.
39. According to Penny in the *Clarion*, Nov. 6, 1903.
40. In the *L.L.*, April 25, 1903.
41. Address to the Council of the Northern Liberal Federation, April 18, as reported in the *Newcastle Daily Chronicle* of April 20, 1903.
42. *Man. Guardian*, Jan. 10, 1906
43. *Newcastle Daily Chronicle*, Dec. 11, 1903.
44. McKinnon Wood to H.G., May 22, 1903. H.G., vol. lxviii, 31.
45. Noting that there appeared to be friction between Rose and the Engineers' Executive, Glasier wrote to Hardie on April 26, 1903: 'Should the E⎡xecu-

tive] C[ouncil] refuse to endorse his [Rose's] candidature he will probably pursue it in defiance of them if he thinks the local societies will stand by him, or he may throw it up and accuse the E.C. of malice or of pursuing some game. The Liberals are in a great state of anxiety over the situation and may perhaps be using their influence at headquarters to prevent Rose from being officially endorsed. For us it would be great business were he—as a Trade Unionist—to fight the Liberal and Tory: on the other hand it would be unfortunate were we placed in the position of having to fight after Rose had thrown the battle up.' Hardie saw Barnes, General Secretary of the Engineers, and pressed upon him not in anyway to discourage Rose's candidature. Hardie to Glasier, April 28, 1903.

46. *Reynolds's*, June 21, 1903.
47. Herbert Memorandum, undated. H.G., vol. cxvi, 36-39.
48. See Penny in the *Clarion*, Nov. 20, 1903.
49. Sir Charles Palmer to C.B., Dec. 21, 1905. C.B., vol. xxxiii, 255.
50. In Sept. 1903, Herbert had written to Gladstone, 'Now that he [MacDonald] has a clear field at Leicester, he ought to do his utmost to do what we ask for.' Jesse Herbert to H.G., Sept. 3, 1903, H.G., vol. xxviii, 157.
51. Herbert Memorandum of interview with MacDonald on Sept. 6, 1903. H.G., vol. cxvi.
52. According to MacDonald. Herbert Memorandum, undated, H.B., cxvi, 36-39.
53. Vivian complained to Winston Churchill, one of the few prominent Liberals to support him, that the London Liberal Federation was encouraging Bowerman and that no London M.P.s were supporting Vivian and asked that Gladstone secure some Liberal M.P.s for him in order to refute the rumour that official Liberalism was against him. Extract from Vivian's letter to Churchill in Churchill to H.G., Nov. 25, 1904, H.G., vol. lxx, 159-161. Bowerman was able to show placards and distribute handbills containing a signed statement of well-known Liberals and Nonconformist ministers in favour of Vivian's withdrawal. *The Times*, July 8, 1906.
54. See comment on Lord Carrington's speech on Liberal-Labour relations in the *L.L.*, Mar. 7, 1903.
55. W. M. Crook to H.G., Nov. 30, 1905. H.G., vol. xix, 224.
56. Crook to H.G., Mar. 21, 1905. H.G., vol. xix, 178.
57. *L.L.*, Feb. 2, 1906.
58. Lulu Harcourt to H.G., Feb. 5, 1904. H.G., vol. xxii, 53.
59. Burns in his public appeal for Vivian's withdrawal at Deptford had said that it might result in Labour's withdrawal at Croydon where the Liberal 'had the best and the only chance of winning.' *Reynolds's*, Jan. 14, 1906. MacDonald at first thought the L.R.C. not at all keen about Croydon. According to Herbert Memorandum undated, H.G., vol. cxvi, 36-39.
60. Crook to H.G., Oct. 8, 1903. H.G., vol. xix, 37-38.
61. Crook to H.G., Nov. 15, 1904. H.G., vol. xix, 167-168.
62. Hardie to Glasier, July 10, 1903.
63. Glasier to Hardie, Aug. 2, 1903.
64. *The Times*, Jan. 11, 1906.
65. Interview with Thomas, *Man. Guardian*, Jan. 2, 1906.
66. Darlington and South West Manchester.
67. Barrow, East Leeds and Chatham.

68. He was Thomas Ashton, President of the Oldham Spinners Association, *L.L.*, Nov. 3, 1905. His society was very slow in seeking a replacement, and eventually the Liberals decided to place a man in the vacancy, much to the annoyance of Philip Snowden. Snowden in *The Leicester Pioneer*, Nov. 18, 1905.
69. J. T. MacPherson of the Steelsmelters in Preston had 1600 more votes than his Liberal partner in victory. Snowden in Blackburn, only slightly behind the other winner, a Conservative, had 1500 plumpers.
70. G. H. Stuart in *The Postman's Gazette*, Feb. 3, 1906. The L.R.C. Executive regretted Crooks' action and expressed the opinion 'that no representative of the L.R.C. should interfere in a constituency where a Labour candidate is running without first communicating with the Labour candidate.' L.R.C. Minutes, Feb. 14, 1906. A postman had no large body of fellow trade unionists to back him nor was Stuart a public figure who could rally support of varied elements in a composite constituency such as York.
71. H.G. to C.B., Jan. 21, 1906. C.B., vol. xii, 294-295. In a typewritten memorandum, undated, Gladstone writes that in preparation for the General Election of 1906 Liberal organization 'apart from routine was specially concerned with ed[ucation], free trade, finance and with the successful working out of an understanding with the Labour party. To this last was due the abnormality of the Liberal victory.' H.G., vol. xxxiv, 162.
72. Jesse Herbert to H.G., Feb. 16, 1906. H.G., vol. xxix, 182-183.

# CHAPTER XVI

# The Advent of the Labour Party

IT is no use disguising from ourselves that the election has been an enormous victory for Liberalism, and that the Socialists have done all they could to make it so. On the war question, on the Education question, on the Free Trade question, they rushed to the heels of Mr. Lloyd George and shouted for Peace, Retrenchment, Reform, Passive Resistance, and the great historic delusion of the Big Loaf-versus-the Little Loaf louder than all the Radicals. . . . They made Socialist and Independent Labour candidates more dependent on Liberal votes than ever. . . . They have no guarantee whatever that the new Labour Party will be anything more than a nominally Independent Trade Unionist and Radical group.

So wrote George Bernard Shaw in the *Clarion* on the morrow of the election,[1] when he, and it seemed everyone else, was rushing into print to explain the significance of Labour's triumph.

Adopting the name 'The Labour Party' and dropping the old title of Labour Representation Committee, the twenty-nine L.R.C. victors took their seats on the opposition side of the House. Symbolically this asserted their independence, but, in any case, there would have been no room on the Liberal side, which was filled to overflowing. Entirely occupying the two benches below the gangway to the left of the Speaker, the Labour men in Parliament bulked in the eye out of all proportion to their real numbers. If seniority and reward for the long fight meant anything, Hardie was the most likely choice as chairman, but Glasier urged Hardie to refuse the post even if it were offered to him with enthusiasm and unanimity. 'It is much more important—much more important indeed to our side of the movement,' he wrote, 'that you should be *free to lead the Socialist policy*, than that you should be stuck in the official Chairmanship where you would be bound for unity and decorum's sake to adopt a personal attitude acceptable to the moderates. . . . If you and our men can lead the Socialist line, then in a few years the party will be a Socialist party and your Chairmanship be not only a fact but a national achievement. In this Parliament we who are not in it depend upon you. You must stand by us. . . .'[2]

Hardie, despite Glasier's exhortation, accepted the chairmanship, though he was by no means a unanimous choice. Almost equally divided between socialists and radical trade unionists, the party voted Hardie into the leadership by only one vote over Shackleton, who became deputy-chairman. Henderson and MacDonald, who remained secretary, were chosen as whips.[3] The twenty-four 'Lib-Labs' who had been returned, most of them miners, decided to form a separate 'Trade Union Labour Group.' Ready to act with the Independents on Labour questions, this group disappeared after 1909 when the miners finally decided to affiliate with the Labour Party.

With the Irish Home Rule issue having worn thin, many Unionists were all too ready in 1906 to raise the bogey of Socialism. As the Liberal London *Tribune* put it, for 'the vision of Mr. Redmond leading the Irish members to College Green' could now be substituted 'the picture of Keir Hardie erecting a guillotine in Palace Yard.'[4] Though a reading of the speeches of the Labour M.P.s and the slightest familiarity with their careers revealed the ridiculousness of presenting them as a rapacious and reckless element, many Englishmen were almost entirely ignorant of the viewpoints and backgrounds of the newcomers; they had sprung as if from nowhere, and it would require some time to take their full measure. To Balfour the advent of the Labour Party meant much more than the ordinary political change; rather it constituted 'a faint echo of the same movement which had produced massacre at St. Petersburg, riots in London, and Socialist processions in Berlin.'[5] It meant, he thought, the eventual break-up of the Liberal party.[6]

The Liberal press and the Liberal leaders tried to be reassuring and ridiculed such dark predictions. 'If these good people knew how much more serious a respect for property and society is to be learnt in the offices of a great trade union than in the fifth form of a public school and at a second-rate Oxford College,' commented the *Manchester Guardian,* 'they would not vex their hearts with these dim fancies.'[7] According to Campbell-Bannerman the Labour members would add ability, intelligence and efficiency to the House.[8] While insisting on change, they would know what was 'reasonable and practicable,'[9] argued Grey. Morley spoke more candidly than his colleagues; there would be some things Labour would ask for that he would do his best to prevent them from having.[10] Meanwhile, however, he was writing to his friend Lord Minto, the Viceroy in India, 'There will be some wild-cat talk, but I represented workmen in Newcastle for a dozen years, and I always felt that the British workmen are essentially bourgeois, without a bit of the French Red and the Phrygian cap about them.'[11] Of all the Cabinet spokesmen, Lloyd George seemed the least cautious. Labour would help force the pace in Parliament, he said. Without overthrowing order, without doing injustice to anybody, there was to be 'a quiet but a certain revolution.'[12]

In the new Parliament, as MacDonald had foreseen, those Labour M.P.s who had benefited from the electoral pact were ready to work in close harness with their Liberal partners in victory. Gladstone felt certain that the awareness of the part that Liberal votes had played in their election would have a 'steadying influence' upon the Labour members, that they would be a 'good element.'[13] Herbert observed that the policy of Liberal headquarters had made them 'strongly favourable to the Government.' 'There are not more than seven irreconcilables,' he noted, 'Even they are friendly to me. There is no reason to anticipate any change in their attitude if the same policy is continued, but will it be?'[14]

\* \* \*

Though often severely tested and the subject of mounting criticism in both parties, this electoral collaboration was to continue until World War I. Partly out of fear lest the Conservatives reap an advantage, Liberals and Labourites remained anxious to avoid broad challenges to one another at the polls and were drawn together in matters of programme and policy in the Commons. Their mutual dependence facilitated the passage of far-reaching social reform measures prior to 1914, many of which were introduced by the Liberal ministry under Labour prodding. The formation of a single Progressive party composed of former Liberals and Labourites was a distinct possibility so long as this collaboration was maintained. Its electoral basis, however, remained extremely precarious. The 1903 type of agreement, while it held for eleven years,[15] was based mainly on clandestine negotiations between the party managers. At no time was it an open agreement formally binding on the rank and file. That it proved so effective in spite of this would indicate that Liberal headquarters and key men like MacDonald in the Labour party machine exercised a much greater influence and discipline over the constituency bodies than has commonly been supposed.

During the war, such agreement was precluded by an electoral truce affecting all parties. After the war, Liberal divisions and Lloyd George's enthusiasm for a Conservative-Liberal coalition made any revival of Liberal-Labour cooperation along the old lines patently impossible. In seeking explanations for the Labour party's espousal in 1918 of a clearly socialist programme, serious weight must be given to the fact that the electoral considerations which earlier had encouraged Labour to adjust its tactics and policy to the maintenance of the Liberal connection no longer applied. On the contrary, it had become electorally advantageous for Labour to sharply distinguish itself from official Liberalism. By adopting a socialist basis in 1918 and reorganizing itself nationally for possible contests in every constituency, Labour was asserting a more genuine independence, a determination henceforth to challenge both Liberals and Conservatives alike.

# The Advent of the Labour Party

## NOTES

1. On Feb. 2, 1906.
2. Glasier to Hardie, Feb. 11, 1906.
3. *Reynolds's*, Feb. 18, 1906; Labouchere had written to Dilke on Jan. 14, 1906, 'I should think that the Labour M.P.s would if numerous form a party with whips—Keir Hardie they all personally detest. But then they are all jealous of each other.' Dilke Papers, vol. xxxii, 138.
4. *Tribune*, Jan. 26, 1906.
5. Balfour to Viscount Esher, Jan. 17, 1906: *Journals and Letters of Reginald, Viscount Esher*, ed. Maurice Brett, London, 1934, 2 vols., vol. ii, 136; Blanche Dugdale, *Arthur James Balfour*, New York, 1937, 2 vols., vol. i, 135.
6. Balfour to Austen Chamberlain, Jan. 17, 1906, Sir Charles Petrie, *Life and Letters of Austen Chamberlain*, London, 1939, 2 vols., vol. i, 176.
7. *Man. Guardian*, Jan. 19, 1906.
8. Speech at Inverness on Jan. 18, *The Times*, Jan. 19, 1906.
9. Speech at Berwick-on-Tweed on Jan. 19, *The Times*, Jan. 20, 1906.
10. Speech at Montrose on Jan. 17, *The Times*, Jan. 18, 1906.
11. John Morley, *Recollections*, New York, 1917, 2 vols., vol. ii, 157.
12. *Clarion*, Jan. 26, 1906.
13. H.G. to C.B., Jan. 21, 1906. C.B., vol. xii, 294-295.
14. Jesse Herbert to H.G., Feb. 16, 1906, H.G., vol. xxix, 182-183.
15. See Herbert Gladstone, *After Thirty Years*, London, 1928, 378.

The *Liberal–Labour Electoral Pact of 1903 as it related to the L.R.C. wins in 1906*

(Seats where there was Liberal opposition are underlined)
* Two-member seats

| | No difficulty anticipated | Some difficulty anticipated | Serious difficulty anticipated | Clear runs obtained after 1903 or not mentioned in 1903 |
|---|---|---|---|---|
| Lancashire: | Blackburn* | Manchester, Southwest | | Barrow-in-Furness |
| | Bolton* | | | |
| | Clitheroe | | | |
| | Gorton | | | |
| | Ince | | | |
| | Manchester, North East | | | |
| | Newton | | | |
| | Preston* | | | |
| | St. Helens | | | |
| | Stockport* | | | |
| | Westhoughton | | | |
| Yorkshire: | Halifax* | | Bradford, West | Leeds, East |
| Northumberland: | Newcastle* | | | |
| Durham: | Barnard Castle | | | |
| | Sunderland* | | | |
| Staffordshire: | Wolverhampton, West | | | |
| Leicestershire: | Leicester* | | | |
| London: | Deptford | | | |
| | Woolwich | | | |
| Essex: | South West Ham | | | |
| Norfolk: | Norwich* | | | |
| Kent: | Chatham (spoken of as possible L.R.C. seat in 1903 but no candidate then fixed) | | | |
| Wales: | | | | Merthyr |

S

## The Liberal-Labour Electoral Pact of 1903 as it related to the L.R.C. losses in 1906

(Seats where there was Liberal opposition are underlined)
* Two-member seats

| | No difficulty anticipated | Some difficulty anticipated | Serious difficulty anticipated | Spoken of as possible L.R.C. seats but no candidate fixed in 1903 | Seats not mentioned 1903 |
|---|---|---|---|---|---|
| Lancashire: | Liverpool (Kirkdale) Liverpool (West Toxteth) | | | Eccles | |
| Yorkshire: | York* | | | Leeds, South Wakefield | Dewsbury Huddersfield |
| Durham: | | Jarrow | Darlington Stockton | | |
| Lincolnshire: | | | | | Grimsby |
| Warwickshire: | Birmingham (Bordesley) Birmingham (East) | | | | |
| Surrey: | | | | | Croydon |
| Kent: | | | | | Gravesend |
| Hampshire: | | | Portsmouth* | | |
| Wales: | | | | | Monmouth |

BIBLIOGRAPHY

## I. *Primary Sources*

A. Official Documents:
  1. Parliamentary Debates, 4th series, House of Commons.
  2. Annual Reports of the Labour Representation Committee, the Independent Labour Party, the Social Democratic Federation, the Fabian Society, the Trades Union Congress and the National Liberal Federation.
  3. Minutes of the Executive of the Labour Representation Committee, the National Administrative Council of the Independent Labour Party, the Executive of the Fabian Society, and the Executive of the London Trades Council.
  4. Annual Reports and monthly journals of various trade unions.
  5. Quarterly Circular of the Labour Representation Committee.

B. Manuscript Correspondence and Diaries:
  1. J. Bruce Glasier: Papers, and correspondence, primarily with James Keir Hardie. Courtesy of Mr. Francis Johnson.
  2. Herbert John Gladstone (later Viscount): Correspondence and papers, primarily those dealing with his tenure as Liberal Chief Whip. British Museum.
  3. John Burns: Diary and Correspondence. British Museum.
  4. Labour Representation Committee: Correspondence, primarily consisting of letters of the Secretary, J. Ramsay MacDonald.
  5. Fabian Society: Correspondence, including letters of George Bernard Shaw, Sidney Webb, James Ramsay MacDonald, H. W. Massingham, Edward R. Pease, S. G. Hobson, Hubert Bland, Sydney Olivier, Herbert Samuel and D. G. Ritchie.
  6. Beatrice Webb: Diaries. Courtesy of the Passfield Trustees.
  7. Sir Henry Campbell-Bannerman: Correspondence and papers. British Museum.
  8. George Lansbury: Correspondence and papers. British Library of Political Science.
  9. Frederic Harrison: Correspondence with John Morley. Courtesy of Mr. Herbert McCready.
  10. Lord and Lady Courtney: Papers and correspondence. British Library of Political Science.
  11. Sir Charles Dilke: Papers and correspondence. British Museum.
  12. John Alfred Spender: Correspondence. British Museum.
  13. Alfred Mattison: Diaries and correspondence. Courtesy of Mrs. Mattison.
  14. The Henry Broadhurst Collection. British Library of Political Science.

C. Newspapers:
  Of Labour and socialist newspapers, the most important cited are: the *Labour Leader;* the *Clarion; Justice;* the *Woolwich Pioneer;* the *Leicester Pioneer.* Labour and socialist monthly newsletters and periodicals include: the *Fabian News;* the *I.L.P. News;* the *Labour Annual* (after 1900, the *Reformers' Year Book*); the *Labour Church Record;* the *Labour Prophet;*

275

# Bibliography

the *Labour Record and Review;* the *Social Democrat;* the *Socialist Review.* The main London newspapers cited, other than Labour are: *The Times;* the *Echo;* the *Tribune; Reynolds's Newspaper;* the *Westminster Gazette;* the *Speaker;* the *Daily Chronicle;* the *Daily News.* Newspapers other than Labour outside London include: the *Glasgow Herald;* the *Newcastle Daily Chronicle;* the *Newcastle Leader,* the *Leeds and Yorkshire Mercury;* the *Yorkshire News;* the *Eastern Morning Gazette* (Norwich); the *Shields Daily News;* the *Barrow-in-Furness Dalton News;* the *North Western Daily Mail* (Barrow); the *Wakefield Express.*

D. Tracts and Leaflets of the Labour Representation Committee, the Independent Labour Party, the Social Democratic Federation, and the Fabian Society.

E. Autobiographies, Memoirs and Published Correspondence:

1. Adderley, James, *In Slums and Society: Reminiscences of Old Friends,* London, 1916.
2. Alcock, G. M., *Fifty Years of Railroad Trade Unionism,* London, 1922.
3. Asquith, H. H., *Memoirs and Reflections,* 2 vols., Boston, 1928.
4. Barnes, George, *From Workshop to War Cabinet,* London, 1924.
5. Bernstein, Edouard, *My Years in Exile,* New York, 1921.
6. Broadhurst, Henry, *Autobiography,* London, 1901.
7. Burt, Thomas, *Autobiography,* London, 1924.
8. Chamberlain, Austen, *Politics from Inside,* London, 1936.
9. Clynes, J. R., *Memoirs,* 2 vols., London, 1937.
10. Esher, Reginald, Viscount, *Journals and Letters,* 2 vols., edited by Maurice Brett, London, 1934.
11. Herbert Gladstone, *After Thirty Years,* London, 1928.
12. Haldane, Elizabeth, *From One Century to Another,* London, 1937.
13. Haldane, Richard Burton, *An Autobiography,* London, 1929.
14. Hewins, W. S., *Apologia of an Imperialist,* 2 vols., London, 1929.
15. Hobson, S. G., *Pilgrim to the Left,* London, 1938.
16. Hodge, John, *Workman's Cottage to Windsor Castle,* London, 1931.
17. Howell, George, *Labour Legislation, Labour Movements and Labour Leaders,* London, 1902.
18. Hyndman, H. M., *Further Reminiscences,* London, 1912.
19. Hyndman, H. M., *The Record of an Adventurous Life,* New York, 1911.
20. Lansbury, George, *My Life,* London, 1928.
21. Mann, Tom, *My Memoirs,* London, 1923.
22. Marx, Karl, and Engels, Friedrich, *Briefe und Auszuge,* Stuttgart, 1921. Translated into English as *Selected Correspondence 1846-1895,* New York, 1943.
23. Morley, John, *Recollections,* 2 vols., New York, 1917.
24. Redfern, Percy, *Journey to Understanding,* London, 1946.
25. Salt, Henry S., *Seventy Years Among Savages,* New York, 1921.
26. Samuel, Herbert, *Memoirs,* London, 1945.
27. Sanders, Stephen, *Early Socialist Days,* London, 1927.
28. Sexton, James, *Sir James Sexton, Agitator: The Life of the Docker's M.P., An Autobiography,* London, 1936.
29. Shaw, G. B., *Sixteen Self Sketches,* New York, 1949.

# Bibliography

30. Snowden, Philip, Viscount, *Autobiography*, 2 vols., London, 1934.
31. Thompson, Alexander M., *Here I Lie*, London, 1937.
32. Thorne, Will, *My Life's Battles*, London, 1925.
33. Tillett, Ben, *Memoirs and Reflections*, London, 1931.
34. Trevor, John, *My Quest for God*, London, 1897.
35. Webb, Beatrice, *Our Partnership*, edited by Barbara Drake and Margaret Cole, London, 1948.
36. Wells, H. G., *Experiment in Autobiography*, 2 vols., London, 1934.

F. Contemporary Works and Articles:
1. Blatchford, Robert, *Merrie England*, London, 1895.
2. Blatchford, Robert, *Britain for the British*, London, 1907 ed.
3. Chesterton, Cecil, *Gladstonian Ghosts*, London, 1905.
4. Ensor, R. C. K., ed., *Modern Socialism*, London, 1903.
5. Harrison, Frederic, 'The end of Trade Unionism,' *The Review of Reviews*, Sept. 14, 1901.
6. Hobson, John A., *Imperialism*, London, 1912 ed.
7. MacDonald, J. R. and Hardie, J. Keir, 'The I.L.P. Programme,' *Nineteenth Century*, Jan. 1899.
8. MacDonald, J. R., *Socialism and Society*, London, 1905.
9. MacDonald, J. R., *The Zollverein and British Industry*, London, 1903.
10. Macrosty, Henry W., *Trusts and the State: A Sketch of Competition*, London, 1901.
11. Mantoux, Paul, *L'eveil du parti ouvrier en Angleterre*, Paris, 1903.
12. Mantoux, Paul and Alfaria, Maurice, *La crise du trade unionisme*, Paris, 1903.
13. Noel, Conrad, *The Labour Party, What It is, What It Wants*, London, 1906.
14. Pease, Edward, Comments on the advent of the L.R.C. in the *Economic Review*, London, April 1900, 236.
15. Porritt, Edward, 'The Labour Party in English Politics,' *Annual Report of the American Historical Society*, 1894.
16. Shaw, G. B., ed., *The Fabian Essays*, London, 1920 ed.,
17. Smith, H. Llewelyn and Nash, Vaughan, *The Story of the Dock Strike Told by Two East Londoners*, London, 1890.
18. Threlfall, T. R., 'New Departures in Trade Unionism,' *Nineteenth Century*, Oct. 1890.
19. Webb, Sidney, 'Lord Rosebery's Escape from Houndsditch,' *Nineteenth Century*, Sept. 1901.
20. Wells, H. G., *Mankind in the Making*, Tauchnitz ed., Leipzig, 2 vols., 1903.

G. Sources partly or largely primary in nature
1. Cole, Margaret, ed., *The Webbs and Their Work*, London, 1949.
2. Glasier, J. Bruce, *The Meaning of Socialism*, London, 1919.
3. *Independent Labour Party (1893-1943)*, Jubilee Souvenir, London, 1943.
4. Lee, H. W. and Archbold, E., *Social Democracy in Britain*, London, 1935.
5. Lowe, David, *From Pit to Parliament: A Life of Keir Hardie*, London, 1923.

# Bibliography

6. MacDonald, J. R., 'Socialism and the Labour Party,' the *Socialist Review*, Aug. 1908.
7. MacDonald, J. R., *The Socialist Movement*, London, 1911.
8. MacDonald, J. R., *A Policy for the Labour Party*, London, 1920.
9. MacDonald, J. R., Foreword to Compton-Rickett, Arthur, *I Look Back: Memoirs of Fifty Years*, London, 1933.
10. Pease, Edward R., *A History of the Fabian Society*, London, 1925.
11. Rose, Frank, *The Coming Force*, Manchester, 1909.
12. Shaw, G. B., Annotations to the Manuscript of Pease's *History of the Fabian Society*.
13. Watson, Robert Spence, *The National Liberal Federation*, London, 1907.

## II. *Secondary Authorities*

A. Biographies and works biographical in nature:
1. Amery, Julian, *The Life of Joseph Chamberlain*, vol. iv, London, 1952.
2. Asquith, Cyril with Spender, J. A., *Life of Lord Oxford and Asquith*, 2 vols., London, 1932.
3. Bettany, Fred G., *Stewart Headlam*, London, 1926.
4. Brockway, Fenner, *Socialism Over Sixty Years: The Life of Jowett of Bradford*, London, 1946.
5. Burgess, Joseph, John Burns: *The Rise and Progress of a Right Honourable*, Glasgow, 1911.
6. Cole, G. D. H., *James Keir Hardie*. Fabian Society Biographical Series, No. 11, London, 1941.
7. Cole, Margaret, *Beatrice Webb*, New York, 1946.
8. Corder, Percy, *Life of Robert Spence Watson*, London, 1914.
9. Dugdale, Blanche, *Arthur James Balfour*, 2 vols., New York, 1937.
10. Elton, Godfrey, *The Life of James Ramsay MacDonald, 1866-1919*. London, 1939.
11. Fisher, H. A. L., *James Bryce*, 2 vols., New York, 1927.
12. Gardiner, A. G., *Life of George Cadbury*, London, 1922.
13. Gardiner, A. G., *Life of Sir William Harcourt*, 2 vols., London, 1923.
14. Garvin, J. L., *Life of Joseph Chamberlain*, 3 vols., London, 1934.
15. Grubb, Arthur Page, *From Candle Factory to British Cabinet*, London, 1908. On John Burns.
16. Gwynn, Stephen and Tuckwell, Gertrude, *Life of Sir Charles Dilke*, 2 vols., London, 1917.
17. Hamilton, Mary Agnes, *J. Ramsay MacDonald*, London, 1923.
18. Hamilton, Mary Agnes, *Sidney and Beatrice Webb*, New York, 1933.
19. Hamilton, Mary Agnes, *Arthur Henderson*, London, 1938.
20. Hammond, J. L., *C. P. Scott of the Manchester Guardian*, New York, 1934.
21. Harris, Henry Wilson, *J. A. Spender*, London, 1946.
22. Henderson, Archibald, *George Bernard Shaw: His Life and Works*, New York, 1918.
23. Jenkins, Edwin A., *From Iron Foundry to War Cabinet*, London, 1933. Life of Henderson.
24. Kent, William, *John Burns: Labour's Lost Leader*, London, 1950.

# Bibliography

25. Knott, G. H., *Mr. John Burns, M.P.*, London, 1901.
26. Lyons, Neil A., *Robert Blatchford*, London, 1910.
27. Mallet, Sir Charles, *Herbert Gladstone: A Memoir*, London, 1932.
28. Masterman, Lucy, *C. F. G. Masterman*, London, 1939.
29. Mayer, Gustav, *Friedrich Engels*, London, 1936.
30. Pearson, Hesketh, G. B. S.: *A Full Length Portrait*, London, 1942.
31. Pearson, Hesketh, G. B. S.: *A Postscript*, New York, 1950.
32. Petrie, Sir Charles, *Life and Letters of Austen Chamberlain*, 2 vols., London, 1939.
33. Raymond, E. T., *The Man of Promise: Lord Rosebery*, London, 1923.
34. Roberts, Carl, *Philip Snowden*, London, 1929.
35. Spender, J. A., *Sir Robert Hudson: A Memoir*, London, 1930.
36. Spender, J. A., *The Life of Sir Henry Campbell-Bannerman*, 2 vols., London, 1923.
37. Stewart, William, *J. Keir Hardie*, London, 1921.
38. Thompson, Laurie, *Portrait of an Englishman: A Life of Robert Blatchford*, London, 1951.
39. Thorold, Algar Labouchere, *The Life of Henry Labouchere*, London, 1913.
40. Tiltman, H. Hessell, *J. Ramsay MacDonald: Labor's Man of Destiny*, New York, 1929.
41. Tracey, Herbert, *From Doughty Street to Downing Street: The Rt. Hon. J. Ramsay MacDonald*, London, 1924.
42. Tschiffely, A. F., *Don Roberto. Being the Account of the Life and Works of R. B. Cunninghame Graham: 1852-1936*, London, 1937.
43. Weir, L. Macneil, *The Tragedy of Ramsay MacDonald*, London, 1938.

B. Other works:

1. Adams, W. S., *Edwardian Heritage*, London, 1949.
2. Arnot, R. Page, *The Miners: A History of the Miners Federation of Great Britain: 1899-1910*, London, 1949.
3. Beer, Max, *A History of British Socialism*, 2 vols., London, 1948.
4. Binyon, Rev. Gilbert C., *The Christian Socialist Movement in England*, London, 1931.
5. Clayton, Joseph, *The Rise and Decline of Socialism in Great Britain: 1884-1924*, London, 1926.
6. Cole, G. D. H., *A Short History of the Working Class Movement*, London, 1948.
7. Cole, G. D. H., *British Working Class Politics: 1832-1914*, London, 1941.
8. Dangerfield, George, *The Strange Death of Liberal England*, London, 1936.
9. Davis, W. J., *History of the British Trades Union Congress*, 2 vols.
10. Desmond, Shaw, *Labour: The Giant with the Feet of Clay*, London, 1921.
11. Elton, Godfrey, *England, Arise!*, London, 1931.
12. Ensor, R. C. K., *England, 1870-1914*, Oxford, 1946.
13. Fyfe, Hamilton, *Keir Hardie*, London, 1935.
14. Glasier, J. Bruce, *William Morris and the Early Days of the Socialist Movement*, London, 1921.

# Bibliography

15. Greenwood, John H., *The Law Relating to Trade Unions*, London, 1911.
16. Gretton, R. H., *A Modern History of the English People: 1880-1922*, London, 1930.
17. Hearnshaw, F. C., ed., *Edwardian England: 1901-1910*, London, 1933.
18. Hobsbawm, Eric J., ed., *Labour's Turning Point*, London, 1948.
19. Humphrey, A. W., *A History of Labour Representation*, London, 1912.
20. Johnston, Thomas, *The History of the Working Classes in Scotland*, Glasgow, 1920.
21. Laidler, Harry W., *A History of Socialist Thought*, New York, 1927.
22. Pelling, Henry, *The Origins of the Labour Party*, New York, 1954.
23. Raymond, E. T., *Portraits of the New Century*, London, 1928. Has sketches of Hardie and Crooks.
24. Reid, J. H. Stewart, *The Origins of the British Labour Party*, Minnesota, 1955.
25. Spender, J. A., *Great Britain, Empire and Commonwealth: 1886-1935*, London, 1936.
26. Tracey, Herbert, *Book of the Labour Party*, 3 vols., London, 1925.
27. Wagner, Donald O., *The Church of England and Social Reform since 1854*, New York, 1930.
28. Webb, Sidney, *The Story of the Durham Miners: 1662-1921*, London, 1921.
29. Webb, Sidney and Beatrice, *History of Trade Unionism*, 1926 ed., London, 1950.
30. Webb, Sidney and Beatrice, *The Problems of Modern Industry*, London, 1898.
31. Wells, H. G., *An Englishman Looks at the World*, London, 1914.
32. *A History of the London Trades Council*, London, 1950. Published by the London Trades Council.

C. Unpublished works:
1. Crowley, D. W., *Origins of the Revolt of the British Labour Party from Liberalism, 1875-1906*, British Library of Political Science, 1952.
2. Hobsbawm, Eric J., *Fabianism and the Fabians, 1884-1914*, Cambridge University Library, 1950.
3. Lamb, W. K., *British Labour and Parliament, 1865-1893*, British Library of Political Science, 1933.

# Index

# Index

# Index

THE END

# ERRATA

Page 49, line 29, read *13,000* in place of *20,000*.

Page 95, line 32, read *in 1904* in place of *just after the 1906 Election*.

Page 150, lines 1 and 2, read *United Textile Workers* in place of *Lancashire Textile Operatives*.

Page 262, lines 20 and 25, insert *August* before *1903*.

Page 273 after heading *List A* and page 274 after heading *List B* insert *(based on Gladstone's list of August 7, 1903)*.

Page 273 underline *Deptford*.

Page 274 read *Monmouth Boroughs* in place of *Monmouth*.